M O O T
CORP ®

New Venture Modules

Gary M. Cadenhead, Ph.D.
The University of Texas at Austin

Raymond W. Smilor, Ph.D.
Center for Entrepreneurial Leadership
Ewing Marion Kauffman Foundation

KENDALL/HUNT PUBLISHING COMPANY
4050 Westmark Drive   Dubuque, Iowa 52002

Neither The Center for Entrepreneurial Leadership Inc., The University of Texas at Austin, or the program(s) make any representations or warranties, express or implied, as to any matter respecting this video presentation including but not limited to, the implied warranties of merchantability and fitness for a particular purpose.

Dedication

to George Kozmetsky

for championing the

MOOT CORP® Program,

exemplifying entrepreneurship,

and inspiring our interest in

entrepreneurship education.

Contents

Expert
Application
Systems
Incorporated

CONFIDENTIAL BUSINESS PLAN

Copy 7 of 7

April 3, 1992

Expert Application Systems, Incorporated

Our Vision:

Expert Application Systems, Incorporated provides the best compliance software systems, seeks to learn from and provide knowledge to customers, and creates and preserves employee and customer satisfaction.

Management Team

Margarita Ash	David Beuerlein
Patricia Mack	Deborah Sallee

Expert Application Systems, Incorporated
8920 Business Park Drive
Austin, Texas 78759

Table of Contents

Appendices

Executive Summary

Our Mission:

Expert Application Systems, Incorporated will outperform any and all competitors in the compliance software systems industry.

The Company

Expert Application Systems, Incorporated (EASI) develops compliance software systems for growth markets. EASI's systems are designed to be extremely user-friendly, accurate, and portable among computer platforms. Today's manufacturers must comply with a host of regulations and standards arising from the joint actions of governmental regulatory and private standards organizations. In the United States, many electronic products must be listed by one of *several* private Nationally Recognized Testing Laboratories (NRTLs) as meeting certain product safety standards. This certification helps companies avoid criminal, civil, and private actions. EASI's initial product is a software system that guides users through the Underwriters Laboratories (UL) product safety compliance process. UL, one of several NRTLs, is the world's largest independent testing laboratory. Its client base represents one of the largest markets for EASI's products. Expert Application Systems, Inc. has received a strong Letter of Endorsement from UL and is formalizing a strategic alliance with Underwriters Laboratories that will continue to give EASI significant access to UL resources. EASI is also currently developing key strategic alliances within the European Community (EC) and with the Canadian Standards Association (CSA). In addition, UL has proposed including EASI products in their marketing plan and distributing EASI's software through their existing channels. EASI's strong relationship with UL is a significant competitive advantage that will contribute to our success in the marketplace. This has generated tremendous interest for EASI's compliance software in the product safety industry.

The Market

Interviews, surveys and trade articles all confirm that companies resent the time and expense involved in obtaining UL listing/recognition. Currently, 95% of products covered by UL Standard 1950 (UL 1950) fail to receive listing/recognition on the first submittal to UL and only 50% succeed

i

9

after the second submittal. UL clients complain that the Standards are confusing, not user-friendly, and difficult to integrate into the product development cycle. However, obtaining the UL mark is a competitive necessity. The 592 UL Standards, in addition to similar international standards, represent an expanding and lucrative market opportunity for compliance software systems. EASI's UL products target an untapped global market of $1.5 billion in program sales and $248 million in annual update sale . Our initial product is targeted to approximately 5,700 domestic manufacturers and represents total potential sales in excess of $10 million in program sales and $1.7 million in annual update sales. We are pursuing an aggressive marketing strategy designed to establish a strong foothold for EASI.

Products

EASI is developing multiple products for the product safety industry. EASI's software systems provide easy-to-use, efficient guidance through compliance processes. The benefits achieved using our systems include higher probability of first-time listing/recognition, reduced expense, shortened product time-to-market, and improved access to standards updates. EASI's initial product, *UL Solutions - 1950*, targets the Underwriters Laboratories Standard that generates the largest user demand and greatest revenue for UL - UL Standard 1950: Safety of Information Technology Equipment Including Electrical Business Equipment. Potential customers are currently reviewing an alpha version of the system. Several Fortune 500 companies, in addition to Underwriters Laboratories, have agreed to serve as beta sites for *UL Solutions - 1950*. Customers have been involved at every stage of the development process and continue to provide valuable feedback regarding the key features that should be integrated into our product. This interaction is ongoing and customer input continues to drive our product development. The experience of EASI personnel is leveraged with object-oriented expert systems development tools to create high-quality, customer-driven products at lower costs than those of conventional software developers.

Key Management Personnel

The EASI management team is well balanced in talents and experience and is supported by a highly qualified Board of Advisors. In addition, EASI has a broad network of contacts in all areas of business.

ii

Patricia Mack - President: Ms. Mack founded a software company that continues to operate successfully. Her experience includes profit and loss responsibility, risk management, and process testing. Ms. Mack is responsible for positioning EASI as an industry leader and developing corporate strategies.

Margarita Ash - VP of Product Development: Ms. Ash has seven years of product research and development experience with IBM, including product safety compliance and certification processes for the U.S., Japan, and Europe. Ms. Ash's responsibilities include determining appropriate development tools and strategies that meet customer needs and the planning of software production.

David Beuerlein - Vice President of Finance and Operations: Mr. Beuerlein has a wide range of operational and financial systems experience with General Dynamics including financial forecasting in New Product Development. Mr. Beuerlein is responsible for financial planning and control and the implementation of software production and customer support systems.

Deborah Sallee - VP of Sales and Marketing: Ms. Sallee has over six years of engineering experience with Powerex, Inc. and Harris Corporation and has worked extensively in the area of technical marketing. Ms. Sallee has also previously worked with UL compliance needs. Ms. Sallee's responsibilities include directing the planning and implementation of all sales and marketing efforts.

Financial Summary

Revenue projections for the five years shown below include sales for *UL Solutions - 1950*, subsequent products, and update subscriptions. The values shown are for fiscal years ending on September 30. To attain projected revenues of $32 million in year 5, EASI will require an investment of $600,000. In return for this investment, EASI is offering 25% equity in the company. Projections indicate an annual rate of return of 104% to the investor(s).

easi	1993	1994	1995	1996	1997
Revenue	$383,572	$3,224,166	$10,658,376	$20,641,964	$32,297,999
Net Income	($343,040)	$657,817	$1,889.520	$3,625,386	$5,605,144

iii

The Company

1.1 Company Background

Expert Application Systems was incorporated in Texas as a C corporation on September 10, 1991 with 1,000,000 shares of common stock authorized. The EASI management team is capitalizing on the lucrative business opportunity of creating compliance software systems to aid manufacturers. EASI's products will help companies gain competitive advantage in the marketplace since our products will shorten the time-to-market cycle for companies. EASI will take advantage of untapped global growth markets for compliance software systems that address a number of standards in a variety of industries. EASI has been accepted into the Austin Technology Incubator (ATI), which fosters the development of high-tech start-up companies, and began operations at that location on January 20, 1992. This, combined with the management team and business opportunity, has generated tremendous interest for EASI's compliance software in the product safety industry.

1.2 Company Objectives

EASI will be the market leader in the compliance software systems market. EASI uses extensive alpha and beta testing to ensure the user-friendliness and accuracy of its software systems prior to their introduction into the marketplace. One of EASI's top priorities is creating and preserving customer satisfaction. Customers are involved at every stage of the development process in order to determine their needs and the key features to be integrated into our products. Establishing and monitoring customer requirements is the foundation for EASI's Quality Program and provides objective measures of EASI's performance. EASI will continue to work with, and listen to, our customers with a focus on ensuring that their satisfaction remains a top corporate priority.

EASI executives are responsible for creating and sustaining a clear and visible Quality Program, along with a supporting management system, to guide all activities of the company. EASI is dedicated to maintaining an environment that is conducive to full employee participation, continuous improvement, and personal and organizational growth. EASI plans to compete in the Small Business Division of the Malcolm Baldrige National Quality Award after establishing a quality track record.

1 - 1

The Market

2.1 The Opportunity

Compliance software systems represent an untapped market of approximately 330,000 manufacturers worldwide (see Appendix A). EASI's products target specific niches within this worldwide market, such as the Underwriters Laboratories (UL) compliance market. EASI projects that these niche markets include at least 50% of the worldwide market, or 165,000 manufacturers. The average manufacturer complies with five safety standards and accompanying updates, resulting in a total worldwide market potential of $1.5 billion in program sales and $248 million in annual update sales (see Appendix A). Because of increased federal emphasis on product safety standards, there is enormous growth potential for EASI. According to the American Tort Reform Association, the number of product liability cases filed has increased by 700% during the past decade. High dollar damages because of unsafe products has promoted a worldwide focus on product safety. Many countries have passed legislation mandating product safety certification prior to product introduction. The U.S. is considering such legislation, which is already mandated in certain areas of the country. With product liability costs rising, companies such as IBM consider the issue important enough to restructure their organization and give the product safety departments direct communication with the CEO. Additionally, universities are now offering specialized Product Safety classes. For example, EASI is currently talking with Dr. Way Johnston of Texas A&M regarding joint projects between the company and the university. This interaction could include the use of EASI's software in the Product Safety curriculum, which would result in the acceptance of EASI's software systems by future product safety engineers before they enter the workplace. These trends illustrate the immense opportunity for EASI's compliance software systems in the marketplace.

2.2 Industry Description

Manufacturers must comply with a host of regulations and standards. In the United States, certain electronic products must be listed by one of *several* Nationally Recognized Testing Laboratories (NRTLs), such as UL, as complying with appropriate product safety standards. This certification helps companies avoid criminal, civil, and private legal actions. UL is the world's largest independent

2 - 1

15

testing laboratory, holding the vast majority of U.S. safety certifications for electronic products. UL engineers test products to meet one or more of the 592 UL Standards.

In the United States, there are over 45,000 equipment manufacturers whose products are covered by one or more UL Standards. Of these, over 5,700 comply with <u>UL 1950: Safety of Information Technology Equipment Including Electrical Business Equipment</u>. This results in domestic market potentials of $405 million in program sales and $68 million in annual update sales for all UL Standards, and over $10 million in program sales and $1.7 million in annual update sales for UL 1950. This market is growing at a rate exceeding 10% per year. Internationally, over 8,500 manufacturers comply with UL 1950 when selling their products in U.S. markets (see Appendix A).

2.3   Customer Need

According to the American Electronics Association's 1991 Productivity Survey, quality, product reliability, and time-to-market are the most important factors for success in high-tech markets. Obtaining product recognition is a time-consuming and costly process that can affect product quality, design time, and cost. For example, the cost of a typical UL product submittal averages between $3,000 and $10,000. According to the August 1991 issue of <u>PC Magazine</u>, the total cost of achieving UL listing/recognition for a complete computer system starts at approximately $10,000 and can spiral upward if the original design is particularly poor with respect to product safety. UL reports that 95% of initial submittals for UL 1950 require changes, resulting in a long listing/recognition cycle (see Appendix B). Avoiding this costly process is not an option since listing/recognition is a competitive necessity. The UL mark significantly broadens a product's potential market by creating competitive advantages over non-listed products. However, UL Standards, as well as other government regulations and standards, are often extremely difficult to interpret and incorporate into the design process. In fact, due to the complexity of UL 1950, Underwriters Laboratories offers a two-day seminar to clarify the Standard. The cost is $695 per participant and, when offered, these seminars are typically filled to capacity. The seminar is a "one-time-only" situation and customers usually need extended instruction. Therefore, a two-day seminar on UL 1950 does not meet the needs of most

2 - 2

manufacturers. *Companies are in need of faster, more efficient compliance processes that will save them time and money and EASI's compliance software systems fill this need.*

To define our customers' needs, EASI recently surveyed 200 manufacturers nationwide (see complete details in Appendix C). The intent of the survey was to make a low-cost, preliminary estimate of market need rather than provide detailed statistical data. The response rate to this "blind" survey was a remarkably high 28%. The survey confirmed that manufacturers devote substantial manpower and funds to the UL compliance process. Responding companies reported frustration with the UL Standards documentation, the frequent changes to standards, and lengthy paperwork requirements. As illustrated in the following graph, 80% of the responding companies that submit products to UL expressed strong interest in an easy-to-use and accurate software package to guide and assist them with the compliance process. In fact, one-third of responding companies have at some point hired a UL consultant to assist them with the process.

Market Survey: Interest in EASI Software

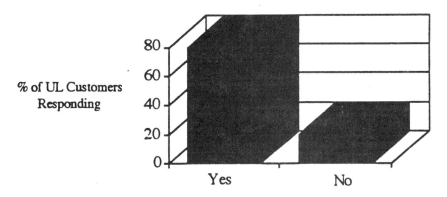

To meet our customers' needs, EASI's product test sites are actively involved in the development process and continue to provide valuable feedback regarding key features that should be integrated into our product. This interaction is ongoing and customer input will continue to drive our product development. We will also conduct follow-up surveys to further define customer needs, and will continue to research target markets as our product line expands.

2.4   Target Marketing

EASI will use target marketing as a means to leverage marketing and sales resources, build early volume, and develop customer relationships. EASI's software products will be targeted at all manufacturers requiring product recognition by testing laboratories. Our first product, *UL Solutions - 1950*, is a software system designed to assist in the UL 1950 compliance process. This product is targeted to approximately 5,700 domestic manufacturers and represents potential sales in excess of $10 million in program sales and $1.7 million in annual update sales (see Appendix A). We will initially target companies through alpha and beta testing in order to establish market presence and gain additional credibility. EASI will then market to small- and medium-sized businesses, those most often confused by compliance requirements.

Although large manufacturers typically have a distinct department that handles all regulatory and standards compliance, they still face delays in bringing a product to market. Large manufacturers will use EASI's products during the design process to reduce the need for costly change after completion of the design. For small- and medium-sized companies an in-house staff is cost-prohibitive, so a design or manufacturing engineer usually handles standards compliance in addition to other duties. This individual is often unfamiliar with compliance specifications, which may result in lengthy product compliance processes and product changes. Letters from CompuAdd, National Instruments, and Rochelle Communications, Inc. all confirm that *companies are in need of faster, more efficient compliance processes that will save them time and money* (see Appendix D). *EASI's compliance software systems fill this need.*

2.4.1 Alpha Testing

Alpha sites provide customer feedback during the early-to-mid stages of product development. EASI is customer driven and, therefore, alpha sites serve an important role in the company's development. We have obtained verbal alpha site commitments from several companies in Austin for their review of, and feedback on,*UL Solutions - 1950*. To date, Rochelle Communications, Inc., Applied Heater Technologies, and OptoMed, Inc. have reviewed the product and provided valuable feedback for the development process.

2 - 4

2.4.2 Beta Testing

Beta sites provide customer feedback during the mid-to-later stages of product development. We have obtained verbal beta site commitments for the testing of *UL Solutions-1950*, from Underwriters Laboratories, Inc., IBM Corporation, CompuAdd, Dell Computer Corporation, National Instruments, and 3M. CompuAdd, Dell Computer Corporation, and National Instruments have already returned written beta site agreements (see Appendix E) and the remaining companies are anticipated to do so in the near future. We will also test applicable products with ECB S.A., a computer manufacturer in Madrid, Spain. The product safety managers at these companies have expressed great interest in our product and have agreed to test the beta version and provide feedback to EASI. Each member of EASI's management team is involved with the company's alpha and beta sites. We view the customer feedback from these sites as crucial to the design and development of our product and the involvement of each team member in this process guarantees a continued focus on customer wants and needs.

2.5 Competition

At present, there is no commercially available software guidance system for product safety standards. Indirect competition (or "alternatives") may exist in five forms: 1) NRTLs, 2) compliance consultants, 3) Information Handling Services, Inc. (IHS), 4) large manufacturers' in-house staff, and 5) compliance seminars. NRTLs offer manufacturers product safety certification services. At present, NRTLs do not offer guidance through the compliance process or provide timely updates. Expansion into these service areas by NRTLs could reduce EASI's market.

If a manufacturer does not wish to commit internal resources to manage the compliance process, he or she may hire a compliance consultant. These consultants provide a manufacturer with guidance and technical expertise. Typically, the fee for a consultant will add between $3,000 and $4,000 per product to the overall cost of obtaining product certification. Large companies under a time deadline may view this as necessary to keep a product introduction on schedule, however, smaller companies typically cannot afford the additional cost of a consultant.

IHS is licensed by UL to market the full set of UL Standards on CD-ROM. This product retails for $4,000. IHS customers complain that the visual quality of the electronic information presented is poor and that the "zoom" feature designed to address this concern is insufficient. This has led some IHS customers to cancel their contracts with the company. IHS does not sell individual standards and their products do not offer guidance to assist users through the compliance process.

Large manufacturers frequently have sizable internal departments that handle all regulatory and compliance requirements for the company. Our marketing survey indicates that these companies would be interested in EASI's software as a time-saving tool for their staff and to promote concurrent/simultaneous engineering in the design process.

Compliance seminars are a "one-time-only" situation and do not provide the extended instruction customers require.

Competitive Analysis

	Improve Manual Access	Guidance Through Process	Increase Success Rate	Reduce Time	Provide Timely Updates	Cost
easi	✓	✓	✓	✓	✓	$3000 Total
NRTLs	✓					$3,000 - $10,000 per Product
Compliance Consultants		✓	✓	✓		$3,000 - $4,000 per Product
IHS	✓					$4,000 Total
In-house Staff		✓	✓			Total Employee Salaries
Compliance Seminars			✓			$1,700 per Person per Class

The fact that *at present there are no direct competitors offering a software based guidance system for product safety standards* is a distinct competitive advantage for EASI. This will make it difficult for competitors to enter the market since companies looking to purchase compliance software systems for product safety standards will tend to follow the example set previously by industry leaders. These industry leaders will have been exposed to EASI's products through our alpha and beta site arrangements and will be familiar with their features and benefits. EASI's initial customers will serve as a "word-of-mouth" salesforce to future customers.

2 - 6

Products

3.1 Benefits for the Customer

EASI's products guide the user through the many compliance standards, assisting in the product certification compliance process by reducing cost, improving accuracy, and providing a useful tool for experts who need quick access to the details of the standards. Additional benefits include shortened product time-to-market and timely standards updates. Our products save time and money by decreasing the probability of failed product submittals and the necessary repeat submittals. Currently 95% of products covered by UL 1950 fail to receive listing/recognition on the first submittal and only 50% succeed after the second submittal (see Appendix B). Our first product, *UL Solutions - 1950* , is designed to guide users through the UL 1950 Standard and reduce manufacturers' failure rates.

3.2 Description of Products

Much of the value of EASI's systems are that they make the compliance process easier and faster for our clients. Our product is an object-oriented expert system implementation of product safety standards. Object-oriented software consists of modules of code which can be modified and rearranged quickly, enabling a shortened development time for products. An expert system is a software package that communicates the knowledge of an expert to the user. Interpretation and understanding of standards is difficult for non-experts because of the legalistic language and cumbersome format of the documents. Our products provide information to the customer in an easy to understand format, using straightforward language and illustrative graphics (see Appendix F).

Regarding the user interface, customers have indicated that they want a point-and-click graphics-based format as opposed to a keyboard command-based system. Microsoft Windows is the computer environment of choice for the majority of our initial customer base, as indicated by our survey results. However, the need for portability among computer platforms is increasing and EASI is positioned to meet this customer need when necessary. Additional features of EASI's products include checklists to track progress through the specifications and the ability to generate test reports to send to product certification agencies. The report generation feature allows product certification agencies to track who is submitting EASI-based applications and feed that information back to EASI for tracking

3 - 1

the certification success rate and reasons for failure. This information is useful for advertising and product improvement. The complete text of standards, and product documentation, is integrated into EASI's products allowing the user to locate pertinent information quickly and easily. Finally, updates to EASI's software will be available to customers on a subscription basis. *All of the previously mentioned features are direct results of customer feedback.*

3.2.1 Initial Products

The decision to develop a product is based on market need and demand. Our initial product, *UL Solutions - 1950*, is a PC-based (personal computer based) application developed for the Windows environment. It is based on the most frequently used UL Safety Standard, UL 1950. This standard generates the most revenue for UL and thus represents *one* of the largest markets for EASI. The customer package includes the software diskettes and User's Manual. As an option, a CD-ROM Directory of Recognized UL Components will be available. Appendix G is EASI's Product Price List.

3.2.2 Follow-on Products

EASI will continue to explore other product and service opportunities as they develop. Other testing laboratories and standards organizations, including the European Community (EC), the Canadian Standards Association (CSA), German Verband Deutscher Electrotechniker (VDE), and ETL Testing Laboratories (ETL) represent additional market opportunities for EASI. The five planned follow-on products listed below are in the same category of product safety standards as UL 1950. EASI's first three products, *UL Solutions - 1950*, *IEC Solutions - 950*, and *CSA Solutions 22.2 - 220* are based on virtually identical standards which are implemented in different countries.

1. **IEC No. 950** is the European Community (EC) equivalent of UL 1950. Manufacturers must comply with this Directive before entering the EC market.

2. **CSA 22.2 No. 220** is the Canadian Standard based entirely on UL 1950.

3. **FCC Part 15** is the FCC emission requirement pertaining to products covered by UL 1950. FCC Part 15 is currently a serious concern for electronic manufacturers due to its confusing terminology and the difficulty associated with its implementation within the European Community.

4. **UL 1459** is the telecommunication/telephone Standard required by the National Electric Code.

3 - 2

5. **CSA 22.2 No. 0.7** is the Canadian Standard based entirely on UL 1459.

3.3 Customer Support

Customers insist on access to qualified technical support for their software products. Support for EASI's products will include a 24-hour toll-free customer service and order line with a 24-hour turnaround time on customer problems. EASI's customer support staff will also maintain an ongoing relationship with each of our customers by making periodic calls to solicit feedback regarding EASI's products and services. In addition, EASI will maintain a restricted access electronic Bulletin Board System (BBS) for our customers. This service will ensure access to the most up-to-date standards and software improvements through a service that the customer may access at any time. Using the BBS, customers will be able to interact with EASI's support staff, other customers, and other industry experts. EASI will mail updates to those subscription customers without access to the BBS to ensure that all customers are kept up-to-date on the latest standards.

3.4 Risk Analysis

Two potential risks for EASI'S products are the illegal copying and use of the software and product liability. EASI is working with the law firm Winstead Sechrest & Minick in Austin, Texas, to address the these issues. EASI's products will be protected under all applicable trade secret and copyright laws. Copyright registration of *UL Solutions - 1950* is in process. Customers are required to abide by EASI's software licensing agreement that prohibits the licensee from copying the program except for backup and archival purposes. Because of the report generation feature in EASI's *UL Solutions - 1950* product, UL can track who is submitting EASI software generated applications and feed that information back to the company. This will assist EASI in tracking down illegal copies of its software programs. Additionally, proper security measures, specifically the signing of non-disclosure and non-compete agreements, have been taken to protect trade secrets. In regard to product liability, EASI will utilize product disclaimers and purchase the appropriate insurance to protect itself against legal claims. EASI has spoken with Bankers Trust and a preliminary cost estimate has been quoted.

3 - 3

Marketing Plan

4.1 Overall Marketing Strategy

The key to EASI's success will be reaching the product safety and compliance engineers at small- and medium-sized businesses. This is where the majority of sales opportunities exist. EASI will penetrate each target market through direct mailings, niche advertising, and telemarketing. To accomplish this we will initially target the large, market leaders in each industry through beta testing in order to establish market presence and increase EASI's credibility. In addition, the previously mentioned arrangement between UL and EASI presents an opportunity for creating customer awareness. UL has proposed including EASI's name in UL's Catalog of Standards for Safety and having EASI product literature included in the UL submittal package sent to potential customers. Another integral element of EASI's strategy is to be responsive to all regulatory and Standards changes in our target industries. We have also initiated discussions with representatives of the Computer and Business Equipment Manufacturers Association (CBEMA) and are establishing networks with CBEMA members who are interested in EASI's products, or who can put us in touch with others who may be interested in our products.

4.2 Strategic Alliances

EASI is currently developing several key strategic alliances. In addition to obtaining permission to publish the European Community (EC) Directives in electronic format and corresponding with John McCarthy, Vice President of Standards for the Canadian Standards Association (CSA), we are currently formalizing a strategic alliance with Underwriters Laboratories. UL requested a proposal for an agreement under which UL would contribute funding toward EASI's software development in return for a share of revenues. Appendix H includes a letter regarding this arrangement from Robert Williams, Corporate Manager of Standards at Underwriters Laboratories. A meeting will be held on April 9, 1992 at EASI's office in Austin, Texas at which time Robert Williams, Gary Schremppe (Field Site Representative for Underwriters Laboratories), and EASI's management team will negotiate the details of the agreement.

4 - 1

UL is currently providing EASI with technical expertise to aid in product development and has provided Standards in both printed and electronic formats. EASI's evolving strategic alliance with UL indicates UL's belief that the EASI management team can develop a "saleable" product . Unlike UL, EASI's management team possesses the necessary expertise to develop compliance software systems successfully. EASI's strong relationship with UL is a significant competitive advantage that will contribute to our success in the marketplace. EASI's UL contacts and relationships cannot be duplicated in a short period of time. Therefore, any potential competitor to EASI would have to overcome a significant barrier to entry upon entering the market.

4.3   Initial Sales and Promotion

In order to penetrate the market quickly and provide a catalyst for future "word-of-mouth" sales, EASI will saturate our initial target market of 5,700 domestic manufacturers complying with UL 1950 through a direct mailing. Each direct mail packet will include a product demonstration disk and product literature. In addition, EASI will offer a substantial introductory discount during the first 6 months of initial product release. EASI will also establish a toll-free number for orders and service.

Industry surveys indicate that the majority of manufacturers complying with product safety standards read the same trade publications. EASI will advertise extensively in publications including Compliance Engineering, Design News and Electronic Buyers News in order to maximize product exposure and sales. EASI personnel will actively submit technical articles regarding the company's products, and their features and benefits, to these trade publications. EASI will also target its promotional efforts at relevant trade shows, CBEMA conferences, and compliance seminars. For example, the use of EASI's products during UL seminars will serve as a third party endorsement by UL and will allow us to directly reach UL clients. This strategy will give us the best access to engineers responsible for a company's product safety design and compliance requirements.

4.4   Distribution

There are four typical channels for the distribution of software products: 1) software retailers, 2) value-added resellers (VARs), 3) direct sales, and 4) mail-order. EASI's software is an industrial niche product. Since software retailers typically handle consumer-oriented mass market products, distributing through this channel presents no advantage. VARs are typically independent businesses that provide customers with integrated hardware and software systems. EASI's software is designed to run on multiple computer platforms and thus our customers do not have the need for the skills of a VAR. EASI will use direct sales only to establish market presence in the Austin-Houston-Dallas market.

EASI will distribute its products primarily through Nationally Recognized Testing Laboratories (NRTLs) and mail-order channels. NRTLs provide EASI with a direct link to manufacturers testing products to comply with particular safety standards. *Specifically, UL has proposed distributing EASI's software in conjunction with UL Standards manuals and diskettes.* This will give us direct access to UL clients. Mail-order sales provide an efficient means of reaching our target customer base. EASI has acquired High Tech Texas, an extremely valuable database of Texas high-tech manufacturing and service organizations produced by TINS (the Texas Innovation Network). It will serve not only as a mailing list for our initial product, but for future products as well. It will also assist in our direct sales effort in the Austin-Houston-Dallas market.

4.5 Pricing Strategy

Based on feedback from our alpha and beta sites and our market survey, we have identified a typical submittal profile for manufacturers. This shows most companies submit between three and five products per year to UL for approval and spend 180 man-hours per product submittal. This includes time spent on documentation, standards interpretation, product redesign, and testing. As the cost of a typical UL product submittal averages between $3,000 and $10,000, a company's overall cost in obtaining a UL mark may reach $15,000 per product when internal costs are included. EASI's software is designed to provide the customer with considerable cost savings.

EASI is in a market which is currently void of direct competition. In this situation, the benefits of EASI's products must be weighed against the benefits of "alternatives" available to the customer in order to determine price (see "Competitive Analysis" chart in Section 2.5). EASI's initial product, *UL Solutions - 1950*, will be marketed at a price of $3,000 per copy and we expect future products to be similarly priced, on average. This price allows our customers to realize both manpower and cost

4 - 3

savings (see Appendix I). Preliminary results from a pricing survey, and interviews with customers, indicate that a price of $3,000 is actually below what some customers will pay for this product.

The software program, User's Manual, and a one-year subscription to updates of the standard for which a particular program is designed will be included in the initial purchase price. Standards updates to be used with EASI's software will be available to customers on a subscription basis. A subscription for updates to the standard in subsequent years will be priced at $500 per standard per year and will be available for distribution through a restricted access electronic Bulletin Board System (BBS). Interviews with product safety managers have revealed that UL frequently revises its Standards without notifying affected customers. EASI will be able to provide timely Standards revisions due to our strong relationship, and emerging strategic alliance, with UL. EASI's BBS will assure for the timely distribution of updates to the Standards. Therefore, manufacturers have a vested interest in maintaining a yearly update subscription with EASI. Finally, EASI will provide its customers with a 30-day moneyback guarantee. All of these factors serve to alleviate any potential customer reluctance associated with trying EASI's products.

4.6   International Markets

As U.S. sales' levels approach maturity, EASI will seek new markets for our products. The largest market outside the U.S. for information technology is the Japanese market, with approximately 4,700 manufacturers (see Appendix A). EASI has developed a three-phase proactive plan for entry into this market: 1) initial market research, 2) suitability of the product, and 3) formation of an alliance (or alliances) with a Japanese distributor(s). Initially, EASI will study Japanese business practices, make contact and network with other companies doing business in Japan, and investigate growth in this market. Next, EASI will examine the suitability of our products for Japanese manufacturers. Linguistic, cultural, customer support, and computer platform portability concerns will be addressed. Finally, EASI will review our market research and propose an alliance with a Japanese distributor. EASI will select this distributor from those we have identified as serving the Japanese market leaders in the information technology industry. EASI will consider, among other attributes, the distributor's ability to monitor competition and its ability to provide venture capital, if required.

4 - 4

Product Development and Operations

Feedback from customers and marketing surveys indicate that our production function needs to possess 4 main characteristics: 1) quality, 2) ease of use, 3) customer support, and 4) competitive price. Quality management will occur in all phases of EASI's development, production, and distribution. Our software industry contacts have been key in assisting EASI in identifying quality suppliers and production methods suitable for all phases of company growth. Our products provide the customer with an easy to understand, straightforward software system using illustrative graphics and animation. EASI's customers insist on access to qualified technical support for their software products. Therefore, the company has developed a support strategy to meet this customer need. Finally, EASI's customers want an economical product. Once again, our software industry contacts have put us in contact with the low-cost, high-quality suppliers of computer disks, CD-ROM, packaging, etc. Further, the sequenced introduction of our products allow each new product to build on the structure and organization of previous ones. In this way, development time and cost will decrease steadily as new products are introduced, as illustrated in the development schedule.

5.1 Product Development

EASI will continue to investigate and employ product development strategies that contribute to meeting customer requirements in a superior manner.

5.1.1 Development Tool Selection

After establishing customer requirements, the initial phase of product development centered on the selection of a software development tool. Our most important criteria for this tool were that it be flexible, powerful, and object-oriented. *UL Solutions - 1950* must be easily portable between computing platforms. In addition, EASI's development strategy includes using a tool that leverages the management teams' significant development experience. Expert system shells allow for rapid, high-quality product development. Similarly, there are many advantages of object-oriented programming. This new philosophy of software development provides numerous benefits, including at least a 40% reduction in lines of code (lower cost), extensive reuse of modules, and increased developer productivity. After evaluating current market offerings, we selected *KnowledgePro*, an

5 - 1

object-oriented expert system shell with hypertext and hypermedia capabilities allowing text and graphics to be accessed through a point-and-click mouse interface.

5.1.2 KnowledgePro

KnowledgePro contains several tools that leverage the developer's productivity, including screen designers, code generators, and built-in debugging tools. In addition, *KnowledgePro* is object -oriented. In contrast to conventional programming, EASI's software developers use a mouse and *KnowledgePro*'s graphical interface to assemble objects into the knowledge base, rather than typing in lines of code. This allows them to focus on the *design* of the program and the *structuring* of the knowledge rather than on the semantics of the programming language. This also allows for easy modification of the program as customer requirements, and compliance standards, change.

5.1.3 Development Strategy: Rapid Prototyping and Phased Development

Using *KnowlegePro* allows us to bring prototypes, or product models, to customers very quickly. The continual feedback process generated by prototyping is designed to keep us responsive to our customers and ensure that they are driving the design of the product. By phasing the delivery of system modules to the beta sites we ensure that each "building block" of our program is meeting customer requirements. The following diagram illustrates this concept:

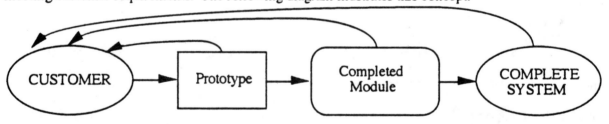

5.1.4 Development Status

Potential customers are currently reviewing the alpha version of *UL Solutions - 1950*. This alpha version is a prototype containing the overall design for the product and a fully-functional section of the UL 1950 manual (Section 4 - Physical Requirements). EASI's alpha sites are scheduled to complete these reviews by April 17, 1992. Customer feedback is currently being incorporated into *UL Solutions - 1950* in the form of requested features and modifications. The product beta version is

5 - 2

30

scheduled for release on June 1, 1992. Documentation for the product is occurring real-time and initial versions of the *UL Solutions - 1950* Users Manual are included with the alpha and beta versions.

5.2   Operations

EASI is developing multiple products for the product safety industry. The development schedule and status is illustrated below for 1991 through 1993. *UL Solutions - 1950* will require considerably more design effort than subsequent products. Once the product design is established, it is a relatively simple process to transfer this knowledge to the development of additional products.

Development Milestones: 1991 - 1993

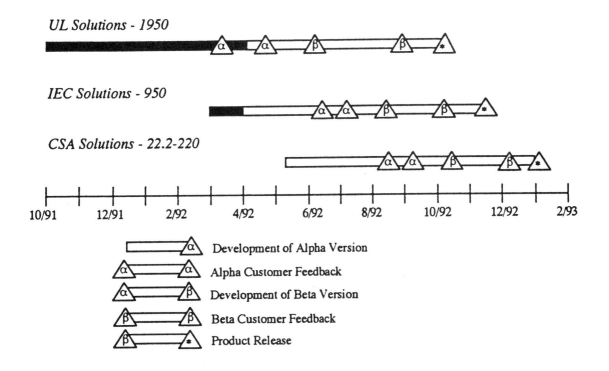

Schedule Assumptions:

1. EASI's first three products are based on nearly identical standards.

2. EASI is currently working with two software developers on initial product design and development.

Management and Organization

6.1 Key Management Personnel

The Expert Application Systems, Incorporated management team consists of individuals with key talents and experience. The team is supported by a highly qualified Board of Advisors. Each member of the management team serves a critical role in the development, marketing, and distribution of EASI's innovative products. The involvement of each team member in all aspects of EASI's business guarantees a continued focus on customer wants and needs. The management team will draw reduced salaries until EASI's revenues permit otherwise. See Appendix J for detailed management resumes.

Patricia M. Mack - President

Ms. Mack founded a software company that continues to operate successfully. Her experience includes profit and loss responsibility, risk management, and process testing within both established and start-up organizations. As President, Ms. Mack's responsibilities include positioning Expert Application Systems, Inc. as an industry leader and developing corporate strategies.

Margarita R. Ash - Vice President of Product Development

Ms. Ash has seven years of product research and development experience with IBM, including product certifications for the U.S., Japan, and Europe. As Vice President of Product Development, Ms. Ash is responsible for determining appropriate development tools and strategies that meet customer needs and the planning of software production.

David Beuerlein - Vice President of Finance and Operations

Mr. Beuerlein has a wide range of operational and financial systems experience with General Dynamics including financial forecasting in New Product Development. Mr. Beuerlein is responsible for financial planning and control and the implementation of software production and customer support systems.

Deborah Sallee - Vice President of Sales and Marketing

Ms. Sallee has over seven years of engineering experience with Powerex, Inc. and Harris Corporation and has worked extensively in the area of technical marketing. Ms. Sallee has also previously worked with UL compliance needs. Ms. Sallee's responsibilities include directing the planning and implementation of all sales and marketing efforts.

6 - 1

6.2 Board of Directors

EASI's Board of Directors provides critical input to the setting of corporate growth strategies and policies. Currently, the Board of Directors consists of the four members of the management team. Three additional board members will be selected by initial investor(s).

6.3 Board of Advisors

Expert Application Systems, Incorporated is supported by a team of thirteen highly qualified advisors who have extensive experience in areas including product safety compliance requirements, object-oriented expert systems software development, quality control, finance, and international business. Appendix K contains detailed information on the Board of Advisors. In addition, an important part of the success of EASI is a broad network of contacts. These individuals have provided valuable advice in their areas of expertise and continue to make themselves available to EASI.

6.4 Company Structure and Ownership

EASI's management team consists of four key individuals, and two software developers, as detailed in the organizational chart in Appendix L. Each member of EASI's management team has taken an equity position in the company, prior to the involvement of outside investors, as follows: Margarita Ash: 29%, Patricia Mack: 31%, David Beuerlein: 20%, and Deborah Sallee: 20%. An initial investment of $59,000 has been made and the management team has agreed to invest $53,000 of additional capital to fund EASI's aggressive marketing and initial product development.

6.5 Future Staffing

Within five years, EASI plans to grow to 160 employees. These employees are divided into Marketing (including sales and support), Research and Development, and Administration. Key among these new members will be the near term addition of an experienced financial officer as the focus of the financial responsibilities move away from financial projections and more heavily to financial control. To maximize customer support and sales potential, as the company expands Marketing becomes the focus of staffing expansion, with half of the employees working in this area by 1996 (see Appendix M). In addition, EASI will be working closely with the Standards experts at UL and will seek out product safety experts who are near retirement age and desire new challenges.

Financial Plan

EASI's financial planning is centered around rapid growth in order to penetrate the untapped market quickly. Twenty-two products will be introduced during the first five years addressing different compliance standards. Projections indicate that EASI will break-even in August, 1993. Detailed financial projections are included in Appendix N. Note that all projections are for fiscal years ending on September 30.

7.1 Sources and Uses of Funds

EASI is seeking investors to provide cash in exchange for equity positions in the corporation. This cash will be used to enable rapid growth in the untapped compliance software market. An initial investment of $59,000 has been made and the management team has agreed to invest $53,000 of additional capital to fund the development of *UL Solutions - 1950* and other initial products. Outside investors are sought to contribute $600,000. These funds will be used to market *UL Solutions - 1950* and develop subsequent products.

7.2 Income Statement

Pro Forma Income Statement	Fiscal Year Ending September 30				
	1993	1994	1995	1996	1997
Revenues					
Software Sales Revenue	$374,700	$3,166,580	$10,226,260	$18,998,640	$28,197,760
Subscription Revenue	$0	$50,500	$413,000	$1,586,500	$3,966,500
Interest	$8,872	$7,086	$19,116	$56,824	$133,739
Total Revenue	$383,572	$3,224,166	$10,658,376	$20,641,964	$32,297,999
Expenses					
Cost of Goods Sold	$21,750	$164,720	$560,770	$1,151,060	$1,933,660
Sales and Marketing Expenses	$425,855	$1,060,753	$3,191,778	$6,175,542	$9,649,278
Research and Development	$160,845	$643,416	$2,127,852	$4,117,028	$6,432,852
General and Administrative	$118,162	$535,302	$1,915,067	$3,705,325	$5,789,567
Total Expenses	$726,612	$2,404,191	$7,795,467	$15,148,955	$23,805,357
Profit (Loss) Before Income Tax	($343,040)	$819,975	$2,862,909	$5,493,009	$8,492,642
		30%	30%		
Income Tax	$0	$162,158	$973,389	$1,867,623	$2,887,498
Net Income	($343,040)	$657,817	$1,889,520	$3,625,386	$5,605,144

7 - 1

The revenue projections in the income statement reflect a 35% market penetration by year 5. Expenses are reduced during the first 6 months of development due to low salaries. Salaries are brought to competitive levels in the following months so EASI can attract and retain the quality personnel necessary to provide high levels of customer satisfaction. Following negotiations with investors, a stock option pool will be established to tie management compensation to overall company success.

7.3 Cash Flow Statement

Strict cash flow management will be critical to the success of the rapid growth plan for EASI. Low levels of inventory and utilization of the Austin Technology Incubator serve to minimize cash outlays during the product introduction. For planning purposes, purchases and operational expenses are assumed to be primarily cash transactions while sales are on accounts receivable. The capital investment of $600,000, in conjunction with steadily increasing revenues, ensure EASI's liquidity.

Pro Forma Cash Flow Statement	Fiscal Year Ending September 30				
	1993	1994	1995	1996	1997
Cash Flow From Operations					
Net Income	($343,040)	$657,817	$1,889,520	$3,625,386	$5,605,144
Depreciation	$950	$2,450	$8,100	$9,200	$20,800
Increase in Accts Receivable	($86,873)	($487,695)	(1,036,593)	(1,548,701)	(2,119,512)
Increases in Accts Payable	$6,833	$51,274	$87,711	$88,488	$121,824
Increases in Inventories	($5,320)	($22,530)	($47,900)	($57,277)	($78,280)
Net Cash from Operations	($427,450)	$201,315	$900,837	$2,107,896	$3,529,176
Cash Flow From Investing					
Purchase of Equipment	($6,000)	($15,000)	($27,000)	($48,000)	($64,000)
Net Cash from Investing	($6,000)	($15,000)	($27,000)	($48,000)	($64,000)
Cash Flow From Financing					
Equity	$600,000	$0	$0	$0	$0
Debt	$0	$0	$0	$0	$0
Net Cash from Financing	$600,000	$0	$0	$0	$0
Net Cash Flow	$166,550	$186,315	$873,837	$2,059,896	$3,465,176
Beginning Cash	$5,000	$171,550	$357,865	$1,231,702	$3,291,598
Ending Cash	$171,550	$357,865	$1,231,702	$3,291,598	$6,756,775

7 - 2

7.4 Balance Sheet

The balance sheet reflects the low overhead advantages of a software company such as EASI.

Projected Balance Sheet	Fiscal Year Ending September 30				
	1993	1994	1995	1996	1997
Assets					
Cash	$171,550	$357,865	$1,231,702	$3,291,598	$6,756,775
Accounts Receivable	$86,873	$574,568	$1,611,162	$3,159,863	$5,279,375
Inventory	$5,320	$27,850	$75,750	$133,027	$211,307
Total Current Assets	$263,743	$960,284	$2,918,614	$6,584,488	$12,247,456
Equipment at Cost	$11,030	$26,030	$53,030	$101,030	$165,030
(Accumulated Depreciation)	($2,350)	($4,800)	($12,900)	($51,124)	($122,354)
Book Value of Equipment	$8,680	$21,230	$40,130	$49,906	$42,676
Total Assets	$272,423	$981,514	$2,958,744	$6,634,394	$12,290,132
Liabilities & Equity					
Current Liabilities	$6,833	$58,107	$145,817	$234,305	$356,130
Total Liabilities	$6,833	$58,107	$145,817	$234,305	$356,130
Stock & Paid-in Capital	$712,000	$712,000	$712,000	$712,000	$712,000
Retained Earnings	($446,410)	$211,407	$2,100,927	$5,688,088	$11,222,002
Total Equity	$265,590	$923,407	$2,812,927	$6,400,088	$11,934,002
Total Liabilities and Equity	$272,423	$981,514	$2,958,744	$6,634,394	$12,290,132

7.5 The Investment Opportunity

The initial investor(s) will receive 25% equity in exchange for their cash infusion of $600,000. The remaining stock will be retained by the management team. After 5 years, the investor(s) will have the option to remain in the company or have EASI repurchase their shares at fair market value. Terms for repurchase will be negotiated with the investor(s). Based on a projected P/E = 15, the investors' share is projected to be worth $21 million, providing a 104% annual return on investment.

600,000

25 X 15,000,000

NI in y5
5.6 million
X 10 X 25% = 21 million

7 - 3

37

Appendix A

The Market

Worldwide Equipment Manufacturers Whose Products Are Covered by One or More UL Standards for Safety

Country	Equipment Manufacturers	Office Equipment Manufacturers (UL 1950)
Australia	3,499	1,027
Austria	1,211	0
Belguim	1,552	0
Brazil	9,515	0
Canada	5,425	187
China	67,342	174
Columbia	502	9
Costa Rica	204	13
Denmark	1,292	39
Finland	880	30
France	unknown	unknown
Germany	6,577	178
Greece	729	6
Hong Kong	6,880	101
Hungary	692	0
India	11,714	153
Ireland	570	40
Italy	5,426	74
Japan	82,341	4,670
Korea	8,847	196
Malaysia	567	8
Mexico	369	23
Netherlands	176	0
New Zealand	3,630	135
Norway	795	18
Peru	1,079	33
Phillipines	451	6
Poland	947	12
Russia	9,247	0
Spain	15,629	37
Sweden	1,668	59
Switzerland	1,390	23
United Kingdom	32,807	1,199
United States	45,000	5,700
Yugo	514	56
TOTALS	329,467	14,206

Worldwide Market Estimates

Market	# of Manufacturers	Percent of Manufacturers who Purchase	# of Standards Purchased (at $3,000 per program)	Estimated Total Market Potential	# of Updates Purchased (at $500 per standard)	Estimated Annual Update Market
Worldwide Standards	165,000 (330,000 X 50%)	60%	5	$1,485,000,000	5	$247,500,000
U.S. UL Standards	45,000	60%	5	$405,000,000	5	$67,500,000
U.S. UL 1950	5,700	60%	1	$10,260,000	1	$1,710,000

Domestic Equipment Manufacturers Whose Products are Covered by One or More UL Standards For Safety:

(Industries covered by UL 1950 are listed in boldface)

Industry	Manufacturers	
	Total	Large
Plastic Plumbing fixtures	350	40
Industrial valves	450	90
Valve/Pipe fittings	850	160
Lawn & Garden equiment	350	50
Power-driven handtools	350	45
Food Products Machinery	1000	90
Pumps & Pumping Machinery	900	120
Air & Gas Compressors	500	50
Indus/Commercial Fans/Blowers	1000	70
Electronic Computers	**1500**	**200**
Computer Storage Devices	**500**	**75**
Computer Terminals	**450**	**50**
Computer Peripheral Equip	**2500**	**150**
Calculating/Accting Equipment	**300**	**20**
Office Machines	**500**	**50**
Automatic Vending Machines	200	25
Commercial Laundry Equipment	200	15
Refrig/Heating Equipment	1550	275
Measuring/Dispensing Pumps	100	20
Service Industry Machinery	1950	130
Motors & Generators	1050	170
Relays & Industrial Controls	1700	150
Electrical Industrial apparatus	400	35
Household Cooking Equipment	150	40
Household Refrig/ Freezers	75	20
Household Laundry Equip	75	15

Industry	Manufacturers	
	Total	Large
Electric Housewares/Fans	400	75
Household Vacuum Cleaners	150	20
Household Appliances	200	25
Electric Lamps/Bulbs/Tubes	350	70
Current Carrying Wiring Devices	650	160
Resid Electric Lighting Fixtures	900	85
Comm Elec Lighting Fixtures	500	55
Lighting Equipment	700	55
Household Audio/Video Equip	1100	55
Telephone/Telegraph Equip	1200	170
Radio/TV Communication Equip	1850	190
Electronic Coils/Transformers	500	55
Electronic Connectors	250	55
Storage Batteries	300	65
Dry/Wet Primary Batteries	150	30
Electrical Equipment/Supplies	2050	170
Environmental Controls	750	70
Industrial Process Control Instr	1950	110
Electricity Measuring Instrument	1550	150
Measuring/Controlling Devices	1700	100
Printed Circuit Boards	1850	200
Electronic Components (n.e.c.)	3400	400
Dental Equipment/Supplies	950	25
X-ray Apparatus/Tubes	250	20
Electromedical Equipment	400	50
Other - marine,roofing and plastics	2000	
TOTAL	45,000	4,615

Appendix B

UL FAX: Questions Regarding UL 1950

UNDERWRITERS LABORATORIES INC.

c: SC - R. Olesen
   - K. Ravo
   - R. Myers

SANTA CLARA — October 30, 1991

TO: BOB WILLIAMS
            Corporate Manager — Standards
            Standards Department
            NORTHBROOK OFFICE

FROM: RANDI MYERS
            Standards Department

SUBJECT: Questions Regarding UL 1950

The following provides you with our response to your request for input regarding the UL 1950 questions noted in your facsimile dated October 29, 1991. Unfortunately, since we are not familiar with "Expert Software," we do not have any comments relative to those questions (7 — 10).

In formulating our comments, we contacted Kevin Ravo, Associate Managing Engineer and Designated Engineer for UL 1950, regarding the questions. We then coupled Kevin's input with our own experiences with UL 1950.

1) What are the most common complaints regarding UL Standard 1950?

a) The format of the standard has been described as not user-friendly. This comment has been expressed by UL clients familiar with the "standard" format for UL standards. The format of UL 1950 is of course based on the format used in IEC 950, from which UL 1950 was developed.

b) UL 1950 is physically difficult to manage. Perhaps a smaller font and more readable typestyle could be used to reduce the bulky size of the standard.

c) Some clients feel that the UL interpretation of the requirements in UL 1950 may differ from the interpretation made by other international sources.

2) In the 1950 seminar taught by UL, which areas of the standard receive the most attention?

B. Williams
October 30, 1991
Page 2

The requirements for (1) insulation and (2) creepage distances, clearances, and distances through insulation. Specifically, there is a great deal of time spent determining the type insulation (i.e. basic, supplementary, reinforced, or double) that is needed between parts and determining the required creepage distances and clearances. The remainder of the requirements in UL 1950 are considerably more straight forward and receive equal attention during the seminar.

3) How often does the 1950 standard change?

UL 1950 is revised in response to revisions of IEC 950, and when necessary to address requirements that will result in the addition of a deviation from IEC 950. Although there is continuous standards activity related to UL 1950, the standard has been revised only once, December 17, 1991, since its publication on March 15, 1989. We do, however, anticipate issuing a second edition of UL 1950 in 1992 to correlate with the publication of the second edition of IEC 950.

4) Is there a checklist for standard 1950 (and the other UL standards) which is followed and completed as a product is tested? Can EASI obtain copies of these checklists?

There is no such checklist for UL 1950. An internal training manual and the March 1988 proposed draft of UL 1950 are used as reference materials; however, the standard itself is used in a product evaluation.

5) Which part of the UL Listing and/or Recognition process do users have the most difficulty with?

In our experience, users do not have difficulty with interpreting UL 1950. There is, however, difficulty on the part of users in designing products to comply with the new/revised construction requirements in UL 1950. Many design engineers have become accustomed to the construction requirements in UL 114 and UL 478 (which will be superseded by UL 1950) and have not adapted to the requirements in UL 1950. As a result, many manufacturers rely on the use of the D3 deviations in UL 1950 which basically enable the manufacturer to comply with UL 1950 (UL 1950 using D3 deviations is very similar to the fifth edition of UL 478) but do not necessarily enable the manufacturer to comply with IEC 950.

6) How many product submittals are rejected once? twice? etc.? (Most, Few, None)

B. Williams
October 30, 1991
Page 3

Generally, manufacturers submit products to UL 1950 without electing to use the D3 deviations (less stringent requirements that enable the manufacturers to comply with UL 1950, but do not necessarily enable the manufacturers to comply with IEC 950). Approximately 95 % of these submittals do not receive Listing/Recognition.

These manufactures will then resubmit these same products for investigation to UL 1950 using the D3 deviations. In this second iteration, approximately 50 % of the resubmittals do not receive Listing/Recognition.

For those products that again did not receive Listing/Recognition using the D3 deviations in UL 1950, the manufacturers will generally choose to have the products investigated using UL 114 or UL 478, as applicable. It should be noted that the product categories for UL 114 and UL 478 will be eliminated March 15, 2000, at which time the Listings/Recognitions for any products under the categories will be withdrawn by UL. Therefore, the option to have products investigated using UL 114 or UL 478 will not be available after March 15, 2000.

◆   ◆   ◆   ◆   ◆

Please note that an EK project is scheduled to be initiated in 1992 by staff in the SC Electrical Department to develop a handbook for UL 1950. The handbook will describe the methods for conducting the tests in UL 1950, and will provide data sheets for recording test results and guidelines for interpreting test results. The handbook will be prepared on a data base, and will be distributed to staff at all UL offices and will be made available to UL clients.

In addition, as the SC office is the controlling office for UL 1950, the designated engineer needs to be involved in the technical review of any resulting UL-affiliated document relating to UL 1950.

If you need additional information, let us know.

Reviewed by:

RICHARD OLESEN
Associate Managing Engineer
Standards Department

williams.001/wp

Appendix C

Market Survey and Results

The survey included in this appendix was sent to 200 companies: 100 manufacturers in Texas and 100 nationwide. The intent was to perform a low-cost, preliminary estimate of market need, not to provide detailed statistical data. All 200 surveys were sent to companies believed to submit products for UL listing/recognition, with over 50% of these believed to comply with UL 1950. The surveys were simply addressed to the "Product Safety/Compliance Engineer" as company contacts were not available. Six surveys were returned due to incorrect addresses. Of the remaining 194 surveys, 54 were returned, representing a surprisingly high response rate of 28% (industry standard ~5%). The responses given in all returned surveys are summarized on page B-4.

Of the 54 respondents, 17 were from Texas and 37 were from out-of-state companies. Ninety-one percent of the companies submitted products to UL for listing/recognition; of those, 41 (83%) use UL Standard 1950:

Use of UL Standards

Half of the companies estimate that they submit 5 or more products per year, 34% submit 3-4 products per year, and 17% submit 1-2 products:

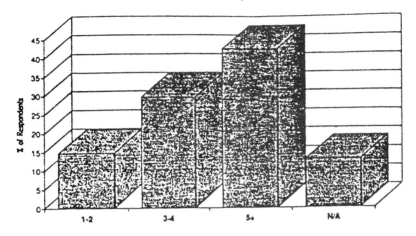

Product Submittals per Year

Most respondents had one or two individuals responsible for the UL submittal process at their companies (89%). These individuals spent an average of 142 hours on the submittal process per product. Sixty percent of the companies completed the UL process in less than 3 months. Thirty-eight percent took 3-6 months to receive the UL mark, and 1 respondent reported that it took over 6 months. Over half of the respondents (54%) estimated that a UL mark cost them $2,000-$5,000 and 41% reported the cost as over $5000 (including internal costs).

Question 9 was intended to determine the area of frustration companies experienced with UL submittals. Respondents were asked to rank the three areas with which they experienced the greatest difficulty. Results showed UL's response time, misinterpretation of standards, and compliance with those standards as the key problem areas. Thirty percent of respondents had hired a UL consultant at some point. Of these 27% had been dissatisfied with the consultant's performance.

Question 11 indicated significant potential for EASI's products. *Eighty percent* of the responding companies that submit products to UL are interested in an easy-to-use and accurate software package to assist them in the submittal process. These companies requested features such as a UL format report generator, a database of UL recognized components, on-line revision support, and glossary of definitions. The most popular computer platform used by respondent companies was the PC, followed by Macintosh and Unix-based systems.

UNDERWRITERS LABORATORIES (UL) SURVEY

Name _____
Title _____
Company _____
Address _____
City _____ State _____ Zip _____
Phone _____

1. Does your company submit products to UL for listing/recognition?   Yes____   No_____

2. If so, how many products are submitted on average in a year?
   1-2 product(s) _____   **3-4 products** ____   **5 or more** ____

3. Which UL standards does your company comply with? _____

4. How many employees are typically assigned to work on a UL submittal? _____ How many
hours does each of these employees typically spend on the submittal? _____

5 How long does it typically take to obtain UL listing/recognition for your products?
   Less than 3 mos. ____   **3-6 mos.** ____   **More than 6 mos.** _____

6. Do your products typically get accepted on the first submittal?
   Almost always ____   **About 50% of time** ____   **Rarely** _____

7. Estimate the total cost of obtaining UL listing/recognition for a new product, including application fees and
internal costs?   **Less than $2000** ____   **$2000-$5000** ____   **$5000+** ____

8. Overall, what is your level of satisfaction with the UL submittal process?
   Outstanding ____   **Acceptable** ____   **Fair** ____   **Unsatisfactory** ____

9. Rank the three most difficult aspects of the UL listing/recognition process for your company:
   ____ **Compliance with a particular UL specification**
   ____ **Frequent changes to UL standards**
   ____ **Misinterpretation of UL documents**
   ____ **Inability to contact UL personnel regarding questions**
   ____ **Slow response time by UL**
   ____ **Other** _____

10. Have your ever hired a UL consultant or product testing facility to assist you in the UL submittal
process? **Yes** ____ **No** ____ If so, which company, and were you satisfied with the outcome?
Company _____   **Satisfied** ____ **Dissatisfied** ____

11. Would you be interested in an easy-to-use, accurate computer-based software package to guide and assist
you in the UL submittal process? **Yes** ____ **No** ____ If so, what features would you like to see included in
such a package? _____

12. Do you currently use any of the following software packages to assist you in the UL submittal process?
   Word ____   **WordPerfect** ____   **Excel** ____   **Lotus 123** ____   **Other** _____

13. What is your company's standard computing platform?
   PC ____   **Macintosh** ____   **VM/MVS** ____   **Vax** ____   **Unix** ____   **Other**

**Please fold, staple or tape closed, and mail promptly. Thank you for your time in
completing this survey.**

Survey Response Key

#6.

    a: almost always
    50% about 50% of the time
    r: rarely

#8

    O: Outstanding
    A: Acceptable
    F: Fair
    U: Unsatisfactory

#9

    a: Compliance with a particular UL specification
    b: Freguent changes to UL standards
    c: Misinterpretation of UL documents
    d: Inability to contact UL personnel regarding questions
    e: Slow response time by UL
    f: Other

#12

    a: Word
    b: WordPerfect
    c: Excel
    d: Lotus 123
    f: Other

#13

    a: PC
    b: Macintosh
    c: VM/MVS
    d: Vax
    e: Unix
    f: Other

Survey No.	Company	1	2	3	4a	4b	5	6	7	8	9	10a	10c	11a	12	13
1	Compaq	Y	5+	1950	2-3	100-150	<3 mos	a	$5K+		cba	N		Y	b	a
2	ODS	Y	5+	1950	1		3-6 mos	a	$2K-$5K	A	e	N		Y		a
3	III Retail Systems	Y	3-4	1950	2	40	3-6 mos	c	$5K+	F	cbf	Y	S	Y	b	a
4	National Instruments	Y	1-2	1950	2	20	3-6 mos	b	<$2K	A	de	N		Y	e	abe
5	Commodore	Y	5+	1950	1	8	<3 mos	a	$2K-$5K	A	abe	N		Y	b	d
6	OMS Inc	Y	5+	1950	2	40	<3 mos	a	$2K-$5K	O	c	N		N	ace	ab
7	Grid System	Y	3-4	1950	1		<3 mos	a	$5K+	F	ceb	N		N	e	a
8	XYCOM	Y	5+	508	1	20-40	3-6 mos	a	$5K+	A	e	N		N		a
9	Dataproducts Inc	Y	5+	1950	1	35-50	<3 mos	a	$2K-$5K	A	eac	N		N	b	a
10	Qantel Corp	Y	3-4	1950	1	10	<3 mos	a	$2K-$5K	A	acb	N		N	de	a
11	Monroe Systems	Y	5+	1950	1		3-6 mos	a		A	cbe	N		N		a
12	Triad Sys.	Y	5+	1950	1	80	<3 mos	a	$5K+	F	cde	Y	D	N	e	ade
13	Leading Edge Prod	Y	3-4	1950			<3 mos	a		A	a	Y	S			a
14	Telxon Corp	Y	1-2	1950	1	40-60	3-6 mos	r	$5K+	F	caf	Y	S	Y	de	a
15	Apple	Y	5+	1950	1	200	<3 mos	a	$5K+	A	f	N		Y	ce	b
16	Itron	Y	3-4	1950	1	40	3-6 mos	a	$5K+	F	bac	N		Y	b	a
17	Modcomp	Y	3-4	1950	1	40	<3 mos	a	$2K-$5K	F	bce	N		Y	c	b
18	NCR	Y	3-4	1950	1	40-50	<3 mos	a	$2K-$5K	A	ea	N		Y	b	e
19	Printronix	Y	5+	1950	1-2	80-120	<3 mos	a	$2K-$5K	F	eta	N		Y	e	d
20	Evans & Sutherland	Y	3-4	1950	1-2	120-160	<3 mos	a	$5K+	F	eca	N		Y	abc	ab
21	Solbourne Computer	Y	3-4	1950	1	80	<3 mos	a	$5K+	U	e	Y	S	Y	e	e
22	Zenith Data System	Y	5+	1950	2-3	40	<3 mos	a	$2K-$5K	O		N		Y	a	a
23	US Integrated Tec	Y	5+	1950	1	6-10	<3 mos	a	$5K+	F	ef	Y	S	Y	b	a
24	General Building Corp	Y	1-2	1950	1	40	3-6 mos	a	$2K-$5K	A	f	N		Y	a	a
25	Encore Computer	Y	5+	1950	1-2	40-150	<3 mos	a		A		Y	S	Y	b	e
26	Tandem Computers	Y	5+	1950	1		<3 mos	a	$2K-$5K	F	cae	N		Y	a	a
27	Harris	Y	5+	1950	1	50-80	<3 mos	a	$8K	F	fca	N		Y		ef
28	Par Microsystems	Y		1950	1	40-80	3-6 mos	a	$5K+	A	fbe	N		Y	ace	a
29	AST Research	Y	1-2	1950	1	16	<3 mos	a	$2K-$5K	F	ec	N		Y	a	d
30	Dictaphone Corp	Y	5+	1950	1	24	3-6 mos	a	$2K-$5K	A	aef	N		Y	b	ad
31	Best Power Tech	Y	5+		3	160	<3 mos	a	$2K-$5K	A	fac	N		Y	b	a
32	Siemens Nixdorf	Y	3-4	1950	4	200	3-6 mos	a	$2K-$5K	F	ced	Y	S	Y	bd	a
33	NCR Corp	Y	3-4	1950	1	80-120	<3 mos	a	$2K-$5K	F	efd	N		Y	b	a
34	Lecroy Corp	Y	1-2	1244	1-2	30-80	3-6 mos	50%	$2K-$5K	F	eac	N		Y	ab	ad
35	Data General	Y	5+	1950	2	30	<3 mos	a	$5K+	U	ecf	N		Y	e	f
36	Arix	Y	1-2	1950	1	150-200	3-6 mos	a	$5K+	F	e	Y	S	Y	a	be
37	NEC Technology	Y	5+	1950	1	20	3-6 mos	a	$2K-$5K	A	ecf	Y	D	Y	e	a
38	Texas company	Y	3-4	1950	1	80	<3 mos	a	$2K-$5K	F	fc	N		N	b	a
39	Texas company	Y	1-2	1950	2	40	<3 mos	a	$2K-$5K	A	cba	Y		Y	e	a
40	PVI Industries	Y	3-4	mult.	1		<3 mos	a	$5K+	A	cae	N		N	bd	a
41	Delta-X Corp	Y	3-4		1	50	>6 mos	r	$5K+	F	aec	N		Y	bd	a
42	Andrew Corp	Y	5+	1950	2		<3 mos	50%	$2K-$5K	F	aed	Y	D	Y		abcd
43	Brinkmann	Y	3-4	mult.	2	40-60	3-6 mos		$2K-$5K	A	acd	N		Y	bd	a
44	Networth Inc	Y	3-4		1	80	3-6 mos	50%	$5K+	U	ead	Y	S	Y	b	a
45	Visentech	Y	5+				3-6 mos	a	$2K-$5K	A		N		Y		ae
46	Northern Telecom	Y	5+	mult.	3	300	3-6 mos	a	$5K+	A	bef	Y	S	Y	ac	abcde
47	Austron	Y	1-2	1459	1	80	<3 mos	50%	$2K-$5K	F	ef	N		Y		
48	FPS Computing	Y	3-4	1950	2	80	3-6 mos	a	$2K-$5K	A	efc	Y	S	Y	ac	b
49	IBM	Y	5+	1950	22	35	<3 mos	a	<$2K	A	ed	N		Y	abcde	a
50	Unisys Defense Sys	N														
51	Senco Products Inc	N														
52	Vitec	N														
53	Loral Space Info	N														
54	Computer Automation Inc	N														

Appendix D

Letters of Support

March 4, 1992

B.J. Poot
CompuAdd Corporation
12303 Technology Blvd.
Austin, Texas 78727

Debbie Sallee
Expert Application Systems, Inc.
8920 Business Park Drive
Austin, Texas 78759

Dear Debbie,

I am very pleased to participate in the development of UL
Solutions-1950. I have enclosed the Beta Test Site Agreement
signed by my manager, and his. Since this Agreement is with
CompuAdd, I felt this was necessary.

Congratulations to the Expert Applications Team: Debra Beard,
Patricia Mack, Margarita Ash, Mark Cooper, and J. Joseph
Loehr for winning the UT Moot Corp. competition. A job well
done! I only have met Debra, but do look forward to meeting
the rest of the team.

Product safety regulations scare most people, because the
terminology is so foreign, and they perceive it to be black
magic of sorts. This software tool you are developing, UL
Solutions-1950, is a wonderful idea and will be so beneficial
in the design process, where it is most needed. All
mechanical, electrical, design, and manufacturing personnel
can benefit from this tool. Mistakes in the design process,
can be very costly to a company. Most companies have too few
Engineers with this Regulatory knowledge, and when they are
absent, there is no where to turn for immediate answers.

Please feel free to contact me with any assistance I may
provide. I am including my business card which gives my phone
and fax numbers. Look forward to hearing from you.

Sincerely,

B.J. Poot

B.J. Poot

6504 Bridge Point Parkway • Austin, TX 78730-5039

Sales/Service (512) 794-0100
other calls (512) 338-9119
Fax (512) 794-8411

March 25, 1992

Expert Application System Inc.

In today's work place, the availability and ease of information is pertinent to the success of a business. In the area of safety compliance, improved information in the development stage can speed a product through release. I believe that your expert system may be a valuable tool in accomplishing these goals.
Compliance begins with proper selection of components. Having the Recognized Component Directory (yellow books) on disk will ease the selection process. Circuit design is crucial for safety approvals. The reader can make many interpretations from the specifications. An expert system would give users an advantage by providing access to simplified interpretations of these highly technical specifications. A check list would allow users to thoroughly test their products for compliance by guaranteeing that the users evaluate all areas of their design. Thus, the expert system combines concurrent engineering with speed of accessing information.
I look forward to using Expert Application Systems Inc.'s software and I hope it will improve National Instruments approval process.

Sincerely,

John A. Nagy
Compliance Coordinator

JAN/cr

Rochelle

March 23, 1992

Ms. Debbie Sallee
Vice President, Marketing and Sales
Expert Application Systems, Inc.
8920 Business Park Drive
Austin, Texas 78759

Dear Debbie:

Thank you for an impressive demonstration of the capabilities of EASI's Compliance Software for UL. It got me excited and convinced that this is a product whose time has come. The increasing complexity and the evolving nature of UL and FCC specifications is stifling the ability of small American manufacturers to bring innovative products to the market. In many cases, the costs of regulatory testing and certification exceed that of product development. I know this because we have just been through it at Rochelle. Small companies just can't afford the in-house staff for this expertise. Often, we are forced to turn to consultants to get the job done. EASI's Compliance Software Solutions promise to present the UL and FCC and CSA specifications in a convenient and simple format. This series will also keep us up to date on the latest changes in the specifications, so we are less likely to be surprised at the test stage. Thank you EASI. You are demystifying UL and FCC!

Please keep us posted on the progress of Compliance Software Solutions.

Sincerely,

Gilbert Amine
President and CEO

ROCHELLE COMMUNICATIONS INC. 4030-1 W. BRAKER LANE, AUSTIN, TX 78759 USA
(512) 794-0088   MCI MAIL 416-9820   FAX(512) 794-0908

56

Appendix E

Signed Beta Site Agreements

BETA TEST SITE AGREEMENT
FOR EXPERT APPLICATION SYSTEMS, INCORPORATED'S
UL SOLUTIONS - 1950

I. INTRODUCTION

This is a beta test site agreement between _CompuAdd Computer_ _Corporation_ ("Tester") and Expert Application Systems, Incorporated ("Owner" or "EASI") in which Tester agrees to test a software program known as *UL Solutions - Std. No. 1950* (Program) and to keep Owner informed of the test results.

II. PAYMENT

Tester agrees to accept as payment in full for his/her services a copy of the Program after final testing. Additionally, the Tester is entitled to a 50% discount on Program updates.

III. DUTIES

Tester agrees to use the Program and report any problems discovered to EASI. Program Report forms will be supplied to the Tester by EASI and are to be completed when any problem is discovered. To the best of the Tester's ability, the completed report is to include documentation of the events that led up to the problem in the Program and the manifestations of the problem.

IV. WARRANTY AND LIABILITY

Tester understands that the Program is experimental and that EASI does not warrant the performance of the Program in any way. All warranties regarding fitness and merchantability are hereby disclaimed. The Program is accepted AS IS, and owing to its experimental nature Tester is advised not to rely exclusively on the Program for any reason. In no event shall Expert Application Systems, Incorporated be liable for any damages arising out of the use or inability to use this software.

V. TRADE SECRETS

In accepting the Program, Tester recognizes that the Program is a trade secret belonging to EASI. Tester hereby agrees not to disclose any information relating to the Program (including its existence) to third parties without written permission from EASI.

VI. LIMITATIONS ON USE

Tester agrees not to sell or transfer any copies of the Program to third parties. Tester accepts the program under the condition that it is for Tester's use only and for no other purpose. Tester hereby acknowledges EASI's copyright in the Program.

_____ Signature

DIR. of ENGR., COMPUADD _____ Title & Company

3/4/92 _____ Date

_____ Signature

Project Design & Development Mgr. Title & Company

3-4-92   COMPUADD   Date

B. J. Post
Regulatory Agency Engineer
3-4-92

Patricia Mack
President, Expert Application Systems, Inc.
3/6/92

BETA TEST SITE AGREEMENT
FOR EXPERT APPLICATION SYSTEMS, INCORPORATED'S
UL SOLUTIONS - 1950

I. INTRODUCTION

This is a beta test site agreement between _National Instruments_ _____ ("Tester") and Expert Application Systems, Incorporated ("Owner" or "EASI") in which Tester agrees to test a software program known as *UL Solutions - Std. No. 1950* (Program) and to keep Owner informed of the test results.

II. PAYMENT

Tester agrees to accept as payment in full for his/her services a copy of the Program after final testing. Additionally, the Tester is entitled to a 50% discount on Program updates.

III. DUTIES

Tester agrees to use the Program and report any problems discovered to EASI. Program Report forms will be supplied to the Tester by EASI and are to be completed when any problem is discovered. To the best of the Tester's ability, the completed report is to include documentation of the events that led up to the problem in the Program and the manifestations of the problem.

IV. WARRANTY AND LIABILITY

Tester understands that the Program is experimental and that EASI does not warrant the performance of the Program in any way. All warranties regarding fitness and merchantability are hereby disclaimed. The Program is accepted AS IS, and owing to its experimental nature Tester is advised not to rely exclusively on the Program for any reason. In no event shall Expert Application Systems, Incorporated be liable for any damages arising out of the use or inability to use this software.

V. TRADE SECRETS

In accepting the Program, Tester recognizes that the Program is a trade secret belonging to EASI. Tester hereby agrees not to disclose any information relating to the Program (including its existence) to third parties without written permission from EASI.

VI. LIMITATIONS ON USE

Tester agrees not to sell or transfer any copies of the Program to third parties. Tester accepts the program under the condition that it is for Tester's use only and for no other purpose. Tester hereby acknowledges EASI's copyright in the Program.

John A. Nagy Signature
Compliance Coordinator Title & Company
_3-24-92_ Date

Michael J. Butler Signature
Mech. Engr. - National Instruments Title & Company
_3/24/92_ Date

Patricia Mock
President, Expert Application Systems, Inc.
_3/24/92_

61

BETA TEST SITE AGREEMENT
FOR EXPERT APPLICATION SYSTEMS, INCORPORATED'S
UL SOLUTIONS - 1950

I. INTRODUCTION

This is a beta test site agreement between _DeLL Computer Corporation_ ("Tester") and Expert Application Systems, Incorporated ("Owner" or "EASI") in which Tester agrees to test a software program known as *UL Solutions - Std. No. 1950* (Program) and to keep Owner informed of the test results.

II. PAYMENT

Tester agrees to accept as payment in full for his/her services a copy of the Program after final testing. Additionally, the Tester is entitled to a 50% discount on Program updates.

III. DUTIES

Tester agrees to use the Program and report any problems discovered to EASI. Program Report forms will be supplied to the Tester by EASI and are to be completed when any problem is discovered. To the best of the Tester's ability, the completed report is to include documentation of the events that led up to the problem in the Program and the manifestations of the problem.

IV. WARRANTY AND LIABILITY

Tester understands that the Program is experimental and that EASI does not warrant the performance of the Program in any way. All warranties regarding fitness and merchantability are hereby disclaimed. The Program is accepted AS IS, and owing to its experimental nature Tester is advised not to rely exclusively on the Program for any reason. In no event shall Expert Application Systems, Incorporated be liable for any damages arising out of the use or inability to use this software.

V. TRADE SECRETS

In accepting the Program, Tester recognizes that the Program is a trade secret belonging to EASI. Tester hereby agrees not to disclose any information relating to the Program (including its existence) to third parties without written permission from EASI.

VI. LIMITATIONS ON USE

Tester agrees not to sell or transfer any copies of the Program to third parties. Tester accepts the program under the condition that it is for Tester's use only and for no other purpose. Tester hereby acknowledges EASI's copyright in the Program.

_____ Signature
Engineering Services Mgr - Dell _ Title & Company
_____3 - 25 - 92_____ Date

_____ Signature
President, Expert Application... _ Title & Company
_____3/25/92_____ Date

Appendix F

Product Screen Samples

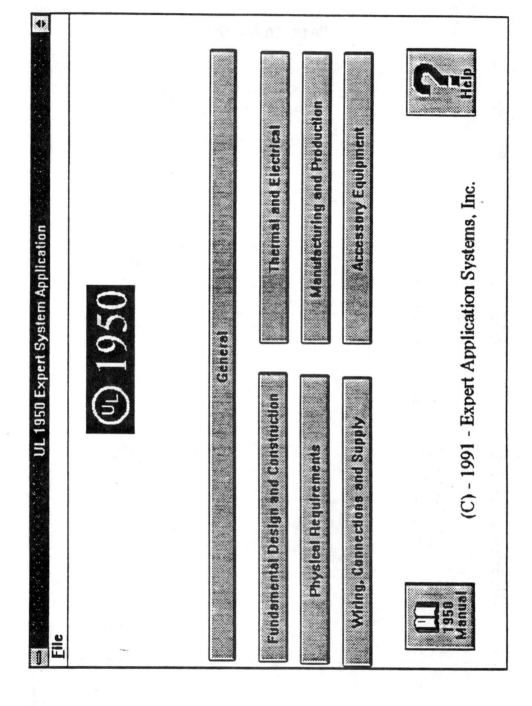

Section 4 - Physical Requirements

4.1 - Stability and Mechanical Hazards

4.2 - Mechanical Strength and Stress Relief

4.3 - Construction Details

4.4 - Resistance to Fire

Appendix G

Product Price List

EXPERT APPLICATION SYSTEMS, INC.
PRODUCT PRICE LIST

Item	Qty	Description	Each
1)	1	*UL - Solutions 1950.* Includes software, User's Manual, port access, and free Standards updates for one year after purchase of software. EASI's product comes with a 30-day moneyback guarantee.	$3,000
2)	1	Yearly update subscription after first year.	$ 500
3)	1	UL Recognized Component Directory on CD-ROM.	$ 300
		Discounted Price if purchased with *UL - Solutions 1950.*	$ 250

Note: Software supplied on either 3.5" or 5.25" disks.

Expert Application Systems, Inc.
8920 Business Park Drive
Austin, Texas 78749
Voice: (512) 794-9994
Fax: (512) 794-9997

Appendix H

Letter of Endorsement from UL

Note: This letter is included with the permission of Underwriters Laboratories.

333 Pfingsten Road
Northbrook Illinois 60062-209
708) 272-8800
FAX No. (708) 272-8129
MCI Mail No. 254-3343
Cable ULINC NORTHBROOK IL
Telex No. 6502543343

Underwriters Laboratories Inc.

November 7, 1991

Ms. Patricia Mack
President
Expert Application Systems, Inc.
2116 Guadalupe, Box 112
Austin, TX 78705

Dear Pat:

I enjoyed meeting with your team in our Northbrook, Illinois
offices recently and was very impressed by the work which you
have completed to date. I look forward to a strong relationship
between Underwriters Laboratories and Expert Application Systems,
Inc.

From the demonstration of your prototype system, I believe that
UL's clients will be extremely interested in your software and
that it has many benefits for them. In my experience, I have
found that any aid to walking a customer through the UL Standards
is "saleable." I want to assure you that you will continue to
have the full support of UL in your development efforts.
Specifically, I would like you to provide the following
information:

*   A proposal for UL to invest in your development efforts in
return for a share of the revenues. Depending on your proposal,
I can envision a relationship where UL and EASI share expenses
and revenues. UL can provide marketing and distribution muscle
to EASI. This arrangement could take the form of EASI providing
consulting services to UL.

*   A complete description of your products and services.

As you know from our discussions, many issues need to be explored
and resolved as the development and marketing of the software
continue. I discussed your software with Mike DeMartini,
Managing Engineer, Electrical, Santa Clara, and he has requested
copies of the documents noted above when available. As we
discussed, UL 1950 may need to be interpreted and Mike expressed
concerns over your interpretation and the use of UL's name.

As I noted in our recent telephone discussion, this letter shall
not be considered as binding upon UL to purchase any products or
services from EASI. This letter is not a contract or letter of
intent and should not be used to obtain financial support from
investors.

Although my schedule does not permit me to be in Austin during EASI's upcoming presentations, I am very excited about continuing to improve our relationship and look forward to receiving your proposals.

Sincerely,

Robert A. Williams
Corporate Manager of Standards
Underwriters Laboratories Inc.

Appendix I

Cost-Benefit Analysis

COST-BENEFIT ANALYSIS
(A Value-added Approach to Pricing)

Facts:

1) Our survey results indicate that manufacturers spend 180 man-hours per product to obtain UL approval.

2) The average engineer's salary (non-management) is $45,000. Benefits and taxes usually double this number. Therefore, the cost associated with one average engineering man-hour is $42.

3) Our survey results and direct customer feedback indicate that the cost of a typical UL product submittal averages between $3,000 and $10,000.

4) Changes/reworks to the initial submittal increase manpower costs for manufacturers.

5) UL resubmittal costs begin at $2,000.

6) UL estimates that 95% of initial submittals to UL 1950 require changes.

7) Our survey results show that over 80% of manufacturers submit more than 3 products per year to for product recognition.

8) EASI's initial product, *UL Solutions - 1950*, will be marketed at a price of $3,000 per copy and we expect future products to be similarly priced, on average. Standards updates to be used with EASI's software will be available to customers on a subscription basis. The software program, User's Manual, and a one-year subscription to updates of the standard for which a particular program is designed will be included in the initial purchase price. A subscription for updates to the standard in subsequent years will be priced at $500 per standard per year.

Assumptions:

1) Information Handling Services (IHS) advertise that their microform services boost productivity by 20%. It is estimated that EASI's software reduces the man-hours required in the submittal process by 20%.

2) It is estimated that EASI's software eliminates the need for a second submittal on 50% of products (50% x 3 products = 1.5 products).

SUMMARY:

Man-hour savings:
3.0* products/yr x (180 man-hours x 20%) x $42 $4,536

Resubmittal costs savings:
1.5 products/year x $2,000 x 95% $2,850

TOTAL COST SAVINGS $7,386

*Three is a conservative estimate of the number of products submitted per year by a manufacturer.

CONCLUSION:

EASI anticipates that our initial product will save our customers in excess of $7,000 per year. Our customers retain over 50% of these cost savings.

Appendix J

Management Team Resumes

Margarita R. Ash

8222 Bent Tree Rd. #236
Austin, Texas 78759
(512) 345 - 4016

EXPERIENCE

9/91 - Present   **Expert Application Systems, Inc.**   Austin, TX
Vice President of Research and Development
- Determining appropriate development tools and strategies that meet customer wants and
   needs and facilitate rapid time-to-market for the company's products.
- Planning software production strategies for the company.

5/91 - 12/91   **Austin Technology Incubator**   Austin, TX
Graduate Research Assistant
- Served as a consultant to start-up technology firms, assisting with market research,
   business plans, financing, and other business activities.

4/90 - 1/92   **Self-Employed Development Consultant**   Wilmington, DE and Austin, TX
- Designed product development solutions to facilitate rapid time-to-market. Most
   solutions were implemented through software interfaces between the departments
   involved. Clients included DuPont, UniSys, Hylunia International, and IBM.

7/83 - 4/90   **IBM Corporation**
Design Engineer - Gallium Arsenide Circuit Design and Test   East Fishkill, NY
- Managed the design and test effort for a set of GaAs fiber-optic communication chips.
   Responsible for transferring pertinent technologies from the IBM Research Labs in
   Zurich, Switzerland and Yorktown Heights, NY to development.
Scientific Engineering Processor Development   Kingston, NY
- Developed logic chips for the Vector Processor of the IBM 3090 Mainframe.
   Coordinated the interfaces of the chips and coordination of team design, resulting in
   the reduction of the planned design time.
Adapter Engineering   Boulder, CO
- Designed and tested microprocessor code and custom hardware for the hard-drive
   controller of the IBM PS/2 model 50. Worked on developing this product with
   engineers in the Fujisawa (Yasu), IBM Japan laboratory.
Future Optical Technology   Boulder, CO
- Designed and tested a low noise detection system for a magneto-optic drive.

EDUCATION

The University of Texas at Austin   Austin, Texas
Master of Business Administration, May 1992
Technology Management

Georgia Institute of Technology   Atlanta, GA
Master of Science in Electrical Engineering, June 1983
Bachelor of Science in Electrical Engineering, June 1982

HONORS, SKILLS AND ACTIVITIES

- IBM SEPD Award 1987 - recognition for significant contributions to the Scientific
   Engineering Processor Development Effort
- President - Innovative Technology Management Association, 1991
- Vice President - Information Systems Management Association, 1990
- Institute of Electrical and Electronic Engineers
- Bilingual - Spanish/English

David L. Beuerlein
7600 Wood Hollow Drive, #914
Austin, Texas 78731
(512) 795-8204

Experience
January 1992
to Present

Expert Application Systems, Inc.   Austin, TX
Vice-President of Finance and Operations
- Responsible for all financial aspects of company including development of financial statements for business plan.
- Identify and review potential suppliers based on price and quality.
- Implement software production and customer support systems.

August 1985 -
August 1991

General Dynamics   Fort Worth, TX
Program Manager of New High Speed Aircraft Programs, 1989-1991.
Experienced in financial planning, program management, technical marketing and program sales, and corporate strategic planning.
- Managed $1.2M market development program and feasibility study.
- Evaluated capital expenditures, development costs, payback periods, and performed risk analysis to support long term corporate planning.
- Part of task force to evaluate expansion into the commercial aircraft business.
- Represented over 300 engineers on board which provided guidance to upper management in employee relations matters.
- Initiated new marketing plan resulting in a broadened $8M customer base.

Aircraft Configuration Designer, 1985-1989.
- Designed aircraft concepts for numerous advanced aircraft programs and presented results to corporate management and customers.
- Extensive experience with workstation based computer aided design systems.

Education

The University of Texas at Austin   May 1993
Master of Business Administration
Concentration in Finance and Accounting

The University of Texas at Arlington   August 1990
Master of Science in Aerospace Engineering

The University of Kansas   May 1985
Bachelor of Science in Aerospace Engineering
Graduated with Distinction

Honors
- Winner of the 1992 Deloitte & Touche Consulting Challenge
- Named Longhorn Scholar by Graduate School of Business, 1991
- Hilltopper Award for campus and community activities, 1985

Activities
- President of the Graduate Consulting Group, Spring 1992
- Toastmasters
- Innovative Technology Management Association
- MBA Marketing Network

Patricia M. Mack

3631 Peregrine Falcon Drive
Austin, Texas 78746
(512) 327 - 0988

EXPERIENCE

9/91 - Present

Expert Application Systems, Inc. Austin, Texas
President
- Developing corporate strategies.
- Positioning company as the industry leader in the development of application software systems for the product safety compliance market.
- Securing capital for company growth.
- Developing strategic alliances to enhance the company's competitive position.

6/91 - 12/91

Austin Technology Incubator Austin, Texas
Research Associate
- Reviewed business plans for technology-based firms, assisted in developing a marketing plan for a manufacturing application, and participated in entrepreneurial workshops.

1/90 - 1/92

FINLE Technologies Plano, Texas
Founder and President
- Developed company strategy and industry image.
- Positioned company as the leader in lithography simulation and consulting.
- Hired employees and handled all financial decisions.
- Explored the market in order to secure customers and market share.

National Security Agency Fort Meade, Maryland

9/89 - 8/90

Project Manager
- Managed a $2,500,000 focused ion beam research and development effort.
- Directed team of four senior level engineers.
- Spearheaded effort to match employees with job assignments to increase productivity.

9/87 - 8/89

Lithography Process Engineer
- Directed a $1,000,000 state-of-the-art lithography operation.
- Served as a technical advisor to assure quality control of integrated circuit production.
- Presented critical strategy and process information to upper management.

8/85 - 8/87

Project Engineer
- Designed experiments to evaluate potential product enhancements.
- Assisted in effort to scale down the dimensions of semiconductor features.

EDUCATION

The University of Texas at Austin   Austin, Texas
Master of Business Administration, December 1991
Master of Science in Manufacturing Systems Engineering, December 1991

The University of Maryland   College Park, Maryland
Master of Science in Electrical Engineering, August 1988

Drexel University   Philadelphia, Pennsylvania
Bachelor of Science in Electrical Engineering, June 1985

HONORS AND ACTIVITIES

- Chairperson of the Board of Directors for FINLE Technologies
- Toastmasters International
- Innovative Technology Management Society

Deborah L. Sallee

7508 Mifflin Kenedy Terrace
Austin, Texas 78749
(512) 288-0309

EXPERIENCE

1/92 - Present	**Expert Application Systems, Inc.**	Austin, Texas

Vice President of Sales and Marketing
- Plan and implement all sales and marketing efforts to meet strategic objectives
- Utilize beta site feedback to enhance product development and promotion

1/92 - Present	**The University of Texas at Austin**	Austin, Texas

Research Assistant
- Research current market pricing and distribution methods

6/89 - 9/90	**Powerex, Inc.**	Youngwood, PA

Joint Venture: Mitsubishi, GE, and Westinghouse
Product Specialist
- Marketed five technical product lines with $4.5 million in sales. Increased sales a minimum of 25% on each product line while maintaining current margins.
- Worked with the product safety engineer to obtain UL listing of components
- Led a multi-functional team to increase production levels and reduce cycle time
- which resulted in a 100% increase in sales within that product line
- Negotiated product prices and provided price strategy support for market planning and forecasting
- Designed and wrote a professional brochure to introduce a new product line
- Initiated and implemented a formalized sampling system which improved response time and generated customer profiles
- Trained outside sales force through presentations and written bulletins

6/83 - 8/88	**Harris Corporation**	Melbourne, FL

Senior Engineer - Electrical
- Managed and completed a $200,000 project ahead of schedule and 20% below budget
- Presented product technical capabilities at military trade shows
- Recommended staffing and generated cost estimates for government bids
- Interviewed and recommended prospective engineers
- Trained and mentored new engineers for two years
- Designed state-of-the-art digital circuits to meet customer needs
- Presented and defended documentation of technical designs
- Developed extensive test software to validate circuit performance
- Designed software and hardware for a control and display system

---

EDUCATION

The University of Texas at Austin	August 1993

Master of Business Administration
Concentration in Marketing and Technology Management

The University of Virginia	May 1983

Bachelor of Science in Electrical Engineering

ACTIVITIES

- Finalist - Marketing Challenge, September 1991
- VP of Placement - Innovative Technology Management Association
- Member - Marketing Network, Students for Students Scholarship Committee

Appendix K

Board of Advisors

Expert Application Systems, Incorporated
Board of Advisors

Mr. Angelos Angelou is Vice President of Economic Development for the Greater Austin Chamber of Commerce and has extensive experience in marketing, new business development, strategic planning, forecasting, international trade, industrial analysis, and regional economics.

Dr. Rayan Bagchi is Chairman of the Department of Management at The University of Texas at Austin, serves on the Austin Quality Council, and has comprehensive experience in the areas of Total Quality Management, quality assurance, and quality control.

Mr. Miguel Bernardini is President of ECB S.A., a computer manufacturer based in Madrid, Spain, and has 23 years experience in product development with Tektronix and Hewlett Packard for the computer-aided testing industry. He will provide feedback on EASI's products designed for the European Community.

Mr. Scott Collier is a venture capitalist with Capital Southwest Corporation in Dallas, Texas and sits on the Board of Directors of a software firm with revenues in excess of $1 million. Mr. Collier's experience includes consulting to technical start-up ventures regarding business planning and early stage operations.

Mr. Lee Cooke is President of Habitek International and former Mayor of Austin, Texas. Mr. Cooke's extensive professional network will provide EASI with access to resources including market research, manufacturing organizations, and key business people.

Mr. Mark Cooper is a consultant to technology-based start-up companies Mr. Cooper has had extensive Information Systems development experience with Andersen Consulting and IBM and will assist in the research and development efforts of EASI.

Mr. Robert Dolson is a Certified Public Accountant in private practice in Austin, Texas. Mr. Dolson has over 17 years of experience in the design and implementation of management information systems and will assist EASI in designing systems that will accommodate the company's expected growth.

Mr. John Fabac is international product safety manager, with 32 years experience, at IBM. He will guide EASI in its product development and will provide the company contacts within the Computer and Business Equipment Manufacturers' Association (CBEMA).

Dr. Ronald Lee is a Professor in the Information Systems Management program at The University of Texas at Austin. Dr. Lee is an experienced expert systems software developer and has created expert systems shells including *XS*. He is also involved with international electronic document interchange (EDI).

Mr. Paul Schultze is President of Access Europe, an international engineering consulting firm. Previously Vice-President of TUV Rheinland, he has over sixteen years of domestic and international product safety experience. Mr. Schultze has experience with compliance issues for European Directives and Standards, technical marketing, product design consulting, and quality assurance.

Dr. Sim Sitkin is a Professor in the Department of Management at The University of Texas at Austin. Dr. Sitkin has extensive knowledge in organizational structure and behavior and will assist in guiding the future personnel growth of EASI.

Mr. Robert Williams is Corporate Manager of Standards at Underwriters Laboratories (UL). Mr. Williams has over 18 years experience with UL and manages the development, printing, and distribution of all UL Standards. He will provide EASI with the necessary contacts in, and resources from, UL.

Mr. Peter Winstead is a lawyer at the firm Winstead, Sechrest & Minick in Austin, Texas. This firm handles legal issues for Dell Computer Corporation and has been involved with the company since its start-up phase. Mr. Winstead will guide EASI in terms of liability issues and contract negotiations.

Appendix L

Organizational Chart

Expert Application Systems, Inc. Organizational Chart

```
                        ┌──────────────────┐
                        │  Patricia Mack   │
                        │    President     │
                        └──────────────────┘
           ┌───────────────────┼───────────────────┐
┌──────────────────┐  ┌──────────────────┐  ┌──────────────────┐
│ David Beuerlein  │  │  Margarita Ash   │  │  Deborah Sallee  │
│  Vice President  │  │  Vice President  │  │  Vice President  │
│Finance and       │  │Product           │  │Sales and         │
│Operations        │  │Development       │  │Marketing         │
└──────────────────┘  └──────────────────┘  └──────────────────┘
              ┌──────────────┴──────────────┐
      ┌──────────────────┐          ┌──────────────────┐
      │    Hua Guo       │          │    Rosa Hoh      │
      │Software Developer│          │Software Developer│
      └──────────────────┘          └──────────────────┘
```

Appendix M

Future Staffing

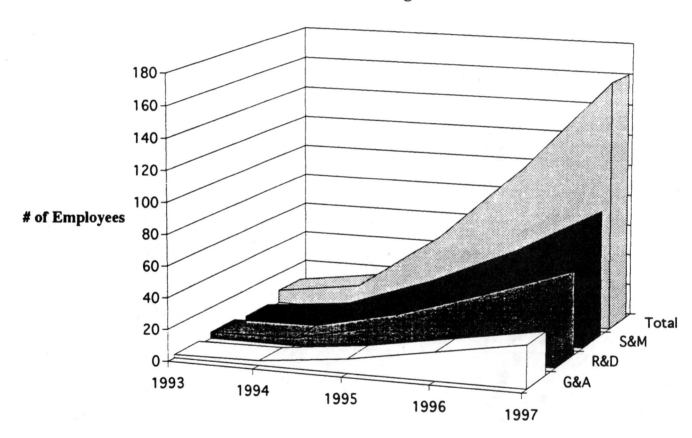

Future Staffing

Appendix N

Detailed Financial Projections

Assumptions For Financial Projections

1. **Market**

   35% market share will be reached in five years and the market will grow annually by 10%.

2. **Revenue**

   The standard purchase price is $3,000, although each new product will be discounted to $2,000 during the first 6 months of its introduction. One free year subscription will be included in the original purchase, further subscriptions will be priced at $500 per year. 70% of those who buy originally will subscribe after the first year, and 90% of the subscribers will renew their subscriptions each year.

3. **Product Cost**

   COGS is $150 per unit: $70 royalties, $30 material, $10 labor, and $40 overhead.

4. **Accounts Payable and Receivable**

   Accounts payable are assumed to be paid 80% in cash, and 20% in 30 days. Sales are assumed to be 25% in cash, 45% on account received within 30 days, 20% in 60 days, and 8% in 90 days. Losses are 2%.

5. **Marketing**

   Sales and Marketing expenses (which include support) will move to 30%, 5% below the industry norm. This is due to primary reliance on direct mail orders resulting in reduced sales force costs

6. **General and Administrative Costs**

   G & A expenses will converge to 18% of revenues, 3% lower than the industry standard. During the initial phase of operation, the business has located in the Austin Technology Incubator and utilizes its services to maintain these costs.

7. **Research and Development**

   R & D expenses will converge to 20%, 3% higher than the industry standard, 17%. This reflects the rapid growth rate and pace of new product introduction forecast for EASI.

8. **Salaries and Wages**

   The founders' salary will grow from $1,250 to $2,500 per month during the first year. Additional compensation will be in the form of stock options.

9. **Travel**

   During the first year, travel expenses average $1,000 per month for R&D, $3,375 per month for Sales and Marketing, and $3,000 per month for G&A.

10. **Banking Services**

    The corporate banking services have been established at Horizon Savings Association in Austin. The projected monthly fee will average $50 over the first year.

11. **Product Liability Insurance**

    Based on an estimate from Bankers Trust, Product Liability Insurance expense is assumed to be 1% of sales revenue.

Pro Forma Income Statements

		Fiscal Year Ending September 30			
	1993	1994	1995	1996	1997
Revenues					
Software Sales Revenue	$374,700	$3,166,580	$10,226,260	$18,998,640	$28,197,760
Subscription Revenue	$0	$50,500	$413,000	$1,586,500	$3,966,500
Interest	$8,872	$7,086	$19,116	$56,824	$133,739
Other					
Total Revenue	$383,572	$3,224,166	$10,658,376	$20,641,964	$32,297,999
Expenses					
Cost of Goods Sold	$21,750	$164,720	$560,770	$1,151,060	$1,933,660
Sales and Marketing Expenses	$425,855	$1,060,753	$3,191,778	$6,175,542	$9,649,278
Research and Development	$160,845	$643,416	$2,127,852	$4,117,028	$6,432,852
General and Administrative	$118,162	$535,302	$1,915,067	$3,705,325	$5,789,567
Total Expenses	$726,612	$2,404,191	$7,795,467	$15,148,955	$23,805,357
Profit (Loss) Before Income Tax	($343,040)	$819,975	$2,862,909	$5,493,009	$8,492,642
Income Tax	$0	$162,158	$973,389	$1,867,623	$2,887,498
Net Income	($343,040)	$657,817	$1,889,520	$3,625,386	$5,605,144

Detail shown in
EVS monthly salaries & Payroll in App. X.
Salary raises at 10% /yr.
Percent of salaries pd = 120%
Product mgrs begin in Q2
Salespeople begin in Q2 (2) and Q3 (2)

Proj & Cost
B/S
CFS Assump

91

Income Statement

FY 1993

	Oct-92	Nov-92	Dec-92	Jan-93	Feb-93	Mar-93	Apr-93	May-93	Jun-93	Jul-93	Aug-93	Sep-93	FY 1993
Revenues													
Software Sales Revenue	2,260	5,260	6,520	13,520	14,780	20,780	31,040	38,300	48,300	50,300	65,560	78,080	374,700
Subscription Revenue	0	0	0	0	0	0	0	0	0	0	0	0	0
Interest													0
Other	13	1,350	1,205	1,095	982	859	738	638	568	519	472	434	8,872
Total Revenue	2,273	6,610	7,725	14,615	15,762	21,639	31,778	38,938	48,868	50,819	66,032	78,514	383,572
Expenses													
Cost of Goods Sold	150	300	450	900	1,050	1,500	1,950	2,400	2,700	2,850	3,450	4,050	21,750
Sales and Marketing	54,178	39,038	27,008	31,578	36,002	38,172	33,132	29,202	29,262	36,332	38,492	33,462	425,855
Research & Development	11,505	11,555	11,555	11,555	14,334	14,334	14,334	14,334	14,334	14,334	14,334	14,334	160,845
General & Administrative	7,596	7,626	7,659	7,749	10,560	10,640	10,763	10,856	11,026	11,066	11,238	11,383	118,162
Total Expenses	73,429	58,519	46,672	51,782	61,946	64,646	60,179	56,792	57,322	64,582	67,514	63,229	726,612
Pre-Tax Profit (Loss)	(71,157)	(51,910)	(38,947)	(37,167)	(46,184)	(43,007)	(28,401)	(17,853)	(8,454)	(13,763)	(1,482)	15,285	(343,040)
Income Tax	0	0	0	0	0	0	0	0	0	0	0	0	0
Net Income	(71,157)	(51,910)	(38,947)	(37,167)	(46,184)	(43,007)	(28,401)	(17,853)	(8,454)	(13,763)	(1,482)	15,285	(343,040)

Income Statement
FY 1994

	Oct-93	Nov-93	Dec-93	Jan-94	Feb-94	Mar-94	Apr-94	May-94	Jun-94	Jul-94	Aug-94	Sep-94	FY 1994
Revenues													
Software Sales Revenue	105,860	132,120	151,900	174,160	196,940	228,200	264,980	309,020	336,540	375,320	417,360	474,180	3,166,580
Subscription Revenue	500	500	1,000	2,000	2,500	3,500	4,500	5,500	6,500	6,500	8,000	9,500	50,500
Interest	429	411	417	444	476	531	589	662	721	768	793	844	7,086
Other													
Total Revenue	106,789	133,031	153,317	176,604	199,916	232,231	270,069	315,182	343,761	382,588	426,153	484,524	3,224,166
Expenses													
Cost of Goods Sold	5,320	6,670	7,790	9,130	10,400	12,190	13,830	16,070	17,560	19,360	21,670	24,730	164,720
Sales and Marketing	40,417	50,396	55,044	63,418	67,810	78,778	86,234	100,646	109,773	122,182	136,115	149,941	1,060,753
Research & Development	21,272	26,524	30,580	35,232	39,888	46,340	53,896	62,904	68,608	76,364	85,072	96,736	643,416
General & Administrative	14,890	19,230	22,935	27,305	31,910	38,231	45,812	40,888	61,747	68,728	76,565	87,062	535,302
Total Expenses	81,899	102,820	116,349	135,084	150,008	175,539	199,771	220,508	257,688	286,634	319,422	358,469	2,404,191
Pre-Tax Profit (Loss)	24,890	30,212	36,968	41,520	49,908	56,692	70,298	94,674	86,073	95,954	106,731	126,055	819,975
Income Tax	0	0	0	0	0	0	0	21,121	29,265	32,624	36,289	42,859	162,158
Net Income	24,890	30,212	36,968	41,520	49,908	56,692	70,298	73,552	56,808	63,330	70,443	83,196	657,817

Pro Forma Cash Flow Statement	Fiscal Year Ending September 30				
	1993	1994	1995	1996	1997
Cash Flow From Operations					
Net Income	($343,040)	$657,817	$1,889,520	$3,625,386	$5,605,144
Depreciation	$950	$2,450	$8,100	$9,200	$20,800
Increase in Accts Receivable	($86,873)	($487,695)	($1,036,593)	($1,548,701)	($2,119,512)
Increases in Accts Payable	$6,833	$51,274	$87,711	$88,488	$121,824
Increases in Inventories	($5,320)	($22,530)	($47,900)	($57,277)	($78,280)
Net Cash from Operations	($427,450)	$201,315	$900,837	$2,107,896	$3,529,176
Cash Flow From Investing					
Purchase of Equipment	($6,000)	($15,000)	($27,000)	($48,000)	($64,000)
Net Cash from Investing	($6,000)	($15,000)	($27,000)	($48,000)	($64,000)
Cash Flow From Financing					
Equity	$600,000	$0	$0	$0	$0
Debt	$0	$0	$0	$0	$0
Net Cash from Financing	$600,000	$0	$0	$0	$0
Net Cash Flow	$166,550	$186,315	$873,837	$2,059,896	$3,465,176
Beginning Cash	$5,000	$171,550	$357,865	$1,231,702	$3,291,598
Ending Cash	$171,550	$357,865	$1,231,702	$3,291,598	$6,756,775

94

Income Statement
FY 1995

	Oct-94	Nov-94	Dec-94	Jan-95	Feb-95	Mar-95	Apr-95	May-95	Jun-95	Jul-95	Aug-95	Sep-95	FY 1995
Revenues													
Software Sales Revenue	528,220	589,260	649,300	697,080	763,120	819,900	879,980	947,280	991,320	1,057,880	1,121,180	1,181,740	10,226,260
Subscription Revenue	12,500	16,000	19,000	22,500	25,500	30,500	35,000	40,500	44,500	49,000	55,000	63,000	413,000
Interest	895	905	967	1,075	1,219	1,372	1,549	1,726	1,944	2,208	2,483	2,775	19,116
Other													
Total Revenue	541,615	606,165	669,267	720,655	789,839	851,772	916,529	989,506	1,037,764	1,109,088	1,178,663	1,247,515	10,658,376
Expenses													
Cost of Goods Sold	27,850	31,190	34,610	37,500	41,070	44,620	48,250	52,170	54,980	58,910	62,750	66,870	560,770
Sales and Marketing	162,216	181,578	200,490	215,874	236,586	255,120	274,494	296,334	310,746	332,064	352,854	373,422	3,191,778
Research & Development	108,144	121,052	133,660	143,916	157,724	170,080	182,996	197,556	207,164	221,376	235,236	248,948	2,127,852
General & Administrative	97,330	108,947	120,294	129,524	141,952	153,072	164,696	177,800	186,448	199,238	211,712	224,053	1,915,067
Total Expenses	395,540	442,767	489,054	526,814	577,332	622,892	670,436	723,860	759,338	811,588	862,552	913,293	7,795,467
Pre-Tax Profit (Loss)	146,075	163,398	180,213	193,841	212,507	228,880	246,092	265,645	278,426	297,500	316,110	334,222	2,862,909
Income Tax	49,666	55,555	61,272	65,906	72,252	77,819	83,671	90,319	94,665	101,150	107,477	113,635	973,389
Net Income	96,410	107,843	118,941	127,935	140,255	151,060	162,421	175,326	183,761	196,350	208,633	220,586	1,889,520

Income Statement
FY 1996 & 1997

	Q1	Q2	Q3	Q4	FY 1996	Q1	Q2	Q3	Q4	FY 1997
Revenues										
Software Sales Revenue	3,936,760	4,477,240	5,024,100	5,560,540	$18,998,640	6,126,320	6,725,500	7,330,800	8,015,140	$28,197,760
Subscription Revenue	247,500	339,000	445,000	555,000	$1,586,500	712,000	885,500	1,082,500	1,286,500	$3,966,500
Interest	9,238	12,162	15,635	19,790	$56,824	24,687	29,950	36,086	43,015	$133,739
Other										
Total Revenue	4,193,498	4,828,402	5,484,735	6,135,330	$20,641,964	6,863,007	7,640,950	8,449,386	9,344,655	$32,297,999
Expenses										
Cost of Goods Sold	227,250	266,460	307,850	349,500	$1,151,060	399,080	452,770	509,900	571,910	$1,933,660
Marketing & Sales	1,255,278	1,444,872	1,640,730	1,834,662	$6,175,542	2,051,496	2,283,300	2,523,990	2,790,492	$9,649,278
R & D	836,852	963,248	1,093,820	1,223,108	$4,117,028	1,367,664	1,522,200	1,682,660	1,860,328	$6,432,852
G & A	753,167	866,923	984,438	1,100,797	$3,705,325	1,230,898	1,369,980	1,514,394	1,674,295	$5,789,567
Total Expenses	3,072,547	3,541,503	4,026,838	4,508,067	$15,148,955	5,049,138	5,628,250	6,230,944	6,897,025	$23,805,357
Pre-Tax Profit (Loss)	1,120,951	1,286,898	1,457,897	1,627,263	$5,493,009	1,813,869	2,012,700	2,218,442	2,447,630	$8,492,642
Income Tax	381,123	437,545	495,685	553,269	$1,867,623	616,716	684,318	754,270	832,194	$2,887,498
Net Income	739,828	849,353	962,212	1,073,993	$3,625,386	1,197,154	1,328,382	1,464,172	1,615,436	$5,605,144

Cash Flow Statement
FY 1993

	Oct-92	Nov-92	Dec-92	Jan-93	Feb-93	Mar-93	Apr-93	May-93	Jun-93	Jul-93	Aug-93	Sep-93	FY 1993
Cash Flow From Operations													
Net Income	(71,157)	(51,910)	(38,947)	(37,167)	(46,184)	(43,007)	(28,401)	(17,853)	(8,454)	(13,763)	(1,482)	15,285	(343,040)
Depreciation	0	50	50	50	100	100	100	100	100	100	100	100	950
Increase in Accts Receivable	(1,695)	(2,928)	(2,071)	(5,973)	(3,276)	(5,708)	(9,891)	(9,419)	(11,120)	(5,847)	(13,811)	(15,134)	(86,873)
Increases in Accts Payable	11,018	(3,012)	(2,399)	932	639	450	(983)	(767)	46	1,422	467	(977)	6,833
Increases in Inventories	(300)	(150)	(450)	(150)	(450)	(450)	(450)	(300)	(150)	(600)	(600)	(1,270)	(5,320)
Net Cash from Operations	(62,134)	(57,950)	(43,818)	(42,308)	(49,172)	(48,616)	(39,626)	(28,239)	(19,577)	(18,687)	(15,326)	(1,996)	(427,450)
Cash Flow From Investing													
Purchase of Equipment	(3,000)	0	0	(3,000)	0	0	0	0	0	0	0	0	(6,000)
Net Cash from Investing	(3,000)	0	0	(3,000)	0	0	0	0	0	0	0	0	(6,000)
Cash Flow From Financing													
Equity	600,000	0	0	0	0	0	0	0	0	0	0	0	600,000
Debt	0	0	0	0	0	0	0	0	0	0	0	0	0
Net Cash Flow	534,866	(57,950)	(43,818)	(45,308)	(49,172)	(48,616)	(39,626)	(28,239)	(19,577)	(18,687)	(15,326)	(1,996)	166,550
Beginning Cash	5,000	539,866	481,916	438,099	392,791	343,619	295,003	255,377	227,138	207,560	188,873	173,546	5,000
Ending Cash	539,866	481,916	438,099	392,791	343,619	295,003	255,377	227,138	207,560	188,873	173,546	171,550	171,550

Cash Flow Statement

FY 1994	Oct-93	Nov-93	Dec-93	Jan-94	Feb-94	Mar-94	Apr-94	May-94	Jun-94	Jul-94	Aug-94	Sep-94	FY 1994
Cash Flow From Operations													
Net Income	24,890	30,212	36,968	41,520	49,908	56,692	70,298	73,552	56,808	63,330	70,443	83,196	657,817
Depreciation	100	150	150	150	200	200	200	200	200	200	350	350	2,450
Increase in Accts Receivable	(27,498)	(30,742)	(27,478)	(28,282)	(29,118)	(36,563)	(43,864)	(52,329)	(43,314)	(47,535)	(53,431)	(67,541)	(487,695)
Increases in Accts Payable	(158)	3,914	2,482	3,479	2,731	4,748	4,519	3,699	7,138	5,429	6,096	7,197	51,274
Increases in Inventories	(1,350)	(1,120)	(1,340)	(1,270)	(1,790)	(1,640)	(2,240)	(1,490)	(1,800)	(2,310)	(3,060)	(3,120)	(22,530)
Net Cash from Operations	(4,017)	2,414	10,783	15,597	21,930	23,437	28,912	23,633	19,032	19,114	20,397	20,083	201,315
Cash Flow From Investing													
Purchase of Equipment	(3,000)	0	0	(3,000)	0	0	0	0	0	(9,000)	0	0	(15,000)
Net Cash from Investing	(3,000)	0	0	(3,000)	0	0	0	0	0	(9,000)	0	0	(15,000)
Cash Flow From Financing													
Equity	0	0	0	0	0	0	0	0	0	0	0	0	0
Debt	0	0	0	0	0	0	0	0	0	0	0	0	0
Net Cash Flow	(7,017)	2,414	10,783	12,597	21,930	23,437	28,912	23,633	19,032	10,114	20,397	20,083	186,315
Beginning Cash	171,550	164,533	166,947	177,730	190,326	212,257	235,694	264,606	288,239	307,271	317,385	337,782	171,550
Ending Cash	164,533	166,947	177,730	190,326	212,257	235,694	264,606	288,239	307,271	317,385	337,782	357,865	357,865

Cash Flow Statement
FY 1995

	Oct-94	Nov-94	Dec-94	Jan-95	Feb-95	Mar-95	Apr-95	May-95	Jun-95	Jul-95	Aug-95	Sep-95	FY 1995
Cash Flow From Operations													
Net Income	96,410	107,843	118,941	127,935	140,255	151,060	162,421	175,326	183,761	196,350	208,633	220,586	1,889,520
Depreciation	350	500	650	650	650	650	650	800	800	800	800	800	8,100
Increase in Accts Receivable	(72,266)	(79,856)	(82,020)	(74,640)	(85,573)	(85,541)	(88,265)	(95,924)	(81,336)	(93,287)	(97,853)	(100,032)	(1,036,593)
Increases in Accts Payable	(8,036)	8,777	8,573	6,974	9,389	8,402	8,783	9,901	6,533	9,664	9,425	9,324	87,711
Increases in Inventories	(3,340)	(3,420)	(2,890)	(3,570)	(3,550)	(3,630)	(3,920)	(2,810)	(3,930)	(3,840)	(4,120)	(8,880)	(47,900)
Net Cash from Operations	13,117	33,844	43,254	57,349	61,171	70,942	79,669	87,292	105,829	109,688	116,885	121,798	900,837
Cash Flow From Investing													
Purchase of Equipment	(9,000)	(9,000)	0	0	0	0	(9,000)	0	0	0	0	0	(27,000)
Net Cash from Investing	(9,000)	(9,000)	0	0	0	0	(9,000)	0	0	0	0	0	(27,000)
Cash Flow From Financing													
Equity	0	0	0	0	0	0	0	0	0	0	0	0	0
Debt	0	0	0	0	0	0	0	0	0	0	0	0	0
Net Cash Flow	4,117	24,844	43,254	57,349	61,171	70,942	70,669	87,292	105,829	109,688	116,885	121,798	873,837
Beginning Cash	357,865	361,982	386,826	430,081	487,429	548,600	619,542	690,211	777,503	883,332	993,020	1,109,904	357,865
Ending Cash	361,982	386,826	430,081	487,429	548,600	619,542	690,211	777,503	883,332	993,020	1,109,904	1,231,702	1,231,702

99

Cash Flow Statement
FY 1996 & 1997

	Q1	Q2	Q3	Q4	FY 1996	Q1	Q2	Q3	Q4	FY 1997
Operations										
Net Income	739,828	849,353	962,212	1,073,993	$3,625,386	1,197,154	1,328,382	1,464,172	1,615,436	$5,605,144
Increase in Accts Receivable	(325,857)	(389,142)	(411,874)	(421,828)	($1,548,701)	(471,654)	(510,228)	(539,998)	(597,630)	($2,119,512)
Increases in Accts Payable	937	28,650	29,596	29,305	$88,488	10,154	35,028	36,371	40,271	$121,824
Increases in Inventories	(13,070)	(13,797)	(13,883)	(16,527)	($57,277)	(17,897)	(19,043)	(20,670)	(20,670)	($78,280)
Operations - Net Cash	401,837	475,064	566,051	664,944	$2,107,896	717,756	834,139	939,874	1,037,407	$3,529,176
Cash Flow From Investing										
Purchase of Equipment	-12,000	-12,000	-12,000	-12,000	-48,000	-16,000	-16,000	-16,000	-16,000	-64,000
Net Cash from Investing	-12,000	-12,000	-12,000	-12,000	-48,000	-16,000	-16,000	-16,000	-16,000	-64,000
Financing										
Equity	0	0	0	0	$0	0	0	0	0	$0
Debt	0	0	0	0	$0	0	0	0	0	$0
Net Cash Flow	389,837	463,064	554,051	652,944	$2,059,896	701,756	818,139	923,874	1,021,407	$3,465,176
Beginning Cash	1,231,702	1,621,539	2,084,603	2,638,654	$1,231,702	3,291,598	3,993,355	4,811,493	5,735,368	$3,291,598
Ending Cash	1,621,539	2,084,603	2,638,654	3,291,598	$3,291,598	3,993,355	4,811,493	5,735,368	6,756,775	$6,756,775

100

FY 1993 Projected Sales Schedule															
Product	Price		Oct-92	Nov-92	Dec-92	Jan-93	Feb-93	Mar-93	Apr-93	May-93	Jun-93	Jul-93	Aug-93	Sep-93	FY 1993
UL Solutions	$3,260	Units Sold	1	1	2	2	3	3	4	5	5	5	6	8	45
-1950		Revenue	2,260	2,260	4,520	4,520	6,780	6,780	13,040	16,300	16,300	16,300	19,560	26,080	134,700
IEC Solutions	$3,000	Units Sold	0	1	1	3	3	4	4	5	6	6	6	8	47
-950		Revenue	0	3,000	2,000	6,000	6,000	8,000	8,000	10,000	18,000	18,000	18,000	24,000	121,000
CSA Solution	$3,000	Units Sold	0	0	0	1	1	3	3	4	4	5	6	6	33
- 22.2 #220		Revenue	0	0	0	3,000	2,000	6,000	6,000	8,000	8,000	10,000	18,000	18,000	79,000
FCC Solutions	$3,000	Units Sold	0	0	0	0	0	0	2	2	3	3	5	5	20
- Part 15		Revenue	0	0	0	0	0	0	4,000	4,000	6,000	6,000	10,000	10,000	40,000
UL Solutions	$3,260	Units Sold	0	0	0	0	0	0	0	0	0	0	0	0	0
-1459		Revenue	0	0	0	0	0	0	0	0	0	0	0	0	0
CSA Solutions	$3,000	Units Sold	0	0	0	0	0	0	0	0	0	0	0	0	0
- 22.2 #0.7		Revenue	0	0	0	0	0	0	0	0	0	0	0	0	0
Product #7	$3,000	Units Sold	0	0	0	0	0	0	0	0	0	0	0	0	0
		Revenue	0	0	0	0	0	0	0	0	0	0	0	0	0
Product #8	$3,000	Units Sold	0	0	0	0	0	0	0	0	0	0	0	0	0
		Revenue	0	0	0	0	0	0	0	0	0	0	0	0	0
TOTAL		Units Sold	1	2	3	6	7	10	13	16	18	19	23	27	145
		Revenue	2,260	5,260	6,520	13,520	14,780	20,780	31,040	38,300	48,300	50,300	65,560	78,080	374,700

FY 1994 Projected Sales Schedule															
Product	Price		Oct-93	Nov-93	Dec-93	Jan-94	Feb-94	Mar-94	Apr-94	May-94	Jun-94	Jul-94	Aug-94	Sep-94	FY 1994
UL Solutions	$3,260	Units Sold	10	11	13	14	16	17	19	21	23	25	28	31	228
-1950		Revenue	32,600	35,860	42,380	45,640	52,160	55,420	61,940	68,460	74,980	81,500	91,280	101,060	743,280
IEC Solutions	$3,000	Units Sold	10	13	14	16	18	20	21	24	26	29	31	35	257
-950		Revenue	30,000	39,000	42,000	48,000	54,000	60,000	63,000	72,000	78,000	87,000	93,000	105,000	771,000
CSA Solution	$3,000	Units Sold	6	8	10	13	14	16	18	20	21	24	26	29	205
- 22.2 #220		Revenue	18,000	24,000	30,000	39,000	42,000	48,000	54,000	60,000	63,000	72,000	78,000	87,000	615,000
FCC Solutions	$3,000	Units Sold	7	9	9	9	10	14	17	19	22	24	27	29	196
- Part 15		Revenue	21,000	27,000	27,000	27,000	30,000	42,000	51,000	57,000	66,000	72,000	81,000	87,000	588,000
UL Solutions	$3,260	Units Sold	1	1	2	2	3	3	4	5	5	5	6	8	45
-1459		Revenue	2,260	2,260	4,520	4,520	6,780	6,780	13,040	16,300	16,300	16,300	19,560	26,080	134,700
CSA Solutions	$3,000	Units Sold	0	1	1	2	2	3	3	4	5	5	5	6	37
- 22.2 #0.7		Revenue	0	2,000	2,000	4,000	4,000	6,000	6,000	12,000	15,000	15,000	15,000	18,000	99,000
Product #7	$3,000	Units Sold	1	1	2	2	3	3	4	5	5	5	6	8	45
		Revenue	2,000	2,000	4,000	4,000	6,000	6,000	12,000	15,000	15,000	15,000	18,000	24,000	123,000
Product #8	$3,000	Units Sold	0	0	0	1	1	2	2	3	3	4	5	5	26
		Revenue	0	0	0	2,000	2,000	4,000	4,000	6,000	6,000	12,000	15,000	15,000	66,000
Product #9	$3,260	Units Sold	0	0	0	0	0	0	0	1	1	2	2	4	10
		Revenue	0	0	0	0	0	0	0	2,260	2,260	4,520	4,520	9,040	22,600
Product #10	$3,000	Units Sold	0	0	0	0	0	0	0	0	0	0	1	1	2
		Revenue	0	0	0	0	0	0	0	0	0	0	2,000	2,000	4,000
TOTAL		Units Sold	35	44	51	59	67	78	88	102	111	123	137	156	1,051
		Revenue	105,860	132,120	151,900	174,160	196,940	228,200	264,980	309,020	336,540	375,320	417,360	474,180	3,166,580

FY 1995 Projected Sales Schedule															
Product	Price		Oct-94	Nov-94	Dec-94	Jan-95	Feb-95	Mar-95	Apr-95	May-95	Jun-95	Jul-95	Aug-95	Sep-95	FY 1995
UL Solutions	$3,260	Units Sold	33	35	36	38	40	41	43	44	44	45	45	46	490
-1950		Revenue	107,580	114,100	117,360	123,880	130,400	133,660	140,180	143,440	143,440	146,700	146,700	149,960	1,597,400
IEC Solutions	$3,000	Units Sold	39	41	44	45	48	50	51	54	55	55	56	56	594
-950		Revenue	117,000	123,000	132,000	135,000	144,000	150,000	153,000	162,000	165,000	165,000	168,000	168,000	1,782,000
CSA Solution	$3,000	Units Sold	31	35	39	41	44	45	48	50	51	54	55	55	548
- 22.2 #220		Revenue	93,000	105,000	117,000	123,000	132,000	135,000	144,000	150,000	153,000	162,000	165,000	165,000	1,644,000
FCC Solutions	$3,000	Units Sold	32	36	39	43	48	53	56	60	61	65	68	70	631
- Part 15		Revenue	96,000	108,000	117,000	129,000	144,000	159,000	168,000	180,000	183,000	195,000	204,000	210,000	1,893,000
UL Solutions	$3,260	Units Sold	10	11	13	14	16	17	19	21	23	25	28	31	228
-1459		Revenue	32,600	35,860	42,380	45,640	52,160	55,420	61,940	68,460	74,980	81,500	91,280	101,060	743,280
CSA Solutions	$3,000	Units Sold	8	10	11	13	14	16	17	19	21	23	25	28	205
- 22.2 #0.7		Revenue	24,000	30,000	33,000	39,000	42,000	48,000	51,000	57,000	63,000	69,000	75,000	84,000	615,000
Product #7	$3,000	Units Sold	10	11	13	14	16	17	19	21	23	25	28	31	228
0		Revenue	30,000	33,000	39,000	42,000	48,000	51,000	57,000	63,000	69,000	75,000	84,000	93,000	684,000
Product #8	$3,000	Units Sold	5	6	8	10	11	13	14	16	17	19	21	23	163
		Revenue	15,000	18,000	24,000	30,000	33,000	39,000	42,000	48,000	51,000	57,000	63,000	69,000	489,000
Product #9	$3,260	Units Sold	4	5	6	6	6	7	10	12	13	16	17	19	121
		Revenue	9,040	16,300	19,560	19,560	19,560	22,820	32,600	39,120	42,380	52,160	55,420	61,940	390,460
Product #10	$3,000	Units Sold	2	2	3	3	4	6	6	6	7	9	11	12	71
		Revenue	4,000	4,000	6,000	6,000	12,000	18,000	18,000	18,000	21,000	27,000	33,000	36,000	203,000
Product #11	$3,000	Units Sold	0	1	1	2	2	3	3	4	5	5	5	6	37
		Revenue	0	2,000	2,000	4,000	4,000	6,000	6,000	12,000	15,000	15,000	15,000	18,000	99,000
Product #12	$3,000	Units Sold	0	0	0	0	1	1	2	2	3	3	4	5	21
		Revenue	0	0	0	0	2,000	2,000	4,000	4,000	6,000	6,000	12,000	15,000	51,000
Product #13	$3,260	Units Sold	0	0	0	0	0	0	1	1	2	2	3	3	12
		Revenue	0	0	0	0	0	0	2,260	2,260	4,520	4,520	6,780	6,780	27,120
Product #14	$3,000	Units Sold	0	0	0	0	0	0	0	0	0	1	1	2	4
		Revenue	0	0	0	0	0	0	0	0	0	2,000	2,000	4,000	8,000
TOTAL		Units Sold	174	193	213	229	250	269	289	310	325	347	367	387	3,353
		Revenue	528,220	589,260	649,300	697,080	763,120	819,900	879,980	947,280	991,320	1,057,880	1,121,180	1,181,740	10,226,260

FY 96&97 Projected Sales Schedule							1					
Product	Price		Q1	Q2	Q3	Q4	FY 1996	Q1	Q2	Q3	Q4	FY 1997
UL Solutions -1950	$3,260	Units Sold	140	144	147	151	582	161	167	176	190	694
		Revenue	456,400	469,440	479,220	492,260	1,897,320	524,860	544,420	573,760	619,400	2,262,440
IEC Solutions -950	$3,000	Units Sold	174	180	181	189	724	196	208	215	232	851
		Revenue	522,000	540,000	543,000	567,000	2,172,000	588,000	624,000	645,000	696,000	2,553,000
CSA Solution - 22.2 #220	$3,000	Units Sold	170	176	180	184	710	190	201	209	220	820
		Revenue	510,000	528,000	540,000	552,000	2,130,000	570,000	603,000	627,000	660,000	2,460,000
FCC Solutions - Part 15	$3,000	Units Sold	223	232	238	246	939	251	257	274	286	1,068
		Revenue	669,000	696,000	714,000	738,000	2,817,000	753,000	771,000	822,000	858,000	3,204,000
UL Solutions -1459	$3,260	Units Sold	104	119	131	136	490	140	144	147	151	582
		Revenue	339,040	387,940	427,060	443,360	1,597,400	456,400	469,440	479,220	492,260	1,897,320
CSA Solutions - 22.2 #0.7	$3,000	Units Sold	99	114	128	134	475	138	144	145	150	577
		Revenue	297,000	342,000	384,000	402,000	1,425,000	414,000	432,000	435,000	450,000	1,731,000
Product #7 0	$3,000	Units Sold	104	119	131	136	490	140	144	147	151	582
		Revenue	312,000	357,000	393,000	408,000	1,470,000	420,000	432,000	441,000	453,000	1,746,000
#8	$3,000	Units Sold	84	104	119	131	438	136	140	144	147	567
		Revenue	252,000	312,000	357,000	393,000	1,314,000	408,000	420,000	432,000	441,000	1,701,000
#9	$3,260	Units Sold	68	92	119	137	416	154	161	165	174	654
		Revenue	221,680	299,920	387,940	446,620	1,356,160	502,040	524,860	537,900	567,240	2,132,040
#10	$3,000	Units Sold	47	63	84	109	303	126	140	148	153	567
		Revenue	141,000	189,000	252,000	327,000	909,000	378,000	420,000	444,000	459,000	1,701,000
#11	$3,000	Units Sold	29	43	57	76	205	99	114	128	134	475
		Revenue	87,000	129,000	171,000	228,000	615,000	297,000	342,000	384,000	402,000	1,425,000
#12	$3,000	Units Sold	16	29	43	57	145	76	99	114	128	417
		Revenue	48,000	87,000	129,000	171,000	435,000	228,000	297,000	342,000	384,000	1,251,000
#13	$3,260	Units Sold	14	19	34	47	114	63	84	104	119	370
		Revenue	45,640	61,940	110,840	153,220	371,640	205,380	273,840	339,040	387,940	1,206,200
#14	$3,000	Units Sold	8	14	19	34	75	47	63	84	104	298
		Revenue	24,000	42,000	57,000	102,000	225,000	141,000	189,000	252,000	312,000	894,000
#15	$3,000	Units Sold	4	8	14	19	45	34	47	63	84	228
		Revenue	12,000	24,000	42,000	57,000	135,000	102,000	141,000	189,000	252,000	684,000
#16	$3,000	Units Sold	0	4	8	14	26	19	34	47	63	163
		Revenue	0	12,000	24,000	42,000	78,000	57,000	102,000	141,000	189,000	489,000
#17	$3,260	Units Sold	0	0	4	8	12	14	19	34	47	114
		Revenue	0	0	13,040	26,080	39,120	45,640	61,940	110,840	153,220	371,640
#18	$3,000	Units Sold	0	0	0	4	4	8	14	19	34	75
		Revenue	0	0	0	12,000	12,000	24,000	42,000	57,000	102,000	225,000
#19	$3,000	Units Sold	0	0	0	0	0	4	8	14	19	45
		Revenue	0	0	0	0	0	12,000	24,000	42,000	57,000	135,000
#20	$3,000	Units Sold	0	0	0	0	0	0	4	8	14	26
		Revenue	0	0	0	0	0	0	12,000	24,000	42,000	78,000
#21	$3,260	Units Sold	0	0	0	0	0	0	0	4	8	12
		Revenue	0	0	0	0	0	0	0	13,040	26,080	39,120
#22	$3,000	Units Sold	0	0	0	0	0	0	0	0	4	4
		Revenue	0	0	0	0	0	0	0	0	12,000	12,000
TOTAL		Units Sold	1,284	1,460	1,637	1,812	6,193	1,996	2,192	2,389	2,612	9,189
		Revenue	3,936,760	4,477,240	5,024,100	5,560,540	18,998,640	6,126,320	6,725,500	7,330,800	8,015,140	28,197,760

Payroll - FY 93

	Oct-92	Nov-92	Dec-92	Jan-93	Feb-93	Mar-93	Apr-93	May-93	Jun-93	Jul-93	Aug-93	Sep-93	FY 1993	Avg Emps
General & Administrative														
President	1,250	1,250	1,250	1,250	2,500	2,500	2,500	2,500	2,500	2,500	2,500	2,500	25,000	1.0
V.P. Finance	1,250	1,250	1,250	1,250	2,500	2,500	2,500	2,500	2,500	2,500	2,500	2,500	25,000	1.0
Other Admin	0	0	0	0	0	0	0	0	0	0	0	0	0	0.0
Subtotal	2,500	2,500	2,500	2,500	5,000	5,000	5,000	5,000	5,000	5,000	5,000	5,000	50,000	
FICA Taxes (7.65%)	191	191	191	191	383	383	383	383	383	383	383	383	3,825	
Work. Comp (1.5%)	38	38	38	38	75	75	75	75	75	75	75	75	750	
Total G&A Payroll	2,729	2,729	2,729	2,729	5,458	5,458	5,458	5,458	5,458	5,458	5,458	5,458	54,575	2.0
Sales & Marketing														
V.P. Sales & Marketir	1,250	1,250	1,250	1,250	2,500	2,500	2,500	2,500	2,500	2,500	2,500	2,500	25,000	1.0
Customer Service	3,750	3,750	3,750	3,750	3,750	3,750	3,750	3,750	3,750	3,750	3,750	3,750	45,000	1.5
Subtotal	5,000	5,000	5,000	5,000	6,250	6,250	6,250	6,250	6,250	6,250	6,250	6,250	70,000	
FICA Taxes (7.65%)	383	383	383	383	478	478	478	478	478	478	478	478	5,355	
Work. Comp (1.5%)	75	75	75	75	94	94	94	94	94	94	94	94	1,050	
Total S&M Payroll	5,458	5,458	5,458	5,458	6,822	6,822	6,822	6,822	6,822	6,822	6,822	6,822	76,405	2.5
R & D														
V.P. R & D	1,250	1,250	1,250	1,250	2,500	2,500	2,500	2,500	2,500	2,500	2,500	2,500	25,000	1.0
V.P. Ops & Quality	1,250	1,250	1,250	1,250	2,500	2,500	2,500	2,500	2,500	2,500	2,500	2,500	25,000	1.0
Senior Programmer	6,667	6,667	6,667	6,667	6,667	6,667	6,667	6,667	6,667	6,667	6,667	6,667	80,000	2.0
Subtotal	9,167	9,167	9,167	9,167	11,667	11,667	11,667	11,667	11,667	11,667	11,667	11,667	130,000	
FICA Taxes (7.65%)	701	701	701	701	893	893	893	893	893	893	893	893	9,945	
Work. Comp (1.5%)	138	138	138	138	175	175	175	175	175	175	175	175	1,950	
Total R&D Payroll	10,005	10,005	10,005	10,005	12,734	12,734	12,734	12,734	12,734	12,734	12,734	12,734	141,895	4.0
TOTALS														
Salaries & Wages	16,667	16,667	16,667	16,667	22,917	22,917	22,917	22,917	22,917	22,917	22,917	22,917	250,000	
FICA and WC	1,525	1,525	1,525	1,525	2,097	2,097	2,097	2,097	2,097	2,097	2,097	2,097	22,875	
Total Payroll	18,192	18,192	18,192	18,192	25,014	25,014	25,014	25,014	25,014	25,014	25,014	25,014	272,875	8.5

Projected Sales Summary

Product		FY 1993	FY 1994	FY 1995	FY 1996	FY 1997
UL Solutions - 1950	Units Sold	45	228	490	582	694
	Revenue	134,700	743,280	1,597,400	1,897,320	2,262,440
IEC Solutions - 950	Units Sold	47	257	594	724	851
	Revenue	121,000	771,000	1,782,000	2,172,000	2,553,000
CSA Solutions - 22.2 #220	Units Sold	33	205	548	710	820
	Revenue	79,000	615,000	1,644,000	2,130,000	2,460,000
FCC Solutions - Part 15	Units Sold	20	196	631	939	1,068
	Revenue	40,000	588,000	1,893,000	2,817,000	3,204,000
UL Solutions - 1459	Units Sold	0	45	228	490	582
	Revenue	0	134,700	743,280	1,597,400	1,897,320
CSA Solutions - 22.2 #0.7	Units Sold	0	37	205	475	577
	Revenue	0	99,000	615,000	1,425,000	1,731,000
Product #7	Units Sold	0	45	228	490	582
	Revenue	0	123,000	684,000	1,470,000	1,746,000
Product #8	Units Sold	0	26	163	438	567
	Revenue	0	66,000	489,000	1,314,000	1,701,000
Product #9	Units Sold	0	10	121	416	654
	Revenue	0	22,600	390,460	1,356,160	2,132,040
Product #10	Units Sold	0	2	71	303	567
	Revenue	0	4,000	203,000	909,000	1,701,000
Product #11	Units Sold	0	0	37	205	475
	Revenue	0	0	99,000	615,000	1,425,000
Product #12	Units Sold	0	0	21	145	417
	Revenue	0	0	51,000	435,000	1,251,000
Product #13	Units Sold	0	0	12	114	370
	Revenue	0	0	27,120	371,640	1,206,200
Product #14	Units Sold	0	0	4	75	298
	Revenue	0	0	8,000	225,000	894,000
Product #15	Units Sold	0	0	0	45	228
	Revenue	0	0	0	135,000	684,000
Product #16	Units Sold	0	0	0	26	163
	Revenue	0	0	0	78,000	489,000
Product #17	Units Sold	0	0	0	12	114
	Revenue	0	0	0	39,120	371,640
Product #18	Units Sold	0	0	0	4	75
	Revenue	0	0	0	12,000	225,000
Product #19	Units Sold	0	0	0	0	45
	Revenue	0	0	0	0	135,000
Product #20	Units Sold	0	0	0	0	26
	Revenue	0	0	0	0	78,000
Product #21	Units Sold	0	0	0	0	12
	Revenue	0	0	0	0	39,120
Product #22	Units Sold	0	0	0	0	4
	Revenue	0	0	0	0	12,000
TOTAL	Units Sold	145	1,051	3,353	6,193	9,189
	Revenue	374,700	3,166,580	10,226,260	18,998,640	28,197,760

R&D Expenses - FY 93

	Oct-92	Nov-92	Dec-92	Jan-93	Feb-93	Mar-93	Apr-93	May-93	Jun-93	Jul-93	Aug-93	Sep-93	FY 1993
R&D Payroll	10,005	10,005	10,005	10,005	12,734	12,734	12,734	12,734	12,734	12,734	12,734	12,734	$141,895
Dues & Subscriptions	75	75	75	75	75	75	75	75	75	75	75	75	$900
Travel	1,000	1,000	1,000	1,000	1,000	1,000	1,000	1,000	1,000	1,000	1,000	1,000	$12,000
Computer Supplies	75	75	75	75	75	75	75	75	75	75	75	75	$900
Computers	*3,000*	*0*	*0*	*3,000*	*0*	*0*	*0*	*0*	*0*	*0*	*0*	*0*	*$6,000*
Computer Depreciation	0	50	50	50	100	100	100	100	100	100	100	100	$950
Telephone	350	350	350	350	350	350	350	350	350	350	350	350	$4,200
Office Rental - Allocated	0	0	0	0	0	0	0	0	0	0	0	0	$0
TOTAL	11,505	11,555	11,555	11,555	14,334	14,334	14,334	14,334	14,334	14,334	14,334	14,334	$160,845

G&A Expenses
FY 1993

	Oct-92	Nov-92	Dec-92	Jan-93	Feb-93	Mar-93	Apr-93	May-93	Jun-93	Jul-93	Aug-93	Sep-93	FY 1993
Accting Services	200	210	220	230	240	250	260	270	280	290	300	310	$3,060
Bank Charges	50	50	50	50	50	50	50	50	50	50	50	50	$600
Property Insurance	100	100	100	100	100	100	100	100	100	100	100	100	$1,200
Copying	100	100	100	100	100	100	100	100	100	100	100	100	$1,200
Dues	75	75	75	75	75	75	75	75	75	75	75	75	$900
Utilities	0	0	0	0	0	0	0	0	0	0	0	0	$0
Product Liability Insurance	23	53	65	135	148	208	310	383	483	503	656	781	$3,747
Entertainment	500	500	500	500	500	500	500	500	500	500	500	500	$6,000
Equipment Maintenance	50	50	50	50	50	50	50	50	50	50	50	50	$600
Equipment Rental	0	0	0	0	0	0	0	0	0	0	0	0	$0
Furniture Rental	0	0	0	0	0	0	0	0	0	0	0	0	$0
G&A Payroll	2,729	2,729	2,729	2,729	5,458	5,458	5,458	5,458	5,458	5,458	5,458	5,458	$54,575
Legal Services	200	210	220	230	240	250	260	270	280	290	300	310	$3,060
Office Maintenance	0	0	0	0	0	0	0	0	0	0	0	0	$0
Office Rental - allocated	0	0	0	0	0	0	0	0	0	0	0	0	$0
Office Supplies	120	100	100	100	100	100	100	100	100	100	100	100	$1,220
Travel & Entertainment	3,000	3,000	3,000	3,000	3,000	3,000	3,000	3,000	3,000	3,000	3,000	3,000	$36,000
Subscriptions	50	50	50	50	50	50	50	50	50	50	50	50	$600
Telephone	400	400	400	400	450	450	450	450	500	500	500	500	$5,400
Total	7,596	7,626	7,659	7,749	10,560	10,640	10,763	10,856	11,026	11,066	11,238	11,383	$118,162

Projected Balance Sheet	Fiscal Year Ending September 30				
	1993	1994	1995	1996	1997
Assets					
Cash	$171,550	$357,865	$1,231,702	$3,291,598	$6,756,775
Accounts Receivable	$86,873	$574,568	$1,611,162	$3,159,863	$5,279,375
Inventory	$5,320	$27,850	$75,750	$133,027	$211,307
Total Current Assets	$263,743	$960,284	$2,918,614	$6,584,488	$12,247,456
Equipment at Cost	$11,030	$26,030	$53,030	$101,030	$165,030
(Accumulated Depreciation)	($2,350)	($4,800)	($12,900)	($51,124)	($122,354)
Book Value of Equipment	$8,680	$21,230	$40,130	$49,906	$42,676
Total Assets	$272,423	$981,514	$2,958,744	$6,634,394	$12,290,132
Liabilities & Equity					
Current Liabilities	$6,833	$58,107	$145,817	$234,305	$356,130
Total Liabilites	$6,833	$58,107	$145,817	$234,305	$356,130
Stock & Paid-in Capital	$712,000	$712,000	$712,000	$712,000	$712,000
Retained Earnings	($446,410)	$211,407	$2,100,927	$5,688,088	$11,222,002
Total Equity	$265,590	$923,407	$2,812,927	$6,400,088	$11,934,002
Total Liabilities and Equity	$272,423	$981,514	$2,958,744	$6,634,394	$12,290,132

Marketing and Sales Expenses - FY 93

	Oct-92	Nov-92	Dec-92	Jan-93	Feb-93	Mar-93	Apr-93	May-93	Jun-93	Jul-93	Aug-93	Sep-93	FY 1993
Marketing Payroll	5,458	5,458	5,458	5,458	6,822	6,822	6,822	6,822	6,822	6,822	6,822	6,822	$76,405
Direct Mailing	22,800	7,600	2,500	2,500	2,500	7,600	2,500	2,500	2,500	2,500	7,600	2,500	$65,600
Brochures	3,000	3,000	0	0	3,000	0	0	0	0	3,000	0	0	$12,000
Travel, Entertainment	3,000	3,000	3,000	3,500	3,500	3,500	3,500	3,500	3,500	3,500	3,500	3,500	$40,500
Trade Shows	4,000	4,000	0	4,000	4,000	4,000	4,000	0	0	4,000	4,000	4,000	$36,000
Telephone & Communicatio	700	730	760	790	820	850	880	910	940	970	1,000	1,030	$10,380
Advertising	15,000	15,000	15,000	15,000	15,000	15,000	15,000	15,000	15,000	15,000	15,000	15,000	$180,000
Other Operating Expenses	220	250	290	330	360	400	430	470	500	540	570	610	$4,970
Office Rental - Allocated	0	0	0	0	0	0	0	0	0	0	0	0	$0
TOTAL	54,178	39,038	27,008	31,578	36,002	38,172	33,132	29,202	29,262	36,332	38,492	33,462	$425,855

Discussion Questions
for
Expert Applications Systems, Incorporated

1. EASI plans to build a business on the idea of developing and selling user-friendly software to assist manufacturers in complying with regulations and standards.

   - What does EASI have to do well to make money with this idea? In other words, what are the critical success factors?

   - How well has EASI established the need for its products?

2. EASI has four founders, all of whom have major responsibilities in the business. How capable is this team of carrying out the business?

   - Who on the team is most critical to EASI's success?

   - What additional talent or skills are critical to EASI?

3. EASI is in negotiations with Underwriters Laboratories, Inc., to establish a working relationship. How critical is this relationship to EASI?

   - What motivation does UL have to pursue an alliance?

4. EASI's pro forma financial statements project sales of $32,000,000 and a net income of $5,600,000 in year 5.

   - Which assumptions are most critical?

   - Are these financials credible?

5. Place yourself in the position of an investor with more than enough resources to provide EASI with $600,000.

   - What do you see as the major strengths and weaknesses of this investment opportunity?

   - What are the major risks?

   - Can any of the weaknesses or risks be reduced by how to deal is structured?

   - Would you expect to earn 104% annual return on this investment?

   - Would you invest?

Company: _____

Please evaluate the <u>business</u> <u>plan</u> on the following aspects:

(Using this rating system: 1 = very poor, 2 = poor, 3 = fair, 4 = adequate, 5 = good, 6 = very good, 7 = excellent)

I. Elements of the Plan (20%)

  1. **Executive Summary**
     (Clear, exciting and effective as a stand-alone
     overview of the plan)   1   2   3   4   5   6   7
     Comments/Questions _____
     _____
     _____

  2. **Company Overview**
     (Business purpose, history, genesis of concept,
     current status, overall strategy and objectives)   1   2   3   4   5   6   7
     Comments/Questions _____
     _____
     _____

  3. **Products or Services**
     (Description, features and benefits, pricing, current
     stage of development, proprietary position)   1   2   3   4   5   6   7
     Comments/Questions _____
     _____
     _____

  4. **Market and Marketing Strategy**
     (Description of market, competitive analysis, needs
     identification, market acceptance, unique
     capabilities, sales/promotion)   1   2   3   4   5   6   7
     Comments/Questions _____
     _____
     _____
     _____

  5. **Management**
     (Backgrounds of key individuals, ability to execute
     strategy, personnel needs, organizational structure,
     role of any non-student executive, which students
     will execute plan)   1   2   3   4   5   6   7
     Comments/Questions _____
     _____
     _____

In rating each of the above, please consider the following questions:
- Is this area covered in adequate detail?
- Does the plan show a clear understanding of the elements that should be addressed?
- Are the assumptions realistic and reasonable?

Please evaluate the <u>financials</u> of the plan:

These should be presented in summary form in the text of the business plan and follow generally accepted accounting principles.

(Using this rating system: 1 = very poor, 2 = poor, 3 = fair, 4 = adequate, 5 = good, 6 = very good, 7 = excellent)

II. Elements of the Plan (20%)

1. **Cash Flow Statement**
    (effective as record of
    available cash and as planning
    tool; Detailed for first two-years,
    quarterly / annually for years 3-5)   1   2   3   4   5   6   7
    Comments / Questions _____
    _____
    _____

2. **Income Statement**
    (consistent with plan and effective
     in capturing profit performance;
    Quarterly for first two years,
    Quarterly / annually for years 3-5)   1   2   3   4   5   6   7
    Comments / Questions _____
    _____
    _____
    _____

3. **Balance Sheet**
    (effective in presenting assets,
    liabilities and owners equity)   1   2   3   4   5   6   7
    Comments / Questions _____
    _____
    _____

4. **Funds Required/Uses**
    (clear and concise presentation
    of amount, timing, type, and use of
    funds required for venture)   1   2   3   4   5   6   7
    Comments / Questions _____
    _____
    _____

5. **Offering**
    (proposal / terms to investors–indicate
    how much you want, the ROI, and the
    structure of the deal; possible exit strategies)   1   2   3   4   5   6   7
    Comments / Questions _____
    _____
    _____

Please evaluate the <u>presentation</u> of the following aspects:

(Using this rating system: 1 = very poor, 2 = poor, 3 = fair, 4 = adequate, 5 = good, 6 = very good, 7 = excellent)

III. Presentation (20%)

1. **Overall organization**
   (materials presented in clear,
   logical and/or sequential form)   1   2   3   4   5   6   7
   Comments/Questions _____
   _____
   _____

2. **Ability to relate need for the company**
   (meaningful examples, practical applications,
   etc.)   1   2   3   4   5   6   7
   Comments/Questions _____
   _____
   _____

3. **Ability to maintain judge's interest**   1   2   3   4   5   6   7
   Comments/Questions _____
   _____
   _____

4. **Responsiveness to judges**
   (answered questions, adapted to judge's
   level, needs, etc.)   1   2   3   4   5   6   7
   Comments/Questions _____
   _____
   _____

5. **Quality of visual aids**
   (slides, outlines, handouts, etc.)   1   2   3   4   5   6   7
   Comments/Questions _____
   _____
   _____

In rating each of the above, please consider the following:

- Do the presenters demonstrate competence in their presentation skills?
- Are they poised, confident and knowledgeable?
- Do they think effectively on their feet?

Strengths of presentation

Weaknesses of presentation

Additional comments

Please evaluate the viability of the company on the following aspects:
(To be completed after reading the plan and viewing the presentation)
(1 indicates definitely no, while 7 indicates definitely yes.)

IV. Viability of Company (40%)

		Definitely No					Definitely Yes	
1.	**Market Opportunity (20%)** (There is a clear market need presented as well as a way to take advantage of that need.)	1	2	3	4	5	6	7
2.	**Distinctive Competence (20%)** (The company provides something novel/unique/ special that gives it a competitive advantage in its market.)	1	2	3	4	5	6	7
3.	**Management Capability (20%)** (This team can effectively develop this company and handle the risks associated with the venture.)	1	2	3	4	5	6	7
4.	**Financial Understanding (20%)** (This team has a solid understanding of the financial requirements of the business.)	1	2	3	4	5	6	7
5.	**Investment Potential (20%)** (The business represents a real investment opportunity in which you would consider investing.)	1	2	3	4	5	6	7

Company Strengths

Company Weaknesses

Additional Comments

116

Independence Marine
Evanston, Illinois 60201

Business Plan

This Plan is Confidential. The reader agrees to hold all aspects
of this plan in the strictest confidence. Use of any materials
contained herein without the expressed written consent of the founders
of Independence Marine is prohibited.

Prepared by
Fred Hagedorn, John Hagey, John Hattery, Caleb Tower and Tom Zant
Independence Marine Founders

Prepared for:

Moot Corp. Competition
Kellogg Graduate School of Management

This is not an offering

April 23, 1993

Executive Summary

Independence Marine seeks $250,000 from outside investors in March, 1994 in exchange for 30% ownership of the company. Prior to this date, the founders will be funding the production tooling, field testing, facilities and equipment and the creation of market awareness. The outside capital infusion will be used for marketing and working capital needs as production levels ramp up. The projected annual internal rate of return to outside investors over five years is conservatively estimated at 51%. *Independence Marine* will develop exit strategies in conjunction with our outside investors at the appropriate time. These options include, but are not limited to, the execution of an IPO, an LBO, an outright redemption buyout or a combination of these.

Independence Marine's strategic goal is to develop, manufacture, and market products that aid in the environmentally sustainable harvest of ocean resources. Our initial product offering, *Whale Away*™, reduces the accidental entrapment (by-catch) of marine mammals, particularly whales, dolphins and porpoises, in commercial fishing equipment. This accessory is attached to fishing nets and emits a signal that alerts marine mammals to the presence of a foreign object in the water. The initial product/technology concept was developed and proven in tests with fishermen in Canada and the United States by Jon Lien, Ph.D., through research at the Whale Research Centre of Memorial University of Newfoundland, Canada.

Independence Marine has taken Dr. Lien's proven technology concept and redesigned it for inexpensive mass manufacture and improved safety-in-use. Initial prototypes have been constructed and will be tested in June and October of 1993 by Dr. Lien and representatives of the National Marine Fisheries Service of the U.S. Government.

The introduction of this product is critical to fishermen as new regulations prohibiting the by-catch of marine mammals will go into effect in October, 1993, threatening to shut down some of their fisheries. In addition to meeting regulations, *Whale Away*™ represents an additional value to fishermen as net damage and loss due to marine mammal entanglement is alleviated. This will reduce operating costs while increasing revenues, since undamaged nets can catch more fish.

The initial target market for *Whale Away*™ is the 2,025 domestic gill net fishermen who will face the regulatory ban on fishing during their peak season, which coincides with whale migrations through the area. Gill net fishermen were chosen because gill nets account for almost 80% of all marine mammal deaths that occur in fishing gear. We project that 150,000 *Whale Away*™ units per year will be required for all domestic gill net fishermen to meet the requirements of the federal regulations. The units are designed to last for one year, after which a replacement unit is needed for each successive year.

Whale Away™ will be introduced in the spring of 1994, coinciding with the beginning of the fishing season. It will be priced and promoted so as to quickly penetrate the market and consolidate our first-mover advantage. *Independence Marine* will promote *Whale Away*™ through trade shows, trade magazines and direct mail. Distribution will be direct via a toll free telephone number and parcel post shipping.

Future growth opportunities include extension of the current product into new markets and the development of product variations for the subsistence fishing markets subsidized by the United Nations. Other potential products include anti-shark and improved "dolphin-free" tuna net devices.

The management team will be a distinctive competence of *Independence Marine*. The founders bring a strong blend of manufacturing, management, marketing and product design experience to the business. This, combined with the fact that all five founders will be graduating from the Masters of Management in Manufacturing program at the J.L. Kellogg Graduate School of Management at Northwestern University, uniquely positions the company to bring *Whale Away*™ and future products to the market. Two of the founders will be running the day-to-day operations while the other three will serve on an external Board of Directors along with representatives of the initial investors. In addition, an advisory board of technical and industry advisors is being recruited to provide scientific advice and to ensure a flow of new product ideas in line with market needs.

Table of Contents

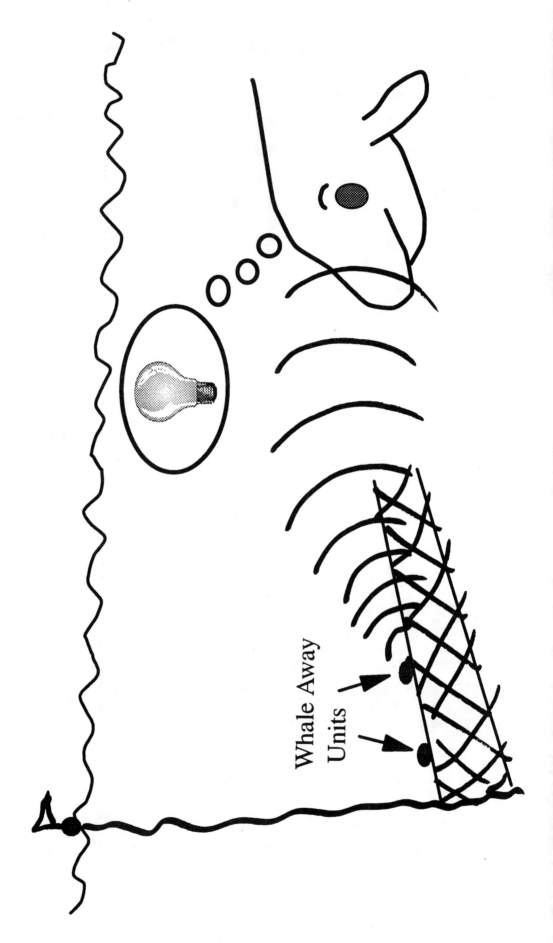

Figure 1: How *Whale Away* Works

Whale Away Units

Product Description and Design

Technology Concept

Whale Away™ works by emitting a signal that alerts cetaceans (marine mammals such as whales, dolphins and porpoises) to the presence of something unusual in the water, similar to the way flashing road lights alert drivers to the presence of danger. The mammal then cautiously approaches the noise and the nets to which the unit is attached. Once the mammal learns of the hazard, it is much less likely to become entrapped in it (please see Figure 1). Also of importance to fishermen, the signal is not audible to fish and therefore does not negatively affect catch yields.

The concept for this product was developed by Jon Lien, Ph.D., through research at the Whale Research Centre at Memorial University of Newfoundland, Canada. Dr. Lien, a preeminent animal behavior researcher and whale expert, began developing this concept over 15 years ago in an effort to assist Newfoundland fishermen in protecting their fishing gear from damage caused by entangled whales. Ten years later, the concept became a reality and underwent testing in Newfoundland, Canada; Queensland, Australia; Natal, South Africa; and New Hampshire, USA, where it was consistently demonstrated to be an effective deterrent to by-catch without negatively affecting the catch yields.

Dr. Lien's device has not been widely disseminated because the actual manufacturing cost of $250 per unit (or $1,250 per net) was greater than the opportunity cost to fishermen of not adopting the technology (i.e. net damage) or of stopping fishing. During the tests, the original prototype design, in addition to being too expensive, was found to be extremely awkward and cumbersome for the fishermen to use. This was a major barrier to commercial development.

After reading about the frustration Dr. Lien was having in making his concept manufacturable, our five person team of graduate students in the Master of Management in Manufacturing program at Northwestern University initiated a series of discussions with him. We subsequently formed *Independence Marine* to commercialize this technology concept.

Design Concept

In an effort to make the commercial product a success, *Independence Marine* worked directly with lead users from Dr. Lein's experimental tests to get feedback on the existing product. These lead users are generally the most successful fishermen in a given port or region and have the economic wherewithal to experiment with new technologies to improve their results. The market research consisted of focus groups conducted by two of

Figure 2: How Gill Nets Work

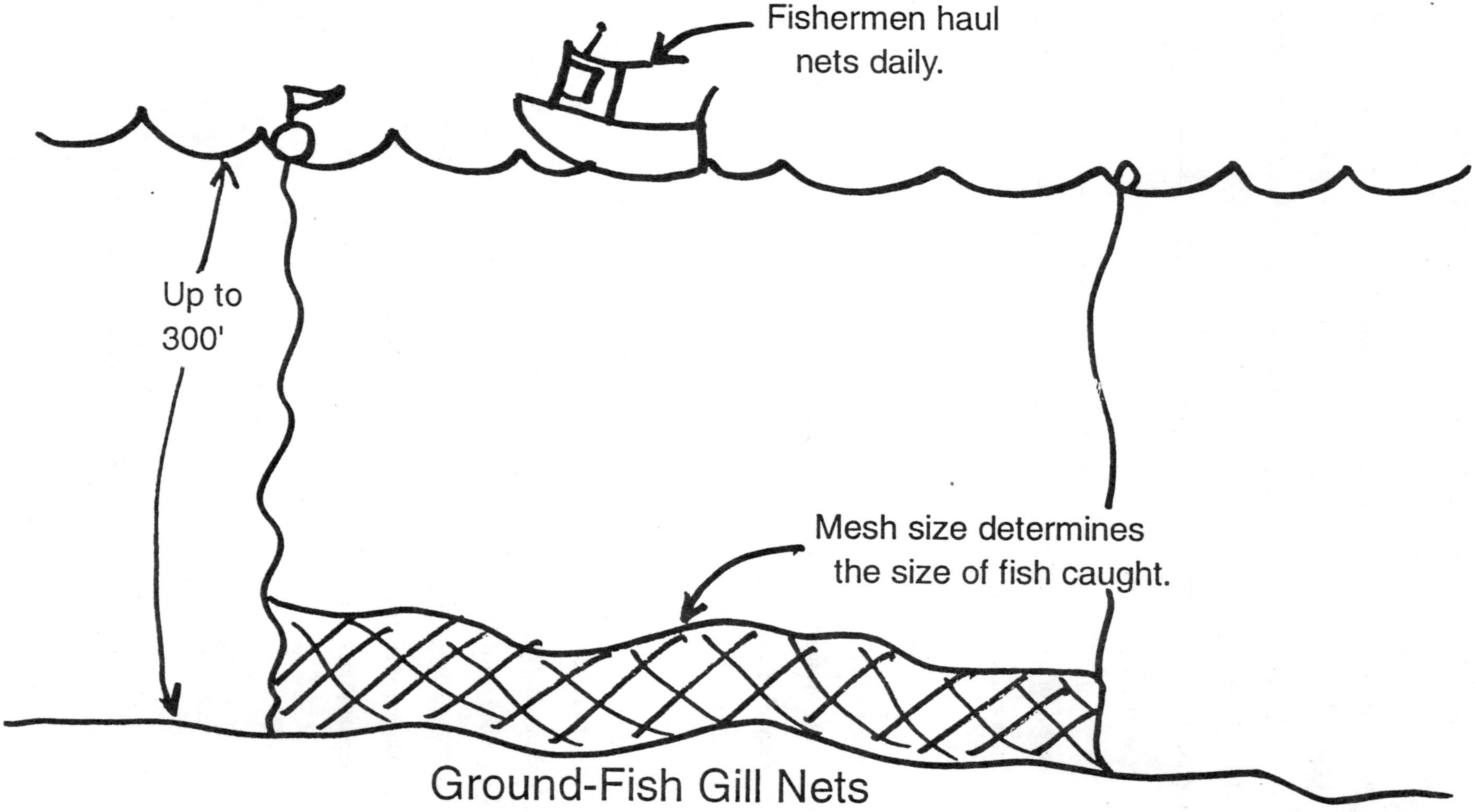

Fishermen haul nets daily.

Mesh size determines the size of fish caught.

Ground-Fish Gill Nets

Up to 300'

the company founders and consisted of the lead users from Dr. Lien's test in Portsmouth, NH. From the research it was determined that the key product attributes were cost, ease of use, safety and compatibility with existing gear. In addition, key internal design parameters were found to be durability, salt water resistance, depth pressure resistance, signal strength and range, power source life and energy consumption.

By working with fishermen on the design, *Independence Marine's* has taken efforts to foster fisherman to "buy-in" to our solution to their problem. With this approach, we will not repeat the experience of the "Turtle Excluder Device" that was mandated a few years ago by the National Marine Fisheries Service (NMFS) for use in the shrimp trawling fisheries along the Gulf Coast of the U.S. The shrimpers were not included in the development process of the product and felt that the product was useless, unusable and a "golden egg" for the manufacturer. *Independence Marine* continues to include lead-users in the development of our products and in the study of the buying and usage behaviors of the vessel owners and fishermen.

Product Attributes and Benefits

Whale Away™ has a distinctive, brightly colored durable plastic exterior. One end has the shape of a whale's head molded in plastic. The device will be noticeable to fishermen who will see the equipment being used by the lead users of each port. The attention that it attracts will encourage imitation, which is a common method of product diffusion in the fishing industry, as well as trial and acceptance of *Whale Away™*. In addition, the colors will be changed from year to year to make it easier for fishermen and regulators to recognize that the fisherman has the most current devices with the latest proven technology (note, however, that user registration will be the primary form of monitoring usage available to regulators).

Whale Away's™ compact, durable, light weight design allows easy, safe use with mechanized fishing equipment (e.g. hydraulic winches and mechanical net spreaders). In some applications, nets are deployed at rates of up to fifteen miles per hour and bang over several metal spreading bars. In this environment, the device must be able to be pulled easily through the system along with the nets. A major problem with the original device was that its weight and bulk required that it be clipped on to nets by a crew member after they had been through the mechanized equipment and were over the side of the boat, resulting in much slower deployment speeds, additional crew members and increased risk of personal injury.

Most importantly, our design is very adaptable to the equipment used in our primary market, the domestic gill net fishing industry, which currently represents 46% of the deployed fishing gear and almost 80% of cetacean by-catch in the U.S. (please see Figure 2 for a description of gill net fishing technology).

Page 5

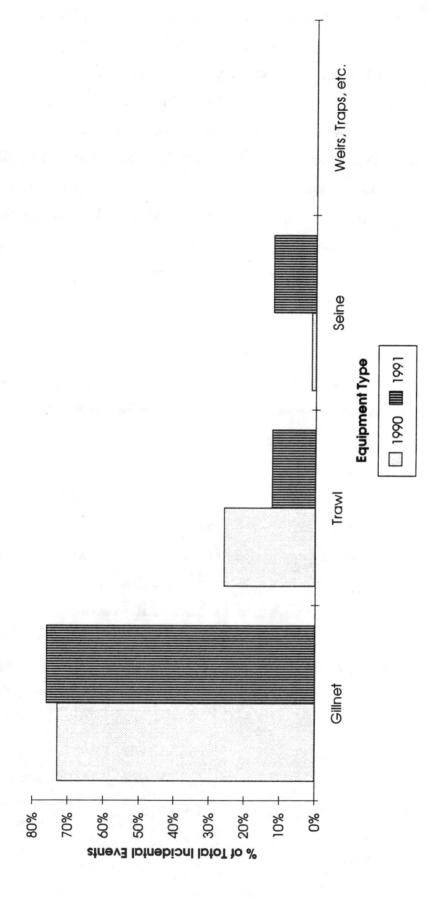

Figure 3: Incidental Cetacean By-catch by Fishing Equipment Type

Source: NMFS Fisheries Statistics Division - Vessel Owner and Observer Data

The power source life is both *Whale Away's*™ greatest constraint and its greatest marketing opportunity. *Whale Away*™ is designed as a disposable, single-season device necessitating annual repurchase. Like many replacement markets (e.g. razor blades), sales will be predictable and the customer base can be developed. In addition to the benefits of planned obsolescence, annual replacement will allow for easy integration of product improvements. Annual color and shape changes will also help government observers to ensure that the latest and best technology is being used. Lastly, the limited life of the current power source is the factor that allows the product to meet the requirements of the fishermen in terms of size and cost.

The color changes will be released in June of each year to coincide with the migratory patterns of cetaceans off the coast of the United States. *Whale Away*™ is designed to function for up to 3 months in the water. Fishermen will attach the devices to their nets only during those times that the cetaceans might reasonably be anticipated in their waters, which is about two months per year. To conserve energy, the design includes a water activated switch to shut the device off when it is out of the water. When dry, the product has a shelf life of almost one year.

Product Name

The product works by warning or alerting cetaceans that there is "something unusual" (a net) in the water. The animal gets curious, and, rather than colliding blindly with the net, learns where it is in the water, and thus avoids entanglement. From the fisherman's perspective, the product keeps cetaceans <u>away</u> from his or her net, thereby protecting the net from damage and keeping the fisherman out of trouble with regulators. Since the best known cetacean is the <u>whale</u>, our product was named *Whale Away*™.

Market Need

Market Drivers

The primary market driver for *Whale Away*™ in the United States is the regulation created by Congress to protect endangered species. Effective October, 1993, regulations promulgated by the National Marine Fisheries Service of the U.S. Department of Commerce to enforce the Endangered Species Conservation Act, the Endangered Species Act, the Marine Mammal Protection Act and the Magnuson Fishery Conservation and Management Act will "disallow any further extensions, waivers, or interim permits" issued to allow the incidental by-catch of marine mammals while fishing in U.S. waters. Currently, regulations protecting these endangered species have been circumscribed by loopholes established to provide a grace period for the U.S. fishing industry

Figure 4

a) Fishing Industry Structure by Equipment Amounts in Use

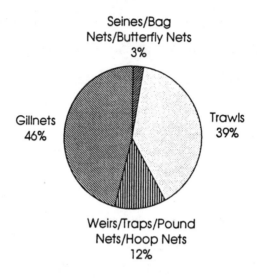

Seines/Bag
Nets/Butterfly Nets
3%

Gillnets
46%

Trawls
39%

Weirs/Traps/Pound
Nets/Hoop Nets
12%

b) Fishing Industry Structure by Vessels Using Equipment Type

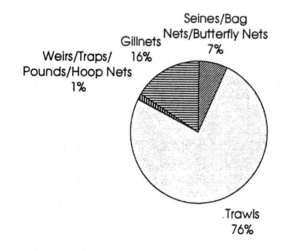

Seines/Bag
Nets/Butterfly Nets
7%

Gillnets
16%

Weirs/Traps/
Pounds/Hoop Nets
1%

Trawls
76%

Source: National Marine Fisheries Service, Fisheries Statistics Division - Fishing Vessels Operating Units Data

128

to develop fishing technologies that protect endangered species. The loopholes have now been closed, and regulations require the use of the "most advanced technology" available to alleviate mammal by-catch. However, no technologies other than *Whale Away*™ currently exist to solve this dilemma.

Under the law, the only alternative to using the "most advanced technology" is the complete cessation of fishing during periods when marine mammals are known to be in a particular fishing area. Ceasing fishing operations over these periods of time will create an economic disaster for fishermen. As an example, over 30% of a the catch of a typical fishery located along the East Coast of the United States is brought in during the two month period in the fall when harbor porpoises migrate. Thus, a significant portion of fishermen's' income is at risk due to regulatory pressure. *Whale Away*™ is the solution for fishermen to meet the regulatory requirements and continue operations.

A second market driver for *Whale Away*™ is that it addresses other important needs of fishermen. The use of Dr. Lien's device has been proven to reduce the number of marine mammal entanglements in fishing nets. This minimizes the amount of damage done to nets, reducing net repair and replacement costs. Also, undamaged nets can catch more fish, thus improving yields. Testing in Newfoundland found these benefits to be economically significant. Our market research with fishermen revealed that they are looking for a ways to improve fishing yields, reduce operating costs, reduce equipment loss and keep the government out of their way. *Whale Away*™ meets the needs of our customers from both a regulatory and an economic perspective.

Market Size

There are roughly 12,500 commercial fishing vessels in the United States. The distribution of the industry by location is shown in Appendix I. Gill net fishing, the industry sector that has the largest by-catch of cetaceans (please see Figure 3 for a breakdown by net type), is the primary target market for *Whale Away*™. Gill nets represent the fishing technology used on 16% of all domestic fishing vessels. Approximately 2,025 domestic vessels deploy about 9 million feet of gill nets, representing 46% of the total commercial fishing equipment in the United States. Gill nets represent a large and highly concentrated target market with a small number of players using most of the equipment (please see Figure 4). In addition, 86% of the domestic gill nets are found along the eastern seaboard (please see Figure 5).

The 9 million feet of gill net translate into roughly 30,000 nets in use domestically. Since five *Whale Away*™ units are required per net, the maximum market volume will be 150,000 units per year. Currently there is no competition in this sector of the market.

Page 7

129

Figure 5: Regional Gill Net Distribution

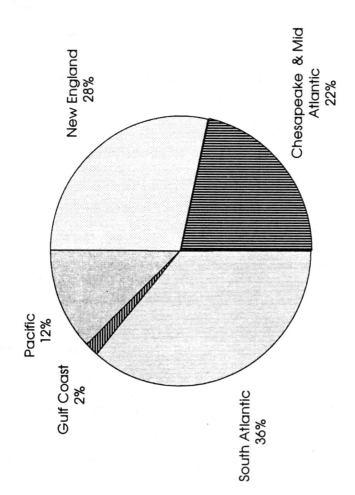

New England
28%

Chesapeake & Mid
Atlantic
22%

Pacific
12%

Gulf Coast
2%

South Atlantic
36%

Source: NMFS, Fisheries Statistics Division - Fishing Vessels Operating Units Data

Marketing

Launch Plan

In 1993, government funded research projects will purchase a total of 5,000 *Whale Away*™ units for field testing. These tests will provide scientific data to validate the effectiveness of our *Whale Away*™ product. If any issues arise during the test phase, time will still be available to address and validate these issues before full market roll-out in early to mid-1994. Development money has been included in the budget for just such an occurrence. This test phase will also generate publicity among fishermen for our product. A detailed, promotional launch plan will run as follows:

June 1993	Field Test, Conception Bay, NFLD.	500 units
	Field Test, Placentia Bay, NFLD.	500 units
September 1993	Ad Roll-out in Trade Journals	
October 1993	Market Intro., Fish EXPO, Seattle, WA	
	NMFS Field Test, Portsmouth, NH, USA	4000 units
February 1994	NMFS Field Test Results Available	
March 1994	National Sales Begin, 1994 Fishing Season	
	Sales Projection	72,000 units

Integral to the launch, and the continued success of *Whale Away*™, will be personal contacts with every member of the gill net fishing community (of which there are only about 2,025 vessels domestically). Maintaining close contact with our customers will be the cornerstone of our approach and commitment to the marketplace. To assist this objective, a database of customer information and potential customers will be maintained. Data will be gathered at trade shows, through direct mailings and by visiting ports.

Promotion

Successful adoption of *Whale Away*™ is primarily dependent on building lead-user trial and rapid imitation. To accomplish this, a promotion plan has been developed to stimulate recognition and familiarity on the part of the general fishing population and to target the lead-users in each port. These lead-users will be at the Fish Expo trade show in Seattle (October 1993). We will collect names, phone numbers and addresses of the fishermen attending the show and provide them with promotional materials. At the same time, advertisements and

Page 8

131

Figure 6: Customer/Market Concentrations & Print Media Advertising

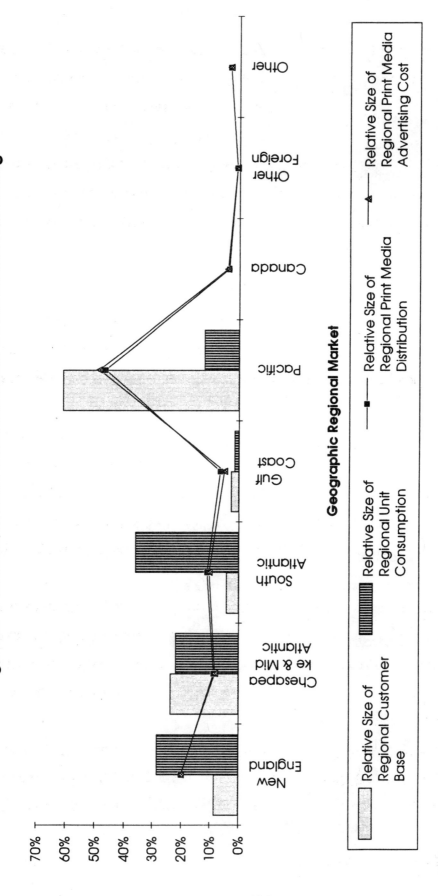

favorable editorials (which are already in the process of being written by independent editors) will be published in leading trade journals.

For ports not covered by Fish Expo attendees, and as a follow up to Fish Expo, we will use direct mailings to stimulate sales prior to the beginning of cetacean migration through each region. In addition, port visits will be conducted by managers and sales representatives and will be timed so as to occur just prior to the arrival of migrating cetaceans in the area in order to promote our company and product coincidentally with demand. Total promotion expenses for 1993 are budgeted at $85,500 (please see Appendix II and Figure 6 for further details).

For a long term market development strategy, public relations will be used to create a consumer demand for "whale-safe" fish, similar to recent demands for "dolphin-free" tuna. This plan will be conducted in coordination with academic and conservation groups.

Distribution

Fishermen are a rugged breed of individuals that are very family-oriented and highly individualistic. People in this industry enjoy the challenge of beating the elements, beating the odds and being in charge of their own destinies (please see Appendix III for a detailed description of our buyer behavior). Most vessels are owner operated.

Initially, fishermen will be encouraged to order *Whale Away*™ directly from *Independence Marine* via a 1-800 toll-free number through direct mailings to Fish Expo contacts. Toll-free numbers are a very common method for equipment procurement in the industry and allow *Independence Marine* to keep control of the channel. Additionally, this distribution channel selection bypasses the strong resistance to new products that exists in other standard industry channels and allows *Independence Marine* to monitor how effectively it is developing a "pull" marketing strategy.

The toll-free number also allows *Independence Marine* to leverage the vessel owners' independent nature and provides another opportunity to learn more about our customers by developing a direct relationship with each of them. This approach is also complementary to the development and monitoring of the customer data base. By being close to the market we will be able to respond immediately and effectively to changing customer needs as sales grow dramatically through 1994.

As the other channels develop an interest in providing *Whale Away*™ based on the "pull" of the marketplace, *Independence Marine* intends to allow movement of *Whale Away*™ through these other channels of equipment distribution. Since these channels provide services that *Independence Marine* cannot (e.g.

Page 9

Figure 7: Value-in-Use Pricing Analysis

Fishing Season at Risk	17% Per NMFS Representative @ Focus Group.			
Fishing Revenue at Risk	30% Per focus group.			
Whale Away unit COGS	$7.75			
	Top 25%	Middle 50%	Bottom 255	Weighted Average
Gross Revenue after Fixed and Personnel Expenses	$60,955	$29,852	$10,968	$32,972
Net Revenue after Fixed and Personnel Expenses	$25,693	$11,056	$1,262	$12,293
Sample Size	12	23	12	47
Profit Margin	42.15%	37.04%	11.50%	37.28%
Potential Revenue Loss	$18,287	$8,956	$3,290	$9,892
Impacted Gross	$42,669	$20,896	$7,678	$23,080
Impacted Net	$17,985	$7,740	$883	$8,605
Operating Loss	$7,708	$3,317	$378	$3,688
Plus Approximate Fixed Costs ($2K/month per focus group)	$4,000	$4,000	$4,000	$4,000
Value-in-Use = Operating Loss + Fixed Cost Coverage	$11,708	$7,317	$4,378	$7,688
Value Based Price = 50% of Value-in-Use (@ National Average 89 unit usage.)	$75.36	$45.64	$25.75	$48.15
Penetration Value-based Price =	**$20.00**			

Source: Focus group research; and Marchek, Suppy and McMullan, "Uncommon Prosperity..."

assembly of finished nets and immediate local access), they will be important assets in our channel strategy to satisfy all segments of our customer base. Volume price discounts will be provided to these channel distributors in order to prevent them from undercutting our price.

Current Industry Channels

Most net manufacturers make fishing nets and equipment as secondary items. They usually fabricate construction nets, safety nets, etc. as their primary product. They sell fishing equipment to distributors of varying sizes who then either sell directly to the fishermen or else assemble the nets for the fishermen. The distributors use direct sales, catalogs, direct mail and toll-free telephone numbers to reach fishermen. The fishermen either buy all the equipment components themselves and have a third party assemble the nets for them, or they have a local shop buy everything and assemble it for them so that they can purchase the net ready to use.

Many small manufacturers receive business because "they have been around for a long time." The fishermen personally know these owners and will give them business because they always have in the past. Some small manufacturers will even make nets to individualized customer orders. When the manufacturers introduce new products, they tend to select a lead-user fisherman in the specific area and give him the equipment to try.

Pricing

In order to create an effective barrier to entry for later competitors, *Independence Marine* will pursue a pricing strategy of market penetration. A low price for *Whale Away*™ will represent an attractive deal for fishermen. For a price, they can continue to fish during the most profitable part of the year uninterrupted. They will also realize savings from lower net damage and experience higher revenues (less damaged and lost nets yield higher catches). One study showed a 300% catch increase with whale alarms because the nets were fully functioning and undisturbed by marine mammals.

To set a price for *Whale Away*™, a value-in-use analysis was performed to determine a rational, market-oriented price point. The additional benefits due to lower net damage were not included in this analysis. The analysis was performed using revenue information provided by fishermen. The variable costs of operation (labor, fuel, gear, food, etc.) were deducted from revenues along with the average fixed costs (boat costs and salaries) to arrive at a "profit" for the owner. Industry data allowed us to divide fishermen into economic quartiles. The value-in-use analysis can be seen in Figure 7. Our calculations show that, for the majority of fishermen, the value of being able to operate while marine mammals are in their area is in excess of $46 per unit.

Page 10

For the lowest quartile, the value is approximately $26 per unit. Again, this does not consider any other economic benefits.

In addition, the focus groups conducted by company management with the lead users in Portsmouth, NH confirmed this price point information for the use of this technology. The lead users suggested that they would be willing to pay as much as $3,000 per boat for the benefits provided. Considering the number of nets these fishermen deployed, this correlated well with the $40 per unit price threshold.

Based on this analysis, *Whale Away*™ will be priced at $20 per unit, undercutting the value-in-use price while still maintaining a healthy contribution margin of 63% (with a delivered unit variable cost of $7.35) for *Independence Marine*. The reason for the low price is to promote rapid product diffusion and to make competitive entry both more difficult and less economically attractive for potential entrants.

Fishermen will need five units per 300 feet of net (which is the common net size), therefore packaged sets of five units will be sold for $100. Individual replacement units will also be sold, but at a price of $22.50 per unit to cover additional shipping costs. As an incentive for trial by lead users, *Independence Marine* will offer a trade discount to first-time buyers, such as a discount toward the next year's purchases (this discount is already factored into the financial statements under the reserve for commissions and promotional discounts).

Sales Projections

For 1993, *Independence Marine* will be manufacturing 5,000 units for field tests in Newfoundland and New Hampshire. Sale of these units to the Whale Research Centre of Memorial University will result in $100,000 in revenue for 1993. Purchasing Dr. Lien's device as originally designed for this test would cost approximately $250,000, so we are already serving the needs of our secondary customer quite favorably.

Beyond 1993, projections are based on a Bass model of new product diffusion. This model is based on assumptions concerning market size, adoption rate and associated revenues, costs, profits, and returns. Federal regulations will help drive trial and adoption rates. In order to assure a conservative approach, the model includes the entry of competitors after *Whale Away's*™ second year in the market. These competitors are assumed to immediately capture one third of the market.

Under these assumptions *Independence Marine's* revenues for the *Whale Away*™ product are projected to grow from $1.2 million in 1994 to $2.0 million by 1998. The five year projections for *Whale Away*™ by region are shown in Appendix IV.

Competitive Strategy

Barriers to entry into our industry are potentially low. Most of the technology is not patentable because much of Dr. Lein's research has been published in the academic press. However, the design can be copyrighted. Capital requirements for entry are modest; however, competitors will face some significant testing and engineering costs that *Independence Marine* is not having to face if they attempt to copy and certify the product.

With regard to the threat of vertical integration into our product category, there are no large equipment manufacturing suppliers to the fishing industry that pose a threat to *Independence Marine*. Fishing equipment is a mature sideline niche for these equipment suppliers.

To establish a stronger market position, *Independence Marine* will use its first mover advantage in the market to create an artificial barrier to entry. *Independence Marine* will quickly "fill the void" in the market by using penetration pricing and positive relationships developed with the NMFS through the test projects in the Fall of 1993 to ensure that *Whale Away*™ is the approved solution to the marine mammal by-catch problem. Approval of our product as the benchmark solution will create a barrier by forcing competitors to demonstrate their products via similar extensive and expensive testing. The NMFS is unlikely to fund additional research on other solutions once ours has already been proven effective.

Despite the relatively small size of this market and our aggressive approach, competitive entry is a possibility. Historically, when a second entrant comes into a new market, the original provider may lose up to one third of its market share. This market share may be somewhat attractive to a competitors, but it will be a lot of work for a small piece of this market, given the low unit price being offered by *Independence Marine*. Our sales projections and financials use the conservative assumption that competitors will enter the market in 1996.

Once established, we will defend our market position by pursuing a low cost manufacturing strategy with continuing refinements to the product design. Efficient design and manufacturing capabilities are the distinctive competencies of the founders. By staying ahead of the competition through innovation and our experience curve, we will discourage entry, or at least keep imitators' profits low.

Another potential threat comes from those fishermen who choose not to comply with the federal regulations that created the impetus for *Whale Away*™. In order to protect our law-abiding customers from unfair competition we will provide local NMFS regulators with lists of registered users from our sales database in order to diminish the impact of cheating within the market. This could be presented as a service to our customers, removing the burden of proof from them and helping the licensing process to run smoothly. We will

Page 12

also promote the importance of lower net damage and loss rates along with higher catch yields for undamaged nets as a significant economic benefit of using *Whale Away*™.

Self-manufacture by fisherman is another competitive threat. However, it is not viewed as very strong because the manufacturing costs associated with self-made units are in excess of the $20 unit price. Dr. Lein at one point circulated an inexpensive "do it yourself" design version. The cost of similar off-the-shelf materials purchased at retail prices is greater than $24, plus the unit was much less effective, less durable and considerably more bulky than our product.

The only similar product we have found in the market is an acoustic alarm sold to frighten seals away from fishing nets in the Pacific Northwest. This device has proven to be a technological failure. No other substitute products or technologies have been developed to date.

Future Growth Opportunities

Independence Marine has several significant opportunities for future growth. These include the extension of the current product into new markets and the development of product variations and line extensions. Presently, the financial projections are based only on sales of *Whale Away*™ to the domestic gill net fishery market, but a considerable amount of money has been budgeted for the research and development of new products. The growth opportunities are further expanded below.

New Markets

We intend to develop new markets for our initial product through international expansion into other developed economic fisheries such as Canada, Europe, South America and Japan. We will be conducting exploratory research into the regulatory and market conditions in these areas. Sales in the Canadian Maritime Provinces are expected to grow since this is where the original need developed as a way to reduce net damage caused by whale collisions. Northern and Western Europe represent attractive, highly regulated economic fisheries markets where gill net fishing is commonly used. Entry into the South American, Japanese and Far East markets will be approached only after additional research into the market and regulatory conditions have been completed.

Page 13

Product Variations / Line Extensions

In addition to incremental improvements to the existing product, we will also be creating new applications for our technology and product line extensions. Some possible line extensions to be explored include longer lasting products, shark deterrents and improved dolphin-free tuna net devices.

For long-lived products there is a vast potential market. The United Nations - Fisheries and Agriculture Organization (UN-FAO) currently equips subsistence-level fishermen in the Third World with gill nets. Gill nets are the most economical and efficient fishing technology available, and as such are the technology of choice for introduction and use in developing countries. To serve this market we will develop a variation of *Whale Away*™ that operates as long as the nets are expected to be in service. This variation is currently in the research phase. This world market has enormous sales potential that can be tapped through a central customer (the UN).

The current prototype device developed by Dr. Lien has been demonstrated to have shark deterrent value during tests in Australia and South Africa. In these countries, anti-shark nets are used to surround and protect beaches used by swimmers. Similar to the marine mammal problems of fishermen, sharks often damage and/or become entangled in the nets. The development of prototype units for shark research are planned for late 1994.

The tuna fishing industry represents another opportunity for devices similar to *Whale Away*™. The rise in demand for "dolphin-safe" tuna is a significant trend that is expected to grow. Currently, dolphins must be chased from the nets with motor boats and divers before the nets are hauled out of the water. This increases the chance of escape for the tuna and places the fishermen at risk. This market will also be explored beginning in late 1994.

Figure 8: Annual Sales Cycle

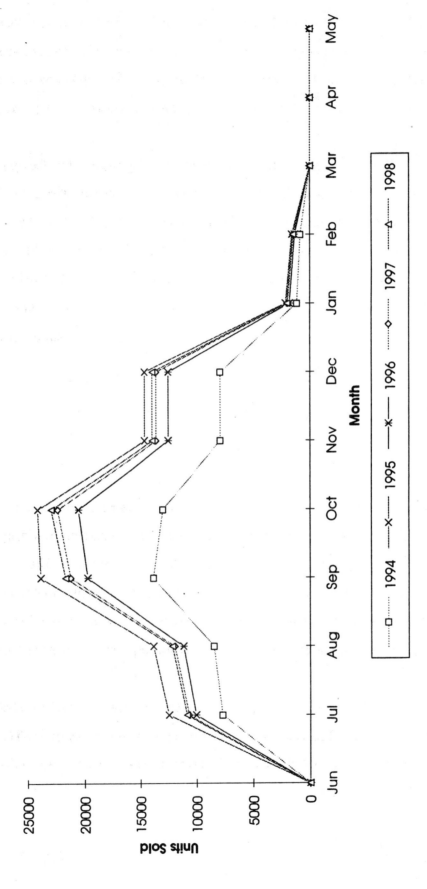

Operations

Major components for *Whale Away*™, such as the circuit board and the molded plastic nose cone, will be subcontracted to outside suppliers in order to keep our capital investment costs low. The components and other raw materials will be shipped to an assembly shop in southern New Hampshire. This region was selected because of its proximity to our customer base and the many unemployed assembly operators desperate for a job opportunity in the area.

The assembly operation will consist of preparing the outer casing, attaching and inserting the signal device, circuit board and power source. Once assembled, the unit is filled with a special polymeric filler and sealed closed. Production will run for about eight months per year and ramp up to meet spikes in August and September caused by the cyclicality of demand (please see Figure 8). Eight hourly employees will be required to staff the operation during the peaks in the production schedules. The hourly employees will be hired on a temporary basis. This will keep costs low by avoiding the cost of fringe benefits and allowing the head count to fluctuate with demand. Since this is a simple assembly operation, there will be no need to retain any highly skilled or highly trained operators. Estimated costs of production are as follows:

Direct Labor	$1.00
Direct Materials	$5.35
Packaging and Shipping	$1.00
Total Variable Cost	$7.35

The manufacture of the control circuit boards is anticipated to be with an electronics subcontracting unit in order to reduce labor costs and therefore piece price. Orders will be placed for monthly batches with an expected lead time of eight weeks. Shipping and duties are included in the total material cost. The out-sourcing of the plastic nose cone will be less complicated and could be contracted with a local injection molding company. Lead times and batch sizes will be smaller, but there will be the requirement of a small investment for tooling. Overall, the choice of subcontracting the major components will keep capital expenses for equipment at a minimum.

Future expansion of capacity will not require any considerable investment other than additional fixtures and increased floor space for materials storage. Ramping up production to meet unexpected demand will be dependent on the ability of subcontractors to meet the new requirements, therefore contingencies for these circumstances will be included in the contracts.

Page 15

Management Team

Our management team is strongly qualified to set up and run the assembly operations as well as the subcontracting arrangements. The founding team has over 35 years of direct manufacturing, design, management, sales and management experience at various sized companies, including both private and publicly traded firms. This experience, combined with professional training in the Masters of Management in Manufacturing program at the J.L. Kellogg Graduate School of Management at Northwestern University, brings an enormous amount of manufacturing and management talent to the company and represents a distinctive competence of *Independence Marine*.

Mr. Tower brings 6 years of experience as a manager and partner at NIMROD Press in Boston, MA. Mr. Hagey brings over 10 years experience as a product development engineer at Hewlett Packard. Mr. Hagedorn has over 10 years of manufacturing and operations management experience. His most recent assignment is as the General Manager of Imaging Services with Bell & Howell's Document Management Products Company. Mr. Hattery brings 8 years of experience in product design and manufacturing engineering at General Motors. In addition, Mr. Hattery is attending the MMM program as a GM Fellow. Mr. Zant participated in manufacturing and design functions in the aerospace industry for three years prior to attending the MMM program at Northwestern University and has been named Manufacturing Program Manager for the Harper-Wyman Division of Oak Industries.

Both Mr. Tower and Mr. Hagey will be compensated for expenses incurred during the first year of operations. After the product launch market rate salaries will be arranged. Both will receive equity incentives based on *Independence Marine's* performance in terms of both profit and capital investment utilization.

In addition to the expertise provided by the founders, *Independence Marine* has strong accounting advice being provided by Bala V. Balachandran, Ph.D., Accounting Center Director at the Kellogg Graduate School of Management, who has agreed to serve on our Board of Directors. We anticipate that further financial advice will be available from both Dr. Balachandran, as well as from an appropriate select group of our investors, as needed.

An Advisory Board is also being formed with the goal of providing *Independence Marine* with access to new product ideas, additional market information and feedback, as well as serving as a source of technical and behavioral information.

With this combination of experts in management, manufacturing, accounting, finance, sales, technology and aquatic mammal behavior, *Independence Marine* is in a unique and unequaled position to capitalize upon the market need that is emerging at this very moment.

Page 16

Figure 9: Cash Management

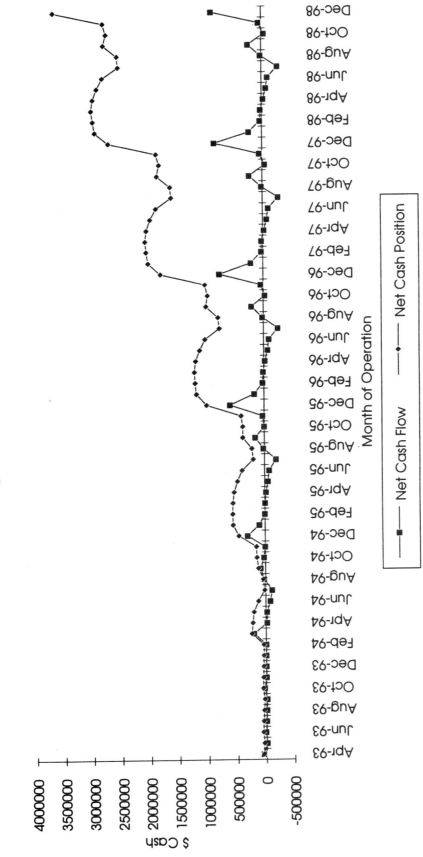

In summary, the management team at *Independence Marine* includes:

Caleb Tower, Managing Director, Chief Financial Officer
John Hagey, Director, Vice President of Product Development

The Board of Directors, in addition to the management team, includes:

Bala V. Balachandran, Outside Director, Accounting Center Director, KGSM
Frederick H. Hagedorn, Founder
John C. Hattery Jr., Founder
Thomas E. Zant, Founder
Outside Director(s), selected by key investors.

The following Board of Technical and Industry Advisors is being recruited:

Glenn Etchegary, Fishery Consultant, Center for Fisheries Innovation, St. Johns, NFLD
John Guzzwell, Acoustical Engineer, Centre for Cold Ocean Resource
                      Engineering, Memorial University, St. Johns, NFLD
Jon Lien, Ph.D., Animal Behaviorist, Whale Research Center,
                      Memorial University, St. Johns, NFLD
Bill Perrin, Marine Mammologist, SW Fisheries Ctr., La Jolla, CA
Tim Smith, Marine Mammal Manager, NMFS-NE, Wood's Hole, MA
Ron Smolowitz, Fishing Gear Designer and Consultant, Wood's Hole, MA

Financial Overview

Capital Needs

Prior to March of 1994, *Independence Marine* will be funded by the founders with an investment of $50,000. These funds will be used for the completion of the product design, production tooling, a limited amount of working capital and primary market development.

In March of 1994, once the field test results have been received and the total viability of the product has **been** verified, a second round of investment will be required. At this point an additional $250,000 will be sought, in exchange for 30% of the firm. These funds will be applied to working capital needs as production expands. The market demand is highly seasonal and requires a relatively high level of working capital so that the net cash position of the firm can be managed effectively, especially during the first two years (see Figure 9). The founders of the firm will retain 50% of the equity. The remaining 20% of the equity is being held in treasury as future incentive for the operating managers.

Page 17

Exit Strategy

We intend *Independence Marine* to be a long term business and will achieve this by expanding beyond our initial product and market. Since there are no firms that currently specialize in serving this industry, there is plenty of room for growth but little potential for a buyout by a larger firm. Our earliest option for exit is a stock repurchase from investors using the considerable amount of cash generated by the firm ($2.2 million by year 5). Eventually a public offering or leveraged buyout can be made when investors want liquidity or the firm needs greater capital access. Valuation of the firm at that point will be based on a fair outside appraisal.

Returns On Investment

Based on the conservative sales and cost estimates and an initial investment of $250,000 (for 30% of the firm's equity), Whale Away™ delivers an expected 43% internal rate of return on investment through year five. At this point the investment value will have increased between 2 and 11 times in the eyes of the investors based on our sensitivity analysis.

Review of Financial Projections

The most important component of the financial projections is the sales forecast. Sales drives our financial results. Our financials are based on our expected market size including the entry of competition in 1995. We have examined several alternative scenarios (best case, worst case). The table below summarizes the results:

Sensitivity to Sales Assumptions:

Scenario	Total Market Size (units per year)	Presence of Competition	1998 Firm Valuation	Net Return on Investment
Expected Case	150,000 per year	yes	$ 4,956,169	43 %
Best Case	18,000 per year	no	$ 7,590,362	62%
Worst Case	75,000 per year	yes	$ 1,805,523	17%
Zero-Profit Case	52,500 per year	yes	$ 866,234	1%

- Competition when present takes up 1/3 of market.
- 1994 capital investment is $250,000 in return for 30% of equity.
- The 1998 firm valuation combines excess cash reserves in 1998 with terminal value based on a 6-X multiple of cash flow and a discount rate of 16.67%.
- Return on investment is for the 1994 outside capital investment

Figure 10: Projected Sales

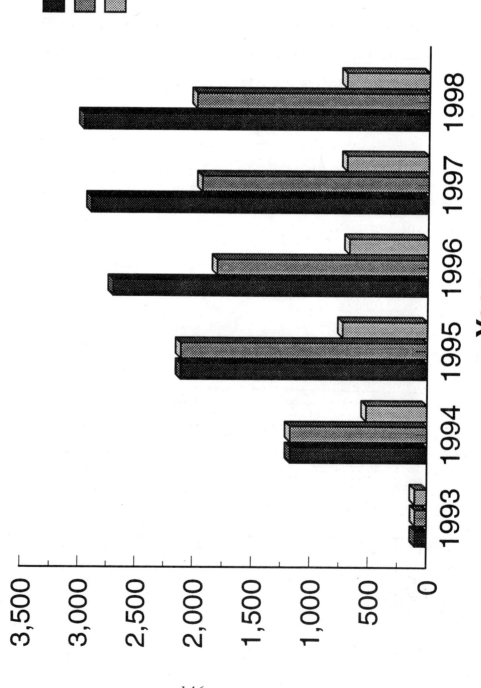

Sales Volume, in $1,000's

- Projected Market
- Projected Sales
- Breakeven Sales

Year

1993 1994 1995 1996 1997 1998

3,500
3,000
2,500
2,000
1,500
1,000
500
0

Figure 10, shows our projected sales in comparison to break-even sales levels. It is clear that expected sales will be well above break-even levels. This is due to the low capital investment manufacturing strategy and the resulting low fixed costs we have employed.

Cash Management

Independence Marine will be a cash machine. With low fixed costs and healthy margins our firm will generate a positive cash flow (and profits) in 1994, the firm's first full year of operation. Because this is the first year of outside investment participation, investors will see red ink only in the first few months of 1994. The reason *Independence Marine* needs investors is not to cover initial losses, but to cover our working capital needs due to our anticipated rapid growth in 1994 -1995. After 1994 *Independence Marine* will experience a cash and earnings build up. During the first year our expected cash position never dips below $35,000. This slack gives *Independence Marine* some flexibility to compensate for unexpected events. For example, if we have underestimated demand, the $35,000 cushion will help cover our additional working capital needs.

Independence Marine's expected return on equity ranges from 81% in 1994 down to 20% in 1998. This is because nonproductive cash builds up, inflating equity and diminishing ROE. Excess cash will either be paid out as dividends and stock repurchases or will be invested in market expansion projects. Actual returns on equity after dividends or investments will range well above 20% minimum.

Our assumptions in building the balance sheet are included with the financials. However, it is important to note that asset and inventory turnovers are realistic. Inventory ranges from 4-8 turns per year depending on the growth rate.

Sources & Uses of Funds

Our anticipated sources and uses of capital for 1993 and 1994 are as follows:

Time Period	Uses			Sources		
	Working Capital	Marketing	Product Development	Investment	Operating Revenues	Loans
June 1993 - Feb. 1994	38,000	46,000	26,000	50,000	60,000	
March 1994 - Dec 1994	494,000	42,000	96,000	250,000	324,000	58,000

Pro Forma Financials

Balance Sheet (attached)

Income Statement (attached)

Statement of Retained Earnings (attached)

Assumptions:

- Market growth and sales: see Appendices IX and X.
- Market development expense schedule: see Appendix VII.
- Salaries:
  - Executive - $120,000 + incentives (after 1993)
  - Operations Manager - $20,000
- Research and development - $25,000 per year
- Rent and utilities - $25,000
- No production learning curve in effect
- Asset assumptions:
  - Accounts receivable - 30 days of sales from previous period
  - Raw materials inventory - two months forward
  - Work-in-process - 5% of next period production (1 day)
  - Finished goods inventory - 30% of next period production (2 days)
  - Pre-paid expenses - $20,000
- Fixed asset spending needs:
  - Tooling - $50,000, three year life
  - Machinery - $25,000
  - Patents and trademarks - $0
- Liability assumptions:
  - Accounts payable - 50% of previous month's expenses
  - Accrued wages - one week
  - Accrued wage taxes - 50% of one month's wages
  - Interest due - $0 (paid every month)
  - Royalties - 2% of sales, accrued and paid quarterly
- Depreciation - three years
- Corporate taxes - 40%

Independence Marine
Pro Forma - Balance Sheet

		Point of Estab.	End Of May-93	End Of Jun-93	2nd Quarter 1993	End Of Jul-93	End Of Aug-93	End Of Sep-93	3rd Quarter 1993	End Of Oct-93	End Of Nov-93	End Of Dec-93	4th Quarter 1993	Annual 1993
ASSETS														
Cash		50000	40242	53483	53483	48407	40282	26457	26457	53632	48007	44882	44882	44882
Accounts Receivable (1-month)		0	0	0	0	0	0	0	0	0	0	0	0	0
Reserve for Bad Debt 5% of A/R	5%	0	0	0	0	0	0	0	0	0	0	0	0	0
Invt. - Raw Matls. (for next 2 months sales)		0	5350	0	0	0	0	21400	21400	0	0	0	0	0
Inv - WIP (5% next period raw matl)	5%	0	0	0	0	0	0	0	0	0	0	0	0	0
Inv - Finished Goods (10% next period FGI)	10%	0	0	0	0	0	0	0	0	0	0	0	0	0
Pre-Paid Expenses (Insurance)		0	0	0	0	0	0	0	0	0	0	0	0	0
Current Assets		50000	45592	53483	53483	48407	40282	47857	47857	53632	48007	44882	44882	44882
Tooling		0	2000	2000	2000	2000	2000	2000	2000	2000	2000	2000	2000	2000
Machinery		0	3000	3000	3000	3000	3000	3000	3000	3000	3000	3000	3000	3000
Patent & Copyright Expenses		0	0	0	0	0	0	0	0	0	0	0	0	0
Accumulated Depreciation		0	-1000	-1000	-1000	-1000	-1000	-5000	-5000	-5000	-5000	-5000	-5000	-5000
Net Property, Plant & Equipment		0	4000	4000	4000	4000	4000	0	0	0	0	0	0	0
TOTAL ASSETS		50000	49592	57483	57483	52407	44282	47857	47857	53632	48007	44882	44882	44882
LIABILITIES														
Accounts Payable Trade (2 Weeks RM, Shipping, Rent & Util.)		0	2675	0	0	0	0	10700	10700	0	0	0	0	0
Accrued Salaries (one Week)		0	0	0	0	0	0	0	0	0	0	0	0	0
Accrued Payroll Taxes (1/2 month's Wages)		0	0	0	0	0	0	0	0	0	0	0	0	0
Income Taxes Payable, Quarterly		0	0	2993	2993	0	0	0	0	0	0	0	0	0
Royalties Payable (quarterly payment)		0	0	0	0	0	0	0	0	0	0	0	0	0
Accrued Interest (paid Promptly)		0	0	0	0	0	0	0	0	0	0	0	0	0
Current Liabilities		0	2675	2993	2993	0	0	10700	10700	0	0	0	0	0
Total Note Due		0	0	0	0	0	0	0	0	0	0	0	0	0
Total Liabilities		0	2675	2993	2993	0	0	10700	10700	0	0	0	0	0
Paid In Capital		50000	50000	50000	50000	50000	50000	50000	50000	50000	50000	50000	50000	50000
Dividends Payable		0	0	0	0	0	0	0	0	0	0	0	0	0
Retained Earnings		0	-3083	4490	4490	2407	-5718	-12843	-12843	3632	-1993	-5118	-5118	-5118
Total Equity		50000	46917	54490	54490	52407	44282	37157	37157	53632	48007	44882	44882	44882
TOTAL LIABILITIES & EQUITIES		50000	49592	57483	57483	52407	44282	47857	47857	53632	48007	44882	44882	44882

149

Independence Marine
Pro Forma - Balance Sheet

	End Of Jan-94	End Of Feb-94	End Of Mar-94	1st Quarter 1994	End Of Apr-94	End Of May-94	End Of Jun-94	2nd Quarter 1994	End Of Jul-94	End Of Aug-94	End Of Sep-94	3rd Quarter 1994	End Of Oct-94	End Of Nov-94	End Of Dec-94	4th Quarter 1994	Annual 1994
ASSETS																	
Cash	41757	38632	245923	245923	228715	208798	137373	137373	43380	69408	126021	126021	152404	154287	403665	403665	403665
Accounts Receivable (1-month)	0	0	0	0	0	0	0	0	153920	168460	276260	276260	259360	157440	157440	157440	157440
Reserve for Bad Debt 5% of A/R) — 5%	0	0	0	0	0	0	0	0	-7696	-8423	-13813	-13813	-12968	-7872	-7872	-7872	-7872
Invt. - Raw Matls. (for next 2 months sales)	0	0	0	0	0	0	86237	86237	118963	143278	111494	111494	84230	355861	10625	10625	10625
Inv - WIP (5% next period raw matl) — 5%	0	0	0	0	0	0	2443	2443	2674	4386	4117	4117	2499	2499	18619	18619	18619
Inv - Finished Goods (10% next period FGI) — 10%	0	0	0	0	0	0	5964	5964	6528	10705	10050	10050	6101	6101	45449	45449	45449
Pre-Paid Expenses (Insurance)	0	20000	20000	20000	20000	20000	20000	20000	20000	20000	20000	20000	20000	20000	20000	20000	20000
Current Assets	41757	38632	265923	265923	248715	228798	252017	252017	337768	407814	534129	534129	511626	688316	647927	647927	647927
Tooling	2000	2000	2000	2000	52000	52000	52000	52000	52000	52000	52000	52000	52000	52000	52000	52000	52000
Machinery	3000	3000	3000	3000	28000	28000	28000	28000	28000	28000	28000	28000	28000	28000	28000	28000	28000
Patent & Copyright Expenses	0	0	0	0	0	0	0	0	0	0	0	0	0	0	0	0	0
Accumulated Depreciation	-5000	-5000	-5000	-5000	-5000	-7083	-9167	-9167	-11250	-13333	-15417	-15417	-17500	-19583	-21667	-21667	-21667
Net Property, Plant & Equipment	0	0	0	0	75000	72917	70833	70833	68750	66667	64583	64583	62500	60417	58333	58333	58333
TOTAL ASSETS	41757	38632	265923	265923	323715	301715	322851	322851	406518	474480	598712	598712	574126	748732	706260	706260	706260
LIABILITIES																	
Accounts Payable Trade (2 Weeks RM, Shipping, Rent & Util.)	0	0	0	0	0	0	43118	43118	59481	71639	55747	55747	42115	177930	5313	5313	5313
Accrued Salaries (one Week)	0	0	0	0	0	0	0	0	2308	2308	2308	2308	2308	2308	2308	2308	2308
Accrued Payroll Taxes (1/2 month's Wages)	0	0	0	0	0	0	0	0	5000	5000	5000	5000	5000	5000	5000	5000	5000
Income Taxes Payable, Quarterly	0	0	0	0	0	0	0	0	0	0	63641	63641	0	0	91344	91344	91344
Royalties Payable (quarterly payment)	0	0	0	0	0	0	0	0	3078	6448	11973	11973	5187	8336	11485	11485	11485
Accrued Interest (paid Promptly)	0	0	0	0	0	0	0	0	0	0	0	0	0	0	0	0	0
Current Liabilities	0	0	0	0	0	0	43118	43118	69867	85394	138668	138668	54610	193574	115449	115449	115449
Total Note Due	0	0	0	0	75000	72917	70833	70833	68750	66667	64583	64583	62500	60417	58333	58333	58333
Total Liabilities	0	0	0	0	75000	72917	113952	113952	138617	152061	203251	203251	117110	253991	173783	173783	173783
Paid In Capital	50000	50000	300000	300000	300000	300000	300000	300000	300000	300000	300000	300000	300000	300000	300000	300000	300000
Dividends Payable	0	0	0	0	0	0	0	0	0	0	0	0	0	0	0	0	0
Retained Earnings	-8243	-11368	-34077	-34077	-51285	-71202	-91101	-91101	-32099	22419	95461	95461	157016	194742	232477	232477	232477
Total Equity	41757	38632	265923	265923	248715	228798	208899	208899	267901	322419	395461	395461	457016	494742	532477	532477	532477
TOTAL LIABILITIES & EQUITIES	41757	38632	265923	265923	323715	301715	322851	322851	406518	474480	598712	598712	574126	748732	706260	706260	706260

- CONFIDENTIAL -

Independence Marine
Pro Forma - Balance Sheet

Item	%	End Of Jan-95	End Of Feb-95	End Of Mar-95	1st Quarter 1995	End Of Apr-95	End Of May-95	End Of Jun-95	2nd Quarter 1995	End Of Jul-95	End Of Aug-95	End Of Sep-95	3rd Quarter 1995	End Of Oct-95	End Of Nov-95	End Of Dec-95	4th Quarter 1995	Annual 1995
ASSETS																		
Cash		489301	489324	480155	480155	459635	406612	336392	336392	177475	191970	312069	312069	320288	341123	830106	830106	830106
Accounts Receivable (1-month)	5%	22800	16920	0	0	0	0	0	0	249080	276060	476420	476420	482000	292580	292580	292580	292580
Reserve for Bad Debt 5% of A/R		-1140	-846	0	0	0	0	0	0	-12454	-13803	-23821	-23821	-24100	-14629	-14629	-14629	-14629
Invt. - Raw Matls. (for next 2 months sales)		4526	0	0	0	0	66629	140475	140475	201288	256377	207200	207200	156530	642273	19747	19747	19747
Inv - WIP (5% next period raw matl)	5%	269	0	0	0	0	0	3954	3954	4382	7563	7652	7652	4645	4645	33471	33471	33471
Inv - Finished Goods (10% next period FGI)	10%	656	0	0	0	0	0	9652	9652	10697	18461	18678	18678	11337	11337	81702	81702	81702
Pre-Paid Expenses (Insurance)		20000	20000	20000	20000	20000	20000	20000	20000	20000	20000	20000	20000	20000	20000	20000	20000	20000
Current Assets		536411	525398	500155	500155	479635	493241	510473	510473	650469	756629	1018197	1018197	970701	1297330	1262977	1262977	1262977
Tooling		52000	52000	52000	52000	52000	52000	52000	52000	52000	52000	52000	52000	52000	52000	52000	52000	52000
Machinery		28000	28000	28000	28000	28000	28000	28000	28000	28000	28000	28000	28000	28000	28000	28000	28000	28000
Patent & Copyright Expenses		0	0	0	0	0	0	0	0	0	0	0	0	0	0	0	0	0
Accumulated Depreciation		-23750	-25833	-27917	-27917	-30000	-32083	-34167	-34167	-36250	-38333	-40417	-40417	-42500	-44583	-46667	-46667	-46667
Net Property, Plant & Equipment		56250	54167	52083	52083	50000	47917	45833	45833	43750	41667	39583	39583	37500	35417	33333	33333	33333
TOTAL ASSETS		592661	579564	552238	552238	529635	541157	556306	556306	694219	798296	1057781	1057781	1008201	1332746	1296311	1296311	1296311
LIABILITIES																		
Accounts Payable Trade (2 Weeks RM, Shipping, Rent & Util.)		2263	0	0	0	0	33314	70237	70237	100644	128189	103600	103600	78265	321136	9873	9873	9873
Accrued Salaries (one Week)		2308	2308	2308	2308	2308	2308	2308	2308	2308	2308	2308	2308	2308	2308	2308	2308	2308
Accrued Payroll Taxes (1/2 month's Wages)		5000	5000	5000	5000	5000	5000	5000	5000	5000	5000	5000	5000	5000	5000	5000	5000	5000
Income Taxes Payable, Quarterly		456	794	794	794	0	0	0	0	4982	10503	141912	141912	9640	15492	191643	191643	191643
Royalties Payable (quarterly payment)		0	0	0	0	0	0	0	0	0	0	20031	20031	0	0	21343	21343	21343
Accrued Interest (paid Promptly)		0	0	0	0	0	0	0	0	0	0	0	0	0	0	0	0	0
Current Liabilities		10027	8102	8102	8102	7308	40622	77545	77545	112933	145999	272851	272851	95213	343936	230167	230167	230167
Total Note Due		56250	54167	52083	52083	50000	47917	45833	45833	43750	41667	39583	39583	37500	35417	33333	33333	33333
Total Liabilities		66277	62269	60185	60185	57308	88539	123379	123379	156683	187666	312435	312435	132713	379352	263500	263500	263500
Paid In Capital		300000	300000	300000	300000	300000	300000	300000	300000	300000	300000	300000	300000	300000	300000	300000	300000	300000
Dividends Payable		0	0	0	0	0	0	0	0	0	0	0	0	0	0	0	0	0
Retained Earnings		226384	217296	192053	192053	172327	152618	132928	132928	237535	310630	445346	445346	575488	653394	732810	732810	732810
Total Equity		526384	517296	492053	492053	472327	452618	432928	432928	537535	610630	745346	745346	875488	953394	1032810	1032810	1032810
TOTAL LIABILITIES & EQUITIES		592661	579564	552238	552238	529635	541157	556306	556306	694219	798296	1057781	1057781	1008201	1332746	1296311	1296311	1296311

151

Independence Marine
Pro Forma - Balance Sheet

	1st Quarter 1996	2nd Quarter 1996	3rd Quarter 1996	4th Quarter 1996	Annual 1996	1st Quarter 1997	2nd Quarter 1997	3rd Quarter 1997	4th Quarter 1997	Annual 1997	1st Quarter 1998	2nd Quarter 1998	3rd Quarter 1998	4th Quarter 1998	Annual 1998
ASSETS															
Cash	997611	869987	831501	1261427	1261427	1400805	1268331	1224234	1695429	1695429	1847167	1713262	1669934	2161249	2161249
Accounts Receivable (1-month)	0	0	394060	249180	249180	0	0	424280	271400	271400	0	0	433460	278280	278280
Reserve for Bad Debt 5% of A/R (5%)	0	0	-19703	-12459	-12459	0	0	-21214	-13570	-13570	0	0	-21673	-13914	-13914
Invt. - Raw Matls. (for next 2 months sales)	0	113393	176464	16826	16826	0	120867	192199	18318	18318	0	123087	197067	0	0
Inv - WIP (5% next period raw matl) (5%)	0	3182	6517	28585	28585	0	3388	7098	30622	30622	0	3449	7277	31386	31386
Inv - Finished Goods (10% next period FGI) (10%)	0	7768	15907	69775	69775	0	8269	17325	74746	74746	0	8418	17764	76611	76611
Pre-Paid Expenses (Insurance)	20000	20000	20000	20000	20000	20000	20000	20000	20000	20000	20000	20000	20000	20000	20000
Current Assets	1017611	1014331	1424746	1633333	1633333	1420805	1420855	1863922	2096944	2096944	1867167	1868216	2323029	2553611	2553611
Tooling	52000	52000	52000	52000	52000	52000	102000	102000	102000	102000	102000	102000	102000	102000	102000
Machinery	28000	28000	28000	28000	28000	28000	53000	53000	53000	53000	53000	53000	53000	53000	53000
Patent & Copyright Expenses	0	0	0	0	0	0	0	0	0	0	0	0	0	0	0
Accumulated Depreciation	-52917	-59167	-65417	-71667	-71667	-77917	-84167	-90417	-96667	-96667	-102917	-109167	-115417	-121667	-121667
Net Property, Plant & Equipment	27083	20833	14583	8333	8333	2083	70833	64583	58333	58333	52083	45833	39583	33333	33333
TOTAL ASSETS	1044694	1035164	1439330	1641667	1641667	1422888	1491688	1928505	2155277	2155277	1919251	1914050	2362612	2586945	2586945
LIABILITIES															
Accounts Payable Trade (2 Weeks RM, Shipping, Rent & Util.)	0	56697	88232	8413	8413	0	60434	96099	9159	9159	0	61544	98534	0	0
Accrued Salaries (one Week)	2308	2308	2308	2308	2308	2308	2308	2308	2308	2308	2308	2308	2308	2308	2308
Accrued Payroll Taxes (1/2 month's Wages)	5000	5000	5000	5000	5000	5000	5000	5000	5000	5000	5000	5000	5000	5000	5000
Income Taxes Payable, Quarterly	0	0	112015	159441	159441	0	0	121199	175555	175555	0	0	125676	180946	180946
Royalties Payable (quarterly payment)	1476	0	16359	18177	18177	1258	0	17522	19798	19798	1370	0	17872	20300	20300
Accrued Interest (paid Promptly)	0	0	0	0	0	0	0	0	0	0	0	0	0	0	0
Current Liabilities	8784	64004	223914	193339	193339	8566	67741	242129	211819	211819	8677	68851	249390	208553	208553
Total Note Due	27083	20833	14583	8333	8333	2083	70833	64583	58333	58333	52083	45833	39583	33333	33333
Total Liabilities	35867	84838	238497	201672	201672	10649	138575	306712	270153	270153	60761	114685	288973	241887	241887
Paid In Capital	300000	300000	300000	300000	300000	300000	300000	300000	300000	300000	300000	300000	300000	300000	300000
Dividends Payable	0	0	0	0	0	0	0	0	0	0	0	0	0	0	0
Retained Earnings	708826	650326	900832	1139994	1139994	1112239	1053114	1321793	1585125	1585125	1558490	1499365	1773639	2045058	2045058
Total Equity	1008826	950326	1200832	1439994	1439994	1412239	1353114	1621793	1885125	1885125	1858490	1799365	2073639	2345058	2345058
TOTAL LIABILITIES & EQUITIES	1044694	1035164	1439330	1641667	1641667	1422888	1491688	1928505	2155277	2155277	1919251	1914050	2362612	2586945	2586945

152

– CONFIDENTIAL –

Independence Marine
Pro Forma - Income Statement

	Per Unit	May-93	Jun-93	2nd Quarter 1993	Jul-93	Aug-93	Sep-93	3rd Quarter 1993	Oct-93	Nov-93	Dec-93	4th Quarter 1993	Annual 1993
Months Per Period		1	1	2	1	1	1	3	1	1	1	3	8
Units Sold per period		0	1000	1000	0	0	0	0	4000	0	0	4000	5000
Price per unit		20	20	20	20	20	20	20	20	20	20	20	20
Total Revenues		0	20000	20000	0	0	0	0	80000	0	0	80000	100000
Break Even Unit Sales Level per period		244	165	667	165	642	563	2237	2698	445	247	5534	8438
Break Even $ Sales Level per period		4875	3294	8169	3294	12846	11265	27404	53953	8893	4941	67787	103360
Per Unit Operating Margin	61.25%												
Costs													
Variable Costs per Unit	Per Unit												
Labor	1.00	0	1000	1000	0	0	0	0	4000	0	0	4000	5000
Components													
Batteries	2.35	0	2350	2350	0	0	0	0	9400	0	0	9400	11750
Electronics	2.00	0	2000	2000	0	0	0	0	8000	0	0	8000	10000
Encasement	1.00	0	1000	1000	0	0	0	0	4000	0	0	4000	5000
Packaging & Shipping	1.00	0	1000	1000	0	0	0	0	4000	0	0	4000	5000
Royalties (0% Of Sales)	0.40	0	0	0	0	0	0	0	0	0	0	0	0
Variable Cost of Production	7.75	0	7350	7350	0	0	0	0	29400	0	0	29400	36750
Depreciation Expense		1000	0	1000	0	0	4000	4000	0	0	0	0	5000
Rent & Utilities	25000	0	0	0	0	0	0	0	0	0	0	0	0
Salaries, before '94 Sales Season	0	0	0	0	0	0	0	0	0	0	0	0	0
Salaries, beginning '94 Sales Season	120000	0	0	0	0	6042	1042	7083	32042	3542	1042	36625	43708
Promotion & Advertising Expenses	1.00 per unit	0	0	0	0	0	0	0	0	0	0	0	0
Commissions/Discounts (5% of Sales)		0	0	0	0	0	0	0	0	0	0	0	0
Reserve for Bad Debt (5% of A/R)		0	0	0	0	0	0	0	0	0	0	0	0
R&D Costs	25000	2083	2083	4167	2083	2083	2083	6250	2083	2083	2083	6250	16667
Total SG&A		2083	2083	4167	2083	8125	3125	13333	34125	5625	3125	42875	60375
Net Operating Costs		3083	9433	12517	2083	8125	7125	17333	63525	5625	3125	72275	102125
Earnings Before Interest		-3083	10567	7483	-2083	-8125	-7125	-17333	16475	-5625	-3125	7725	-2125
Interest Expense, Interest Rate =	10.00%	0	0	0	0	0	0	0	0	0	0	0	0
Earnings After Interest		-3083	10567	7483	-2083	-8125	-7125	-17333	16475	-5625	-3125	7725	-2125
Income Tax, t = 40%	40.00%	0	2993	2993	0	0	0	0	0	0	0	0	0
Tax Loss Carry Forward		-3083	0	0	-2083	-10208	-17333	-17333	-858	-6483	-9608	-9608	-2125
Net Income, with strong competition '96 on		-3083	7573	4490	-2083	-8125	-7125	-17333	16475	-5625	-3125	7725	-2125

Financial Ratios

	May-93	Jun-93	2nd Quarter 1993	Jul-93	Aug-93	Sep-93	3rd Quarter 1993	Oct-93	Nov-93	Dec-93	4th Quarter 1993	Annual 1993
Profit Margin after Interest		52.8%	37.4%					20.6%			9.7%	-2.1%
Profit Margin net of Interest Effects		52.8%	37.4%					20.6%			9.7%	-2.1%
Return on Equity	-6.4%	14.9%	8.6%	-3.9%	-16.8%	-17.5%	-37.8%	36.3%	-11.1%	-6.7%	18.8%	-4.5%
Current	17.0	17.9	17.9			4.5	4.5	5.1			3.4	3.4
Quick	15.0	17.9	17.9			2.5	2.5	2.5				
Operating Cash Flow to Current Liabilities	-3.6	4.7	5.7	-3.4		-2.6	-3.9					
Working Capital	42917	50490	50490	48407	40282	37157	37157	53632	48007	44882	44882	44882
Working Capital Turns	0.0	0.4	0.8	0.0	0.0	0.0	0.0	1.8	0.0	0.0	2.0	2.0
Inventory Turns	0.0	2.0		0.0	0.0	0.0	0.0	2.0	0.0	0.0	2.0	2.0
A/R Turns												4.5

Independence Marine
Pro Forma - Income Statement

	Per Unit	Jan-94	Feb-94	Mar-94	1st Quarter 1994	Apr-94	May-94	Jun-94	2nd Quarter 1994	Jul-94	Aug-94	Sep-94	3rd Quarter 1994	Oct-94	Nov-94	Dec-94	4th Quarter 1994	Annual 1994
Months Per Period		1	1	1	3	1	1	1	3	1	1	1	3	1	1	1	3	12
Units Sold per period		0	0	0	0	0	0	0	0	7696	8423	13813	29932	12968	7872	7872	28712	58644
Price per unit		20	20	20	20	20	20	20	20	20	20	20	20	20	20	20	20	20
Total Revenues		0	0	0	0	0	0	0	0	153920	168460	276260	598640	259360	157440	157440	574240	1172880
Break Even Unit Sales Level per period		247	247	1795	2289	1360	1574	1573	4508	2788	2902	3753	9443	4448	2653	2651	9752	25992
Break Even $ Sales Level per period		4941	4941	35903	45784	27207	31489	31461	90157	55769	58040	75056	188866	88958	53054	53026	195038	519845
Per Unit Operating Margin	61.25%																	
Costs																		
Variable Costs per Unit	Per Unit																	
Labor	1.00																	
Components																		
Batteries	2.35									18086	19794	32461	70340	30475	18499	18499	67473	137813
Electronics	2.00									15392	16846	27626	59864	25936	15744	15744	57424	117288
Encasement	1.00									7696	8423	13813	29932	12968	7872	7872	28712	58644
Packaging & Shipping	1.00									7696	8423	13813	29932	12968	7872	7872	28712	58644
Royalties (0% Of Sales)	0.40									3078	3369	5525	11973	5187	3149	3149	11485	23458
Variable Cost of Production	7.75									59644	65278	107051	231973	100502	61008	61008	222518	454491
Depreciation Expense		0	0	0	0		2083	2083	4167	2083	2083	2083	6250	2083	2083	2083	6250	16667
Rent & Utilities	25000			2083	2083	2083	2083	2083	6250	2083	2083	2083	6250	2083	2083	2083	6250	20833
Salaries, before '94 Sales Season	0	0	0	0	0	0	0	0	0	0	0	0	0	0	0	0	0	0
Salaries, beginning '94 Sales Season	120000			10000	10000	10000	10000	10000	30000	10000	10000	10000	30000	10000	10000	10000	30000	100000
Promotion & Advertising Expenses		1042	1042	8542	10625	3042	3042	3042	9125	3042	3042	3042	9125	13542	1042	1042	15625	44500
Commissions/Discounts (5% of Sales)	1.00									7696	8423	13813	29932	12968	7872	7872	28712	58644
Reserve for Bad Debt (5% of A/R)										7696	8423	13813	29932	12968	7872	7872	28712	58644
R&D Costs	25000	2083	2083	2083	6250	2083	2083	2083	6250	2083	2083	2083	6250	2083	2083	2083	6250	25000
Total SG&A		3125	3125	22708	28958	17208	17208	17208	51625	32600	34054	44834	111489	53644	30952	30952	115549	307621
Net Operating Costs		3125	3125	22708	28958	17208	19292	19292	55792	94328	101416	153968	349712	156230	94044	94044	344317	778779
Earnings Before Interest		-3125	-3125	-22708	-28958	-17208	-19292	-19292	-55792	59592	67044	122292	248928	103130	63396	63396	229923	394101
Interest Expense, Interest Rate =	10.00%	0	0	0	0	0	625	608	1233	590	573	556	1719	538	521	503	1563	4514
Earnings After Interest		-3125	-3125	-22708	-28958	-17208	-19917	-19899	-57024	59002	66471	121736	247209	102592	62876	62893	228361	389587
Income Tax, t = 40%	40.00%									0	11953	48694	60647	41037	25150	25157	91344	155835
Tax Loss Carry Forward		-12733	-15858	-38567	-31083	-55775	-75692	-95591	-88108	-36589	0	0	0	0	0	0	0	0
Net Income, with strong competition '96 on		-3125	-3125	-22708	-28958	-17208	-19917	-19899	-57024	59002	54518	73042	186562	61555	37725	37736	137016	233752
Financial Ratios																		
Profit Margin after Interest										38.3%	39.5%	44.1%	41.3%	39.6%	39.9%	39.9%	39.8%	33.2%
Profit Margin net of Interest Effects										38.6%	39.7%	44.2%	41.5%	39.7%	40.1%	40.1%	39.9%	33.4%
Return on Equity		-7.2%	-7.8%	-14.9%	-18.6%	-6.7%	-8.3%	-9.1%	-24.0%	24.7%	18.5%	20.3%	61.7%	14.4%	7.9%	7.3%	29.5%	81.0%
Current						5.8	5.8	5.8	5.8	4.8	4.8	3.9	3.9	9.4	3.6	5.6	5.6	5.6
Quick						3.6	3.6	3.6	3.6	3.0	2.9	2.9	2.9	7.7	1.7	5.0	5.0	5.0
Operating Cash Flow to Current Liabilities								-3.2	-4.8	-1.6	0.4	0.5	0.0	0.3	0.0	1.6	2.2	2.3
Working Capital		41757	38632	265923	265923	248715	228798	208899	208899	267901	322419	395461	395461	457016	494742	532477	532477	532477
Working Capital Turns		0.0	0.0	0.0	0.0	0.0	0.0	0.0	0.0	0.6	0.6	0.8	2.0	0.6	0.3	0.3	1.2	4.1
Inventory Turns										0.4	0.3	0.5	1.5	0.6	0.2	0.2	1.5	8.4
A/R Turns										2.0	1.0	1.2	4.3	1.0	0.8	1.0	3.6	14.9

- CONFIDENTIAL -

154

Independence Marine
Pro Forma - Income Statement

	Per Unit	Jan-95	Feb-95	Mar-95	1st Quarter 1995	Apr-95	May-95	Jun-95	2nd Quarter 1995	Jul-95	Aug-95	Sep-95	3rd Quarter 1995	Oct-95	Nov-95	Dec-95	4th Quarter 1995	Annual 1995
Months Per Period		1	1	1	3	1	1	1	3	1	1	1	3	1	1	1	3	12
Units Sold per period		1140	846	0	1986	0	0	0	0	12454	13803	23821	50078	24100	14629	14629	53358	105422
Price per unit		20	20	20	20	20	20	20	20	20	20	20	20	20	20	20	20	20
Total Revenues		22800	16920	0	39720	0	0	0	0	249080	276060	476420	1001560	482000	292580	292580	1067160	2108440
Break Even Unit Sales Level per period		1586	1538	1995	5119	1559	1558	1557	4674	3524	3736	5319	12579	6191	3902	3703	13797	36168
Break Even $ Sales Level per period		31712	30755	39910	102377	31187	31159	31132	93478	70485	74723	106373	251581	123829	78043	74063	275934	723370
Per Unit Operating Margin	61.25%																	
Costs	Per Unit 1.00																	
Variable Costs per Unit																		
Labor	1.00	1140	846	0	1986	0	0	0	0	12454	13803	23821	50078	24100	14629	14629	53358	105422
Components	2.35	2679	1988	0	4667	0	0	0	0	29267	32437	55979	117683	56635	34378	34378	125391	247742
Batteries	2.00	2280	1692	0	3972	0	0	0	0	24908	27606	47642	100156	48200	29258	29258	106716	210844
Electronics	1.00	1140	846	0	1986	0	0	0	0	12454	13803	23821	50078	24100	14629	14629	53358	105422
Encasement	1.00	1140	846	0	1986	0	0	0	0	12454	13803	23821	50078	24100	14629	14629	53358	105422
Packaging & Shipping	0.40	456	338	0	794	0	0	0	0	4982	5521	9528	20031	9640	5852	5852	21343	42169
Royalties (0% Of Sales)		0	0	0	0	0	0	0	0	0	0	0	0	0	0	0	0	0
Variable Cost of Production	7.75	8835	6557	0	15392	0	0	0	0	96519	106973	184613	388105	186775	113375	113375	413525	817021
Depreciation Expense		2083	2083	2083	6250	2083	2083	2083	6250	2083	2083	2083	6250	2083	2083	2083	6250	25000
Rent & Utilities	25000	2083	2083	2083	6250	2083	2083	2083	6250	2083	2083	2083	6250	2083	2083	2083	6250	25000
Salaries, before '94 Sales Season	0	10000	10000	10000	30000	10000	10000	10000	30000	10000	10000	10000	30000	10000	10000	10000	30000	120000
Salaries, beginning '94 Sales Season	120000																	
Promotion & Advertising Expenses		1042	1042	8542	10625	3042	3042	3042	9125	3042	3042	3042	9125	13542	3542	1042	18125	47000
Commissions/Discounts (5% of Sales)	1.00	1140	846	0	1986	0	0	0	0	12454	13803	23821	50078	24100	14629	14629	53358	105422
Reserve for Bad Debt (5% of A/R)		1140	846	0	1986	0	0	0	0	12454	13803	23821	50078	24100	14629	14629	53358	105422
R&D Costs	25000	2083	2083	2083	6250	2083	2083	2083	6250	2083	2083	2083	6250	2083	2083	2083	6250	25000
Total SG&A		17488	16900	22708	57097	17208	17208	17208	51625	42116	44814	64850	151781	75908	46966	44466	167341	427844
Net Operating Costs		28407	25540	24792	78739	19292	19292	19292	57875	140718	153871	251546	546136	264767	162224	159924	587116	1269865
Earnings Before Interest		-5607	-8620	-24792	-39019	-19292	-19292	-19292	-57875	108362	122189	224874	455425	217233	130156	132656	480045	838576
Interest Expense, Interest Rate =	10.00%	486	469	451	1406	434	417	399	1250	382	365	347	1094	330	313	295	938	4688
Earnings After Interest		-6093	-9089	-25243	-40425	-19726	-19708	-19691	-59125	107980	121825	224526	454331	216903	129843	132360	479107	833888
Income Tax, t=40%	40.00%	0	0	0	0	0	0	0	0	3372	48730	89811	141912	86761	51937	52944	191643	333555
Tax Loss Carry Forward		-6093	-15182	-40425	-40425	-60150	-79859	-99550	-99550	0	0	0	0	0	0	0	0	0
Net Income, with strong competition '96 on		-6093	-9089	-25243	-40425	-19726	-19708	-19691	-59125	104608	73095	134716	312418	130142	77906	79416	287464	500333

Financial Ratios

	Jan-95	Feb-95	Mar-95	1st Quarter 1995	Apr-95	May-95	Jun-95	2nd Quarter 1995	Jul-95	Aug-95	Sep-95	3rd Quarter 1995	Oct-95	Nov-95	Dec-95	4th Quarter 1995	Annual 1995
Profit Margin after Interest	-26.7%	-53.7%		-101.8%					43.4%	44.1%	47.1%	45.4%	45.0%	44.4%	45.2%	44.9%	39.5%
Profit Margin net of Interest Effects	-25.4%	-52.1%		-99.7%					43.4%	44.2%	47.2%	45.4%	45.0%	44.4%	45.3%	44.9%	39.7%
Return on Equity	-1.2%	-1.7%	-5.0%	-7.9%	-4.1%	-4.3%	-4.4%	-12.8%	21.6%	12.7%	19.9%	53.0%	16.1%	8.0%	8.5%	32.3%	63.9%
Current	53.5	64.8	61.7	61.7	65.6	65.6	65.6	6.6	5.8	5.2	2.9	3.7	10.2	3.8	5.5	5.5	5.5
Quick	53.0	64.8	61.7	61.7	65.6	12.1	10.5	4.6	3.8	3.2	2.9	2.9	8.4	1.9	4.9	4.9	4.9
Operating Cash Flow to Current Liabilities	1.4	0.3	-0.8	1.4	-1.1	-2.1	-3.2	-3.2	-1.6	0.1	0.6	-0.1	0.1	0.1	1.7	0.6	2.6
Working Capital	526384	517296	492053	492053	472327	452618	432928	432928	537535	610630	745346	745346	875488	953394	1032810	1032810	1032810
Working Capital Turns	0.0	0.0	0.0	0.1	0.0	0.0	0.0	0.0	0.5	0.5	0.7	1.7	0.6	0.3	0.3	1.2	2.7
Inventory Turns	0.2	1.7	1.7	0.3	0.3	0.3	0.3	0.3	0.3	0.3	0.5	1.4	0.7	0.2	0.2	1.5	5.4
A/R Turns	0.3	0.9	0.9	0.5	0.5	0.2	0.2	1.3	2.0	1.1	1.3	4.2	1.0	0.8	1.0	3.6	9.4

155

Independence Marine
Pro Forma - Income Statement

	Per Unit	1st Quarter 1996	2nd Quarter 1996	3rd Quarter 1996	4th Quarter 1996	Annual 1996	1st Quarter 1997	2nd Quarter 1997	3rd Quarter 1997	4th Quarter 1997	Annual 1997	1st Quarter 1998	2nd Quarter 1998	3rd Quarter 1998	4th Quarter 1998	Annual 1998
Months Per Period		3	3	3	3	12	3	3	3	3	12	3	3	3	3	12
Units Sold per period		3691	0	40898	45443	90032	3145	0	43806	49495	96446	3424	0	44680	50749	98853
Price per unit		20	20	20	20	20	20	20	20	20	20	20	20	20	20	20
Total Revenues		73820	0	817960	908860	1800640	62900	0	876120	989900	1928920	68480	0	893600	1014980	1977060
Break Even Unit Sales Level per period		5339	4625	11078	1296	33538	5203	4674	11637	13235	34749	5346	4674	11726	13384	35130
Break Even $ Sales Level per period		106780	92490	221565	24919	670753	104065	93478	232738	264708	694987	106924	93478	234512	267685	702598
Per Unit Operating Margin	61.25%															
Costs	Per Unit															
Variable Costs per Unit	1.00															
Labor	1.00	3691	0	40898	45443	90032	3145	0	43806	49495	96446	3424	0	44680	50749	98853
Components																
Batteries	2.35	8674	0	96110	106791	211575	7391	0	102944	116313	226648	8046	0	104998	119260	232305
Electronics	2.00	7382	0	81796	90886	180064	6290	0	87612	98990	192892	6848	0	89360	101498	197706
Encasement	1.00	3691	0	40898	45443	90032	3145	0	43806	49495	96446	3424	0	44680	50749	98853
Packaging & Shipping	1.00	3691	0	40898	45443	90032	3145	0	43806	49495	96446	3424	0	44680	50749	98853
Royalties (0% Of Sales)	0.40	1476	0	16359	18177	36011	1258	0	17522	19738	38518	1370	0	17872	20300	39541
Variable Cost of Production	7.75	28605	0	316960	352183	697748	24374	0	339497	383586	747457	26536	0	346270	393305	766111
Depreciation Expense		6250	6250	6250	6250	25000	6250	6250	6250	6250	25000	6250	6250	6250	6250	25000
Rent & Utilities	25000	6250	6250	6250	6250	25000	6250	6250	6250	6250	25000	6250	6250	6250	6250	25000
Salaries, before '94 Sales Season	0	30000	30000	30000	30000	120000	30000	30000	30000	30000	120000	30000	30000	30000	30000	120000
Salaries, beginning '94 Sales Season	120000															
Promotion & Advertising Expenses		10625	9125	9125	18125	47000	10625	9125	9125	18125	47000	10625	9125	9125	18125	47000
Commissions/Discounts (5% of Sales)	1.00	3691	0	40898	45443	90032	3145	0	43806	49495	96446	3424	0	44680	50749	98853
Reserve for Bad Debt (5% of A/R)		3691	0	40898	45443	90032	3145	0	43806	49495	96446	3424	0	44680	50749	98853
R&D Costs	25000	6250	6250	6250	6250	25000	6250	6250	6250	6250	25000	6250	6250	6250	6250	25000
Total SG&A		60507	51625	133421	151511	397064	59415	51625	139237	159615	409892	59973	51625	140985	162123	414706
Net Operating Costs		95362	57875	456631	509844	1119812	90031	57875	488984	549451	1182249	92753	57875	493505	561678	1205817
Earnings Before Interest		-21521	-57875	361330	399016	680828	-27139	-57875	391137	440449	746572	-24270	-57875	400095	453302	771243
Interest Expense, Interest Rate =	10.00%	781	625	469	313	2188	156	1250	1719	1563	4688	1406	1250	1094	937	4688
Earnings After Interest		-22324	-58500	360861	398603	678641	-27295	-59125	389418	438886	741884	-25685	-59125	399001	452365	766556
Income Tax, t = 40%	40.00%	0	0	112015	159441	271456	0	0	121199	175555	296754	0	0	125676	180946	306622
Tax Loss Carry Forward		-22324	-80824	0	0	0	-27295	-86420	0	0	0	-25685	-84810	0	0	0
Net Income, with strong competition '96 on		-23984	-58500	250506	239162	407184	-27755	-59125	268679	263332	445130	-26635	-59125	274274	271410	459933
Financial Ratios																
Profit Margin after Interest		-30.2%		44.1%	43.9%	37.7%	-43.4%		44.4%	44.3%	38.5%	-37.5%		44.7%	44.6%	38.8%
Profit Margin net of Interest Effects		-29.6%	-6.0%	44.2%	43.9%	37.8%	-43.2%	-4.3%	44.6%	44.4%	38.6%	-36.3%	-3.2%	44.7%	44.6%	38.9%
Return on Equity		-2.3%		23.3%	18.1%	32.9%	-1.9%		18.1%	15.0%	26.8%	-1.4%		14.2%	12.3%	21.7%
Current		115.8	15.8	6.4	8.4	8.4	165.9	21.0	7.7	9.9	9.9	215.2	27.1	9.3	12.2	12.2
Quick		115.8	13.9	5.5	7.9	7.9	165.9	19.0	6.8	9.3	9.3	215.2	25.2	8.4	11.7	11.7
Operating Cash Flow to Current Liabilities		1.5	-3.3	-0.2	2.1	2.2	1.5	-3.3	-0.2	2.1	2.3	1.4	-3.3	-0.2	2.2	2.4
Working Capital		1008826	950326	1200832	1439994	1439994	1412239	1353114	1621793	1885125	1885125	1858490	1799365	2073639	2345058	2345058
Working Capital Turns		0.1	0.0	0.8	0.7	1.5	0.0	0.0	0.6	0.6	1.2	0.0	0.0	0.5	0.5	0.9
Inventory Turns		0.3	0.0	1.4	1.5	3.9	0.3	0.0	1.3	1.6	4.3	0.3	0.0	1.3	1.6	4.6
A/R Turns		0.5		4.2	3.6	6.6	0.5		4.1	3.6	7.4	0.5		4.1	3.6	7.2

156

- CONFIDENTIAL -

Independence Marine
Pro Forma - Statement of Retained Earnings

	Apr-93	May-93	Jun-93	2nd Quarter 1993	Jul-93	Aug-93	Sep-93	3rd Quarter 1993	Oct-93	Nov-93	Dec-93	4th Quarter 1993	Annual 1993
Dividends Payable Declared, Rate = 0.00%		0	0	0	0	0	0	0	0	0	0	0	0
Period Retained Earnings		-3083	7573	4490	-2083	-8125	-7125	-17333	16475	-5625	-3125	7725	-5118
Net Retained Earnings		-3083	4490	4490	2407	-5718	-12843	-12843	3632	-1993	-5118	-5118	-5118

Independence Marine
Pro Forma - Statement of Cash Flows

	Apr-93	May-93	Jun-93	2nd Quarter 1993	Jul-93	Aug-93	Sep-93	3rd Quarter 1993	Oct-93	Nov-93	Dec-93	4th Quarter 1993	Annual 1993
Net Income		-3083	7573	4490	-2083	-8125	-7125	-17333	16475	-5625	-3125	7725	-5118
Add Back Interest Expense		0	0	0	0	0	0	0	0	0	0	0	0
Add Back Depreciation		1000	0	1000	0	4000	0	4000	0	0	0	0	5000
Net Changes in Working Capital													
Change in Current Liabilities		2675	318	2993	-2993	0	10700	7707	-10700	0	0	-10700	0
Change in Non-Cash Current Assets		-5350	5350	0	0	-21400	-21400	-21400	21400	0	0	21400	0
Operating Cash Flow		-4758	13242	8483	-5077	-8125	-13825	-27027	27175	-5625	-3125	18425	-118
Investments													
Tooling		2000	0	2000	0	0	0	0	0	0	0	0	2000
Machinery		3000	0	3000	0	0	0	0	0	0	0	0	3000
Patents & Copy rights		0	0	0	0	0	0	0	0	0	0	0	0
Cash Flow from Investments		-5000	0	-5000	0	0	0	0	0	0	0	0	-5000
Financing													
Loan for Plant, Property & Equipment	0	0	0	0	0	0	0	0	0	0	0	0	0
Payments on Principle on Loan		0	0	0	0	0	0	0	0	0	0	0	0
Interest On Debt		0	0	0	0	0	0	0	0	0	0	0	0
Paid in Capital (Working Cap.)	50000	0	0	50000	0	0	0	0	0	0	0	0	50000
Dividends Paid		0	0	0	0	0	0	0	0	0	0	0	0
Cash Flow From Financing	50000	0	0	50000	0	0	0	0	0	0	0	0	50000
Net Cash Flow	50000	-9758	13242	53483	-5077	-8125	-13825	-27027	27175	-5625	-3125	18425	44882
Net Cash Position	50000	40242	53483	53483	48407	40282	26457	26457	53632	48007	44882	44882	44882
Amortization Schedule for Investments													
Depreciation		1000	0	1000	0	4000	0	4000	0	0	0	0	5000
Period Depreciation		1000	0	1000	0	4000	0	4000	0	0	0	0	5000
Net Depreciation for period		1000	0	1000	0	4000	0	4000	0	0	0	0	5000

157

Independence Marine
Pro Forma - Statement of Retained Earnings

	Jan-94	Feb-94	Mar-94	1st Quarter 1994	Apr-94	May-94	Jun-94	2nd Quarter 1994	Jul-94	Aug-94	Sep-94	3rd Quarter 1994	Oct-94	Nov-94	Dec-94	4th Quarter 1994	Annual 1994
Dividends Payable Declared, Rate = 0.00%	0	0	0	0	0	0	0	0	0	0	0	0	0	0	0	0	0
Period Retained Earnings	-3125	-3125	-22708	-28958	-17208	-19917	-19899	-57024	59002	54518	73042	186562	61555	37725	37736	137016	237596
Net Retained Earnings	-8243	-11368	-34077	-34077	-51285	-71202	-91101	-91101	-32099	22419	95461	95461	157016	194742	232477	232477	232477

Independence Marine
Pro Forma - Statement of Cash Flows

	Jan-94	Feb-94	Mar-94	1st Quarter 1994	Apr-94	May-94	Jun-94	2nd Quarter 1994	Jul-94	Aug-94	Sep-94	3rd Quarter 1994	Oct-94	Nov-94	Dec-94	4th Quarter 1994	Annual 1994
Net Income	-3125	-3125	-22708	-28958	-17208	-19917	-19899	-57024	59002	54518	73042	186562	61555	37725	37736	137016	237596
Add Back Interest Expense	0	0	0	0	0	625	608	1233	590	573	556	1719	538	521	503	1563	4514
Add Back Depreciation	0	0	0	0	0	2083	2083	4167	2083	2083	2083	6250	2083	2083	2083	6250	16667
Net Changes in Working Capital																	0
Change in Current Liabilities	0	0	0	0	0	0	43118	43118	26749	15527	53274	95550	-84058	138964	-78125	-23219	115449
Change in Non-Cash Current Assets	0	0	-20000	-20000	0	0	-94645	-94645	-179744	-44017	-69702	-293464	48886	-174806	289767	163847	-244262
Operating Cash Flow	-3125	-3125	-42708	-48958	-17208	-17208	-68735	-103151	-91319	28684	59252	-3384	29005	4487	251965	285457	129964
Investments																	
Tooling	0	0	0	0	50000	0	0	50000	0	0	0	0	0	0	0	0	50000
Machinery	0	0	0	0	25000	0	0	25000	0	0	0	0	0	0	0	0	25000
Patents & Copy rights	0	0	0	0	0	0	0	0	0	0	0	0	0	0	0	0	0
Cash Flow from Investments	0	0	0	0	-75000	0	0	-75000	0	0	0	0	0	0	0	0	-75000
Financing																	
Loan for Plant, Property & Equipment	0	0	0	0	75000	0	0	75000	0	0	0	0	0	0	0	0	75000
Payments on Principle on Loan	0	0	0	0	0	-2083	-2083	-4167	-2083	-2083	-2083	-6250	-2083	-2083	-2083	-6250	-16667
Interest On Debt	0	0	0	0	0	-625	-608	-1233	-590	-573	-556	-1719	-538	-521	-503	-1563	-4514
Paid in Capital (Working Cap.)	0	0	250000	250000	0	0	0	0	0	0	0	0	0	0	0	0	250000
Dividends Paid	0	0	0	0	0	0	0	0	0	0	0	0	0	0	0	0	0
Cash Flow From Financing	0	0	250000	250000	75000	-2708	-2691	69601	-2674	-2656	-2639	-7969	-2622	-2604	-2587	-7813	303819
Net Cash Flow	-3125	-3125	207292	201042	-17208	-19917	-71426	-108551	-93993	26028	56613	-11352	26383	1883	249378	277644	358783
Net Cash Position	41757	38632	245923	245923	228715	208798	137373	137373	43380	69408	126021	126021	152404	154287	403665	403665	912982
Amortization Schedule for Investments																	
Depreciation	0	0	0	0	0	2083	2083	4167	2083	2083	2083	6250	2083	2083	2083	6250	16667
Period Depreciation	0	0	0	0	0	2083	2083	4167	2083	2083	2083	6250	2083	2083	2083	6250	16667
Net Depreciation for period	0	0	0	0	0	2083	2083	4167	2083	2083	2083	6250	2083	2083	2083	6250	16667

- CONFIDENTIAL -

Independence Marine
Pro Forma - Statement of Retained Earnings

	Jan-95	Feb-95	Mar-95	1st Quarter 1995	Apr-95	May-95	Jun-95	2nd Quarter 1995	Jul-95	Aug-95	Sep-95	3rd Quarter 1995	Oct-95	Nov-95	Dec-95	4th Quarter 1995	Annual 1995
Dividends Payable Declared, Rate = 0.00%	0	0	0	0	0	0	0	0	0	0	0	0	0	0	0	0	0
Period Retained Earnings	-6093	-9089	-25243	-40425	-19726	-19708	-19691	-59125	104608	73095	134716	312418	130142	77906	79416	287464	500333
Net Retained Earnings	226384	217296	192053	192053	172327	152618	132928	132928	237535	310630	445346	445346	575488	653394	732810	732810	732810

Independence Marine
Pro Forma - Statement of Cash Flows

	Jan-95	Feb-95	Mar-95	1st Quarter 1995	Apr-95	May-95	Jun-95	2nd Quarter 1995	Jul-95	Aug-95	Sep-95	3rd Quarter 1995	Oct-95	Nov-95	Dec-95	4th Quarter 1995	Annual 1995
Net Income	-6093	-9089	-25243	-40425	-19726	-19708	-19691	-59125	104608	73095	134716	312418	130142	77906	79416	287464	500333
Add Back Interest Expense	486	469	451	1406	434	417	399	1250	382	365	347	1094	330	313	295	938	4688
Add Back Depreciation	2083	2083	2083	6250	2083	2083	2083	6250	2083	2083	2083	6250	2083	2083	2083	6250	25000
Net Changes in Working Capital																	
— Change in Current Liabilities	-105423	-1925	0	-107347	-794	33314	36923	69443	35388	33066	126852	195306	-177639	248723	-113769	-42684	114718
— Change in Non-Cash Current Assets	197151	11036	16074	224262	0	-66629	-87452	-154081	-298913	-91665	-141470	-532047	55716	-305794	523335	273257	-188610
Operating Cash Flow	88205	2575	-6634	84146	-18003	-50523	-67737	-136263	-156452	16944	122529	-16979	10633	23231	491360	525224	456128
Investments																	
Tooling	0	0	0	0	0	0	0	0	0	0	0	0	0	0	0	0	0
Machinery	0	0	0	0	0	0	0	0	0	0	0	0	0	0	0	0	0
Patents & Copy rights	0	0	0	0	0	0	0	0	0	0	0	0	0	0	0	0	0
Cash Flow from Investments	0	0	0	0	0	0	0	0	0	0	0	0	0	0	0	0	0
Financing																	
Loan for Plant, Property & Equipment	0	0	0	0	0	0	0	0	0	0	0	0	0	0	0	0	0
Payments on Principle on Loan	-2083	-2083	-2083	-6250	-2083	-2083	-2083	-6250	-2083	-2083	-2083	-6250	-2083	-2083	-2083	-6250	-25000
Interest On Debt	-486	-469	-451	-1406	-434	-417	-399	-1250	-382	-365	-347	-1094	-330	-313	-295	-938	-4688
Paid in Capital (Working Cap.)	0	0	0	0	0	0	0	0	0	0	0	0	0	0	0	0	0
Dividends Paid	0	0	0	0	0	0	0	0	0	0	0	0	0	0	0	0	0
Cash Flow From Financing	-2569	-2552	-2535	-7656	-2517	-2500	-2483	-7500	-2465	-2448	-2431	-7344	-2413	-2396	-2378	-7188	-29688
Net Cash Flow	85636	23	-9169	76490	-20520	-53023	-70220	-143763	-158917	14496	120098	-24323	8219	20835	488982	518037	426441
Net Cash Position	489301	489324	480155	989471	459635	406612	336392	845708	177475	191970	312069	821306	320288	341123	830106	1339423	3995998

Amortization Schedule for Investments

	Jan-95	Feb-95	Mar-95	1st Quarter 1995	Apr-95	May-95	Jun-95	2nd Quarter 1995	Jul-95	Aug-95	Sep-95	3rd Quarter 1995	Oct-95	Nov-95	Dec-95	4th Quarter 1995	Annual 1995
Depreciation	2083	2083	2083	6250	2083	2083	2083	6250	2083	2083	2083	6250	2083	2083	2083	6250	25000
Period Depreciation	2083	2083	2083	6250	2083	2083	2083	6250	2083	2083	2083	6250	2083	2083	2083	6250	25000
Net Depreciation for period	2083	2083	2083	6250	2083	2083	2083	6250	2083	2083	2083	6250	2083	2083	2083	6250	25000

159

Independence Marine
Pro Forma - Statement of Retained Earnings

	1st Quarter 1996	2nd Quarter 1996	3rd Quarter 1996	4th Quarter 1996	Annual 1996	1st Quarter 1997	2nd Quarter 1997	3rd Quarter 1997	4th Quarter 1997	Annual 1997	1st Quarter 1998	2nd Quarter 1998	3rd Quarter 1998	4th Quarter 1998	Annual 1998
Dividends Payable Declared, Rate = 0.00%	0	0	0	0	0	0	0	0	0	0	0	0	0	0	0
Period Retained Earnings	-23984	-58500	250506	239162	407184	-27755	-59125	268679	263332	445130	-26635	-59125	274274	271419	459933
Net Retained Earnings	708826	650326	900832	1139994	1139994	1112239	1053114	1321793	1585125	1585125	1558490	1499365	1773639	2045058	2045058

Independence Marine
Pro Forma - Statement of Cash Flows

	1st Quarter 1996	2nd Quarter 1996	3rd Quarter 1996	4th Quarter 1996	Annual 1996	1st Quarter 1997	2nd Quarter 1997	3rd Quarter 1997	4th Quarter 1997	Annual 1997	1st Quarter 1998	2nd Quarter 1998	3rd Quarter 1998	4th Quarter 1998	Annual 1998
Net Income	-23984	-58500	250506	239162	407184	-27755	-59125	268679	263332	445130	-26635	-59125	274274	271419	459933
Add Back Interest Expense	781	625	469	313	2188	156	1250	1719	1563	4688	1406	1250	1094	937	4688
Add Back Depreciation	6250	6250	6250	6250	25000	6250	6250	6250	6250	25000	6250	6250	6250	6250	25000
Net Changes in Working Capital															
Change in Current Liabilities	-221383	55220	159910	-30575	-36828	-184773	59176	174387	-30309	18480	-203142	60174	180538	-40837	-3266
Change In Non-Cash Current Assets	412871	-124343	-448902	221338	60965	351907	-132524	-487163	238172	-29609	381516	-134954	-498941	261533	9153
Operating Cash Flow	174536	-120748	-31767	436488	458508	145784	-124074	-36129	479007	463689	159395	-126405	-36785	499302	495508
Investments															
Tooling	0	0	0	0	0	0	50000	0	0	50000	0	0	0	0	0
Machinery	0	0	0	0	0	0	25000	0	0	25000	0	0	0	0	0
Patents & Copy rights	0	0	0	0	0	0	0	0	0	0	0	0	0	0	0
Cash Flow from Investments	0	0	0	0	0	0	-75000	0	0	-75000	0	0	0	0	0
Financing															
Loan for Plant, Property & Equipment	0	0	0	0	0	0	75000	0	0	75000	0	0	0	0	0
Payments on Principle on Loan	-6250	-6250	-6250	-6250	-25000	-6250	-6250	-6250	-6250	-25000	-6250	-6250	-6250	-6250	-25000
Interest On Debt	-781	-625	-469	-313	-2188	-156	-1250	-1719	-1563	-4688	-1406	-1250	-1094	-937	-4688
Paid in Capital (Working Cap.)	0	0	0	0	0	0	0	0	0	0	0	0	0	0	0
Dividends Paid	0	0	0	0	0	0	0	0	0	0	0	0	0	0	0
Cash Flow From Financing	-7031	-6875	-6719	-6563	-27188	-406	67500	-7969	-7813	45313	-7656	-7500	-7344	-7188	-29688
Net Cash Flow	167505	-127623	-38486	429925	431321	139378	-132474	-44097	471195	434002	151739	-133905	-44129	492115	465820
Net Cash Position	997611	869987	831501	1261427	1261427	1400805	1268331	1224234	1695429	1695429	1847167	1713262	1669134	2161249	2161249
Amortization Schedule for Investments															
Depreciation	6250	6250	6250	6250	25000	6250	6250	6250	6250	25000	6250	6250	6250	6250	25000
Period Depreciation	6250	6250	6250	6250	25000	6250	6250	6250	6250	25000	6250	6250	6250	6250	25000
Net Depreciation for period	6250	6250	6250	6250	25000	6250	6250	6250	6250	25000	6250	6250	6250	6250	25000

160

– CONFIDENTIAL –

Appendix I: Market Definition Analysis

New England	# Vessels	# Gear	Net Feet	Avg Gear	Avg Feet
Seines/Bag Nets/Butterfly Nets	36	168		5	
Trawls	1,151	1,155		1	
Weirs/Traps/Pound Nets/Hoop Nets	8	76		10	
Gillnets	172	8,449	2,544,000	49	301
Gillnet Whale Away Market Size	172	users			
	42,400	units total			
	247	units/user @ 75 ft spacing =			$4,930

Chesapeake	# Vessels	# Gear	Net Feet	Avg Gear	Avg Feet
Seines/Bag Nets/Butterfly Nets	51	111	19,050	2	172
Trawls	313	370	4,867	1	13
Weirs/Traps/Pound Nets/Hoop Nets	122	610		5	
Gillnets	446	2,357	1,730,500	5	734
Gillnet Whale Away Market Size	446	users			
	28,842	units total			
	65	units/user @ 75 ft spacing =			$1,293

Mid Atlantic	# Vessels	# Gear	Net Feet	Avg Gear	Avg Feet
Seines/Bag Nets/Butterfly Nets	3	18		6	
Trawls	302	302		1	
Weirs/Traps/Pound Nets/Hoop Nets	6	253		42	
Gillnets	35	777	233,100	22	300
Gillnet Whale Away Market Size	35	users			
	3,885	units total			
	111	units/user @ 75 ft spacing =			$2,220

South Atlantic	# Vessels	# Gear	Net Feet	Avg Gear	Avg Feet
Seines/Bag Nets/Butterfly Nets	50	352	171,653	7	488
Trawls	1,491	6,380	73,670	4	12
Weirs/Traps/Pound Nets/Hoop Nets	0	5,381			
Gillnets	87	10,458	3,241,592	120	310
Gillnet Whale Away Market Size	87	users			
	54,027	units total			
	621	units/user @ 75 ft spacing =			$12,420

Gulf Coast	# Vessels	# Gear	Net Feet	Avg Gear	Avg Feet
Seines/Bag Nets/Butterfly Nets	263	387	55,631	1	144
Trawls	5,634	12,909	151,424	2	12
Weirs/Traps/Pound Nets/Hoop Nets	0	0			
Gillnets	55	64	141,700	1	2,214
Gillnet Whale Away Market Size	55	users			
	2,362	units total			
	43	units/user @ 75 ft spacing =			$859

Pacific	# Vessels	# Gear	Net Feet	Avg Gear	Avg Feet
Seines/Bag Nets/Butterfly Nets	455	513	67,760	1	132
Trawls	660	1,015	4,589	2	5
Weirs/Traps/Pound Nets/Hoop Nets	21	496		24	
Gillnets	1,230	3,621	1,086,300	3	300
Gillnet Whale Away Market Size	1,230	users			
	18,105	units total			
	15	units/user @ 75 ft spacing =			$294

Total	# Vessels	# Gear	Net Feet	Avg Gear	Avg Feet
Seines/Bag Nets/Butterfly Nets	858	1,549	314,094	2	203
Trawls	9,551	22,131	234,550	2	11
Weirs/Traps/Pound Nets/Hoop Nets	157	6,816		43	
Gillnets	2,025	25,726	8,977,192	13	349
Gillnet Whale Away Market Size	2,025	users			
	149,620	units total			
	74	units/user @ 75 ft spacing =			$1,478

Source: NMFS Fisheries Statistics Division - Fishing Vessels Operating Units Data

Trade Journal Subscription Levels/Ad Rates

Geographic Region	# of Users	% of Users	Journal - Distribution - # of Units	% of Mkt	National Fisheries Product News	National Fisherman	Regional New England Commercial Fisheries News	Regional Pacific The Fishermen's News	Regional Pacific Pacific Fishing	Regional Pacific Alaska Fisherman's Journal	Regional Subscriber Distribution	Regional Advertising Cost	Saturation Regional Cost per User	Regional Cost per Device
New England	172	8%	42,400	28.40%	7,699	9,873	6,675	70	155	92	24,564	$3,529	$20.52	$0.08
Chesapeake & Mid Atlantic	481	24%	32,727	21.85%	3,109	6,253	992	51	97	35	10,537	$1,439	$2.99	$0.04
South Atlantic	87	4%	54,027	36.08%	4,085	8,786	293	130	114	65	13,473	$1,791	$20.59	$0.03
Gulf Coast	55	3%	2,362	1.58%	5,647	2,001	67	77	56	38	7,886	$887	$16.13	$0.38
Pacific	1,230	61%	18,105	12.09%	12,964	9,712	155	12,677	8,873	12,378	56,759	$8,470	$6.89	$0.47
Canada					360	2,314	180	222	1,267	73	4,416	$691	$0.00	$0.00
Other Foreign					106	712	45	37	66	11	977	$143	$0.00	$0.00
Other					1,030	1,807	93	236	442	281	3,889	$550	$0.00	$0.00
Total	2,025		149,620		35,000	41,458	8,500	13,500	11,070	12,973	122,501	$17,500	$8.64	$0.12
4-Color Full-page rate, 12 Issues					$2,000	$4,360	$1,280	$1,510	$1,615	$1,735	12,500			
Cost/reader					$0.06	$0.11	$0.15	$0.11	$0.15	$0.13	$0.10			
Campaign/Artwork Preparation			$5,000											
Total Print Advertising Cost			$17,500											

Trade Journal Subscription Distribution

Geographic Region	# of Users	% of Users	Journal - Distribution - # of Units	% of Mkt	National Fisheries Product News	National Fisherman	Regional New England Commercial Fisheries News	Regional Pacific The Fishermen's News	Regional Pacific Pacific Fishing	Regional Pacific Alaska Fisherman's Journal	Regional Subscriber Distribution	Regional Advertising Cost
New England	172	8%	42,400	28.40%	22%	24%	79%	1%	1%	1%	20%	20%
Chesapeake & Mid Atlantic	481	24%	32,727	21.85%	9%	15%	12%	0%	1%	0%	9%	8%
South Atlantic	87	4%	54,027	36.08%	12%	21%	3%	1%	1%	1%	11%	10%
Gulf Coast	55	3%	2,362	1.58%	16%	5%	1%	1%	1%	0%	6%	5%
Pacific	1,230	61%	18,105	12.09%	37%	23%	2%	94%	80%	95%	46%	48%
Canada					1%	6%	2%	2%	11%	1%	4%	4%
Other Foreign					0%	2%	1%	0%	1%	0%	1%	1%
Other					3%	4%	1%	2%	4%	2%	3%	3%

Total Costs of Promotion

		1993	1994	1995-on
Materials:	Brochures	$8,000	$4,000	$4,000
	Publicity Package	$3,000	$1,000	$1,000
	Print Ad Design	$5,000	$5,000	$5,000
Direct Mail:		$5,000	$5,000	$5,000
Trade Magazine Advertising:		$12,500	$12,500	$12,500
Conventions:	Booth Design	$15,000	$2,500	$2,500
	Space Lease	$5,000	$5,000	$5,000
Port Call Travel:		$12,000	$12,000	$12,000
Public Relations:		$20,000	$25,000	$30,000
Total		$85,500	$72,000	$77,000

162

Source: SRDS Business Publications Vol. 1; and NMFS Fisheries Statistics Division - Fishing Vessels Operating Units Data

APPENDIX III

Buyer Behavior:

Fishermen have distinct buying behaviors. Therefore, in an effort to prepare the product for introduction to the industry, a consumer profile was constructed.

The decision making unit
- Investment decisions are made exclusively by vessel owners.
- Including equipment purchases and repairs.
- Operational decisions are often made in consultation with the crew.

Supplier Relationships
- Supply houses primarily provide materials that are requested.
- New product ideas do not normally come from or through supply houses.
- At times, suppliers will assist manufacturers by identifying lead users.

Industry information sources
- Primary information sources for lead users include Trade Journals, Associations and Shows.
- Lead users within a fleet drive technological dispersal.
- Non-lead user fishermen are innovation averse, and imitation prone.
- Visual cues obtained through observation of other fishermen are primary drivers of imitation.

Communication between industry members
- Nonexistent regarding strategy or technique.
- Responsive to direct questions regarding equipment and technology.
- Open and helpful when centered around equipment repair, family and personal tragedy.

Diffusion of technology
- On average it takes 6-10 years for a new technology to be accepted and diffused.
- When positive economic benefit is observable, acceptance can be twice as fast.
- All fleets (all boats and vessels within a port, regardless of ownership) have lead users who must be accepting of the technology if it is to succeed within the fleet. What one fleet does has little bearing on another fleet's actions.

Financial Characteristics
- Two types of financial risk -- market price of catch and harvest fluctuations.
- Economists commonly segment a fishing fleet into three categories:
- Highliners -- fishermen who fall into the top 25% in earnings;
- Average earners -- fishermen who fall into the middle 50% in earnings;
- Low liners -- fishermen who fall into the lowest 25% in earnings.

Evidence suggests that performance within fishing fleets is highly correlated over time. Fisherman who do well one year tend to do well in following years. A study performed by Patricia Marchik showed that the correlation between a vessel's catch value in 1979 and 1980 was 0.72 for the Pacific Northwest Salmon Fleet. The existence of consistent yearly performance variations sets up a "pecking order" within a fleet. Consistently, high performers are recognized as highliners and tend to lead innovation adoption for the fleet members. Regulatory pressure will significantly affect buying behavior.

Appendix IV: Market Size, Share Revenue and Profits

Annual Market Size	Users	@ 50 ft	% of Mkt
Estimated Wholesale Price =	$20.00		
Estimated COGS w/shipping =	$8.75		
New England	172	42,400	28.40%
Chesapeake	446	28,842	19.26%
Mid Atlantic	35	3,885	2.59%
South Atlantic	87	54,027	36.08%
Gulf Coast	55	2,362	1.58%
Pacific	1,230	18,105	12.09%
Total US	2,025	149,620	

Source: Bass Model constructed using adoption rate of hospital ultrasound equipment.

$$s(t) = pm + (q-p)y(t-1) - (q/m)(y(t-1))^2$$

m = # of Identified Users in Region
p = 0.37
q = 0.37
y(t-1) = Cumulative users through time t-1.
s(t) = New users adopting in time period t.

New England

Year	y(t-1)	s(t)	Market Volumes Incremental	Gross	Market Share	Share Volume	Gross Revenue	Operating Profit	% of Op. Profit
1994	20	63	15,621	20,552	100%	20,552	$411,033	$231,206	33.90%
1995	83	49	12,093	32,645	100%	32,645	$652,900	$367,256	30.47%
1996	132	26	6,431	39,076	67%	26,051	$521,015	$293,071	29.11%
1997	159	10	2,378	41,454	67%	27,636	$552,725	$310,908	28.57%
1998	168	3	696	42,151	67%	28,100	$562,009	$316,130	28.40%

Chesapeake

Year	y(t-1)	s(t)	Market Volumes Incremental	Gross	Market Share	Share Volume	Gross Revenue	Operating Profit	% of Op. Profit
1994	0	167	10,781	10,781	100%	10,781	$215,617	$121,284	17.78%
1995	167	143	9,254	20,035	100%	20,035	$400,700	$225,394	18.70%
1996	310	86	5,560	25,595	67%	17,063	$341,268	$191,964	19.07%
1997	396	35	2,282	27,877	67%	18,585	$371,692	$209,077	19.21%
1998	431	11	706	28,583	67%	19,056	$381,110	$214,375	19.26%

Mid Atlantic

Year	y(t-1)	s(t)	Market Volumes Incremental	Gross	Market Share	Share Volume	Gross Revenue	Operating Profit	% of Op. Profit
1994	0	13	1,452	1,452	100%	1,452	$29,044	$16,337	2.40%
1995	13	11	1,247	2,699	100%	2,699	$53,975	$30,361	2.52%
1996	24	7	749	3,448	67%	2,298	$45,969	$25,858	2.57%
1997	31	3	307	3,755	67%	2,503	$50,067	$28,163	2.59%
1998	34	1	95	3,850	67%	2,567	$51,336	$28,876	2.59%

South Atlantic

Year	y(t-1)	s(t)	Market Volumes Incremental	Gross	Market Share	Share Volume	Gross Revenue	Operating Profit	% of Op. Profit
1994	0	33	20,195	20,195	100%	20,195	$403,896	$227,191	33.31%
1995	33	28	17,335	37,530	100%	37,530	$750,595	$422,210	35.03%
1996	60	17	10,415	47,945	67%	31,963	$639,268	$359,588	35.72%
1997	77	7	4,274	52,219	67%	34,813	$696,258	$391,645	35.99%
1998	84	2	1,323	53,543	67%	35,695	$713,900	$401,569	36.08%

Gulf Coast

Year	y(t-1)	s(t)	Market Volumes Incremental	Gross	Market Share	Share Volume	Gross Revenue	Operating Profit	% of Op. Profit
1994	0	21	883	883	100%	883	$17,656	$9,931	1.46%
1995	21	18	758	1,641	100%	1,641	$32,811	$18,456	1.53%
1996	38	11	455	2,096	67%	1,397	$27,944	$15,719	1.56%
1997	49	4	187	2,283	67%	1,522	$30,436	$17,120	1.57%
1998	53	1	58	2,341	67%	1,560	$31,207	$17,554	1.58%

Pacific

Year	y(t-1)	s(t)	Market Volumes Incremental	Gross	Market Share	Share Volume	Gross Revenue	Operating Profit	% of Op. Profit
1994	0	460	6,768	6,768	100%	6,768	$135,351	$76,135	11.16%
1995	460	395	5,809	12,577	100%	12,577	$251,534	$141,488	11.74%
1996	854	237	3,490	16,067	67%	10,711	$214,227	$120,503	11.97%
1997	1,092	97	1,432	17,499	67%	11,666	$233,325	$131,245	12.06%
1998	1,189	30	443	17,943	67%	11,962	$239,237	$134,571	12.09%

Total US

Year	y(t-1)	s(t)	Market Volumes Incremental	Gross	Market Share	Share Volume	Gross Revenue	Operating Profit	Net Income
1993	20	0	4,500	4,500	0	0	72,000	40,500	-113,783
1994	20	756	55,700	60,630	100%	60,630	1,212,596	682,085	531,363
1995	776	644	46,496	107,126	100%	107,126	2,142,515	1,205,165	1,147,668
1996	1420	383	27,101	134,227	67%	89,485	1,789,692	1,006,702	944,893
1997	1803	156	10,861	145,088	67%	96,725	1,934,503	1,088,158	1,030,709
1998	1959	48	3,322	148,410	67%	98,940	1,978,799	1,113,074	1,070,566

Discussion Questions
for
Independence Marine

1. Independence Marine plans to build a business on the idea of developing and selling devices to frighten whales and other cetaceans away from "gill"-type fishing nets.

   - How good is this idea?

   - What does Independence Marine have to do well to make money with this idea? In other words, what are the critical success factors?

   - How well has Independence Marine established the need for its product?

2. Independence Marine has five founders, two of whom have major responsibilities in the business.

   - How capable is this team of carrying out the business?

   - Who on the team is most critical to Independence Marine's success?

   - What additional talent or skills are critical to Independence Marine?

3. Independence Marine has established a working relationship with the Whale Research Centre (WRC) of Memorial University.

   - How critical is this relationship to Independence Marine?

   - What motivation does the WRC have to pursue an alliance?

4. Independence Marine's pro forma financial statements project sales of $1,800,640 and a net income of $407,184 in 1996.

   - What assumptions are most critical?

   - Are these financials credible?

5. Place yourself in the position of an investor with more than enough resources to provide Independence Marine with $50,000 (in exchange for 6% of its stock).

   - What do you see as the major strengths and weaknesses of this investment opportunity?

   - What are the major risks?

   - Can any of the weaknesses or risks reduced by how the deal is structured?

   - Would you invest?

MOOT CORP®
Company Evaluation

Company: _____

Please evaluate the <u>business plan</u> on the following aspects:

(Using this rating system: 1 = very poor, 2 = poor, 3 = fair, 4 = adequate, 5 = good, 6 = very good, 7 = excellent)

I. Elements of the Plan (20%)

1. **Executive Summary**
   (Clear, exciting and effective as a stand-alone
   overview of the plan)   1   2   3   4   5   6   7
   Comments/Questions _____
   _____
   _____

2. **Company Overview**
   (Business purpose, history, genesis of concept,
   current status, overall strategy and objectives)   1   2   3   4   5   6   7
   Comments/Questions _____
   _____
   _____

3. **Products or Services**
   (Description, features and benefits, pricing, current
   stage of development, proprietary position)   1   2   3   4   5   6   7
   Comments/Questions _____
   _____
   _____

4. **Market and Marketing Strategy**
   (Description of market, competitive analysis, needs
   identification, market acceptance, unique
   capabilities, sales/promotion)   1   2   3   4   5   6   7
   Comments/Questions _____
   _____
   _____

5. **Management**
   (Backgrounds of key individuals, ability to execute
   strategy, personnel needs, organizational structure,
   role of any non-student executive, which students
   will execute plan)   1   2   3   4   5   6   7
   Comments/Questions _____
   _____
   _____

In rating each of the above, please consider the following questions:
- Is this area covered in adequate detail?
- Does the plan show a clear understanding of the elements that should be addressed?
- Are the assumptions realistic and reasonable?

167

Please evaluate the <u>financials</u> of the plan:

These should be presented in summary form in the text of the business plan and follow generally accepted accounting principles.

(Using this rating system: 1 = very poor, 2 = poor, 3 = fair, 4 = adequate, 5 = good, 6 = very good, 7 = excellent)

II. Elements of the Plan (20%)

1. **Cash Flow Statement**
   (effective as record of
   available cash and as planning
   tool; Detailed for first two-years,
   quarterly/annually for years 3-5)   1   2   3   4   5   6   7
   Comments/Questions _____
   _____
   _____

2. **Income Statement**
   (consistent with plan and effective
    in capturing profit performance;
   Quarterly for first two years,
   Quarterly/annually for years 3-5)   1   2   3   4   5   6   7
   Comments/Questions _____
   _____
   _____

3. **Balance Sheet**
   (effective in presenting assets,
   liabilities and owners equity)   1   2   3   4   5   6   7
   Comments/Questions _____
   _____
   _____

4. **Funds Required/Uses**
   (clear and concise presentation
   of amount, timing, type, and use of
   funds required for venture)   1   2   3   4   5   6   7
   Comments/Questions _____
   _____
   _____

5. **Offering**
   (proposal/terms to investors–indicate
   how much you want, the ROI, and the
   structure of the deal; possible exit strategies)   1   2   3   4   5   6   7
   Comments/Questions _____
   _____
   _____

Please evaluate the <u>presentation</u> of the following aspects:

(Using this rating system: 1 = very poor, 2 = poor, 3 = fair, 4 = adequate, 5 = good, 6 = very good, 7 = excellent)

III. Presentation (20%)

1. **Overall organization**
   (materials presented in clear,
   logical and/or sequential form)   1   2   3   4   5   6   7
   Comments/Questions _____
   _____
   _____

2. **Ability to relate need for the company**
   (meaningful examples, practical applications,
   etc.)   1   2   3   4   5   6   7
   Comments/Questions _____
   _____
   _____

3. **Ability to maintain judge's interest**   1   2   3   4   5   6   7
   Comments/Questions _____
   _____
   _____

4. **Responsiveness to judges**
   (answered questions, adapted to judge's
   level, needs, etc.)   1   2   3   4   5   6   7
   Comments/Questions _____
   _____
   _____

5. **Quality of visual aids**
   (slides, outlines, handouts, etc.)   1   2   3   4   5   6   7
   Comments/Questions _____
   _____
   _____

In rating each of the above, please consider the following:

- Do the presenters demonstrate competence in their presentation skills?
- Are they poised, confident and knowledgeable?
- Do they think effectively on their feet?

Strengths of presentation

Weaknesses of presentation

Additional comments

Please evaluate the viability of the company on the following aspects:
(To be completed after reading the plan and viewing the presentation)
(1 indicates definitely no, while 7 indicates definitely yes.)

IV. Viability of Company (40%)

		Definitely No					Definitely Yes	
1.	**Market Opportunity (20%)** (There is a clear market need presented as well as a way to take advantage of that need.)	1	2	3	4	5	6	7
2.	**Distinctive Competence (20%)** (The company provides something novel/unique/ special that gives it a competitive advantage in its market.)	1	2	3	4	5	6	7
3.	**Management Capability (20%)** (This team can effectively develop this company and handle the risks associated with the venture.)	1	2	3	4	5	6	7
4.	**Financial Understanding (20%)** (This team has a solid understanding of the financial requirements of the business.)	1	2	3	4	5	6	7
5.	**Investment Potential (20%)** (The business represents a real investment opportunity in which you would consider investing.)	1	2	3	4	5	6	7

Company Strengths

Company Weaknesses

Additional Comments

170

Breeze

Technology

Incorporated

Presented by

Robert Brough

Peter Homan

Timothy Zwemer

BUSINESS PLAN

1994
INTERNATIONAL MOOT CORP
COMPETITION
UNIVERSITY OF TEXAS, AUSTIN

Bond University

This business plan provides a blueprint for the launch and growth of Breeze Technology Inc. (Breeze). It will also serve to demonstrate the operational and financial viability of Breeze.

Breeze is in the business of commercializing technology for the sports, leisure and recreation markets. Our launch product is a footwear ventilation technology which is applicable to all closed shoes and boots. Breeze will first enter the athletic/casual/outdoor shoe and boot markets, where the technology can be applied immediately. The technology will later be diffused throughout the entire range of footwear products as ongoing R&D and marketing analyses identify further avenues for profitable application of the technology.

The technology consists of an active displacement system which induces a positive flow of fresh air into the shoe while forcibly exhausting the warm and moisture-laden air which has collected inside the shoe. The air is replaced entirely once per stride with fresh air from outside the shoe. The resultant cooling and dehumidifying effect on the feet is substantial. Product testing indicates a reduction in the temperature inside the shoe of 7.3°F and a reduction in the "heat index" within the shoe by 46°F. This has obvious benefits in reducing odor, athlete's foot and other fungal infections. Less obviously, the technology militates against foot fatigue, blistering and discomfort related to the buildup of heat and moisture within the shoe.

The benefits of Breeze technology include significant cushioning advantages over the existing airbag and gel technologies, allowing the user greater comfort and protection from shock-related injuries. Breeze technology can be used in conjunction with existing cushioning systems to improve the functioning of those systems, and potentially can be custom-adjusted by the user to suit different activities and/or users of different weights.

Potential manufacturing cost advantages are also provided by Breeze technology since it renders obsolete the need for ventilation holes and/or porous fabrics (including leather). This in turn permits the use of less expensive manufacturing materials which are both waterproof and stretch resistant, eliminating the need for reinforcing overlays and multiple stitching processes.

Two additional advantages are offered by the use of nonporous and non-stretching materials. First, if water does enter the shoe from around the ankle, the Breeze technology would actively evacuate the water and ultimately dry the foot. Second, non-stretching fabrics in the shoe's upper will significantly extend the useful life of athletic shoes and other footwear (and the period of peak performance), and thus justify a premium price.

173

The market for athletic/casual footwear is colossal. In the US alone, annual retail sales in 1993 were $11.6 billion. Breeze research demonstrates that this market demands comfort, performance, style and value in their footwear. Breeze technology better satisfies these demands.

To serve this market Breeze considered two strategic options: manufacturing and licensing. Manufacturing and marketing the footwear under our own banner involves considerable business risk and funding costs, which may be minimized by licensing. Breeze decided to seek to license the technology to a major athletic footwear manufacturer in a mutually-beneficial strategic alliance. Royalty income from this alliance will provide the necessary funding for ongoing R&D expenditures and patent protection for other technologies which the company intends to commercialize in the sports, leisure, and recreation markets. By year three, revenue flows are expected from licensing and/or manufacturing of subsequent technologies.

Strategy to achieve licensing of the technology is based on personal selling to senior executives of target footwear manufacturer(s) using prototypical models, video, and technical support. Breeze is currently negotiating with a major footwear manufacturing company and expects to soon announce its first licensing agreement for the Breeze technology.

Expected royalties total $3.56 million for calendar 1994, with $30.4 million in royalties expected over the first five years. This income will be applied liberally to R&D, a patent protection fund, and the commercialization of other technologies, as well as to the accumulation of a strategic fund to defend against theft of our intellectual property. It is anticipated that about $4.9 million of royalty income will be paid out as dividends to shareholders over the five years. Cash balances remain positive throughout, and grow to $10.7 million over the five years.

The Breeze management team consists of Bob Brough, Peter Homan, and Tim Zwemer. They bring together complementary skills and a wealth of experience in the management of new and growing businesses. The venture team has successfully funded the development and the protection of the intellectual property. Breeze is not seeking further investor participation nor any debt funding. They expect to fund the continued growth of the company with royalty income from the initial strategic alliance and subsequent commercialization of other technologies.

TABLE OF CONTENTS

1. THE COMPANY

The mission of Breeze is to commercialize technology in the sports, leisure and recreation industries. The management team, Bob Brough, Tim Zwemer, and Peter Homan, have identified several windows of opportunity for the application of new technology in these industries and together constitute the nucleus of the expertise required to take advantage of these opportunities. As early plans developed, a network of complementary expertise was identified and involved. Breeze now has at its disposal the critical mass of talents and individuals necessary for the efficient, speedy and profitable application of advanced technologies in the chosen industries.

A number of proposals were examined during the process of selecting a launch technology. J. Mike O'Dwyer's invention to ventilate and improve the cushioning and performance of footwear was ultimately selected after extensive investigation and independent testing. Breeze Technology Inc. was subsequently formed with O'Dwyer as a 25% shareholder. Bob Brough, Tim Zwemer and Peter Homan each hold one third of Recreation Innovations Inc., which in turn holds 75% of Breeze. The rights to the technology have been assigned to Breeze by the inventor under contract.

O'Dwyer's invention represents a major change in the paradigm of footwear technology and will revolutionize the entire footwear industry. The technology dramatically increases the efficiency of footwear ventilation and improves on current shock absorption technology. The technology will also render unnecessary some of the current materials and manufacturing methods. Porous uppers will no longer be necessary, nor will it be necessary to stitch together multiple porous panels to gain the required support and stability of the uppers. Concurrent with this innovation, shoe manufacturers might use non-stretching uppers to extend the useful life of their shoes.

2. MARKET ANALYSIS

The footwear market currently seeks certain benefits from footwear products. These have been identified through four related streams of research: (i) a 1992 US Athletic Footwear Association report; (ii) focus group interviews; (iii) a competitor content analysis; and (iv) formal discussions with "key informants" i.e., senior executives in the footwear industry.

2.1 Athletic Footwear Association Research

The Athletic Footwear Association undertook a major study in 1992 to determine the decision criteria used by consumers when purchasing athletic footwear. The results demonstrate that nine of out of ten consumers place "comfort, fit, and feel" as the most important characteristics of athletic footwear. Other important criteria identified in the study include "suit active life-style," has performance advantages," and "fashion."

2.2 Focus Group Interviews

To better understand the criteria used by consumers when evaluating and selecting footwear, focus group interviews were conducted utilizing Bond University students. One group consisted of Americans and the second of Australians. Analysis of the focus group protocols provided a rich qualitative assessment of consumer decision behavior in this product category and extends in an important way the results from the Athletic Footwear Association study. Results revealed consistency across respondents in the manner in which they categorized footwear: athletic/casual, outdoor and dress. Agreement was also found when respondents were asked to generate the factors they look for when purchasing footwear. These included quality, comfort, performance, price, and style. Likewise, respondents concurred on the negative aspects of footwear and footwear use. Among the negatives identified were "sweaty feet," "stinky feet," "too warm/hot," "not waterproof," and "materials rip and fall apart."

When asked to identify their "wish list" (i.e., those features or benefits they would like their footwear to have) respondents described the following: waterproofing, ventilation, ability to regulate temperature, no maintenance, and a gel sole conforming to the foot. Virtual unanimity was found among respondents when specifically asked to affirm whether ventilation would be a "significant benefit." Moreover, some respondents stated they would be willing to pay an additional 25% for this feature, while others indicated they would pay as much as US$120 for footwear with this benefit. (See Appendix I for more details).

2.3 Competitor Content Analysis

Content analysis was employed to systematically and objectively identify the specific content (i.e., the features and/or benefits) touted in magazine advertisements for footwear. Current issues of athletic/outdoor magazines were collected and each footwear advertisement was analyzed and its content coded. The footwear categories evaluated were athletic/casual and outdoor. In all, 46 advertisements by 42 manufacturers were evaluated. Claims for "support" were found in 43% of the advertisements, "performance" in 36%, "ventilation/temperature" in 32%, "durability/ruggedness" in 32%, "dryness" in 30%; "comfort" in 21%, "shock absorption" in 15%, and "fashion," in 11%. (See Appendix II for more details).

2.4   Key Informant Analysis

Informal discussions held with senior executives at a major US footwear manufacturer gave Breeze management effective access to the findings of the primary research and market experience of that manufacturer. These discussions confirmed what had been derived from the Athletic Footwear Association study, the focus group interviews, and the competitor content analysis.

Users require comfort, performance, style and value from their footwear. "Comfort" is a combination of cushioning, dryness and ventilation. "Performance" includes shock absorption, rebound (energy return) and the maintenance of optimal foot support. "Style" includes the myriad design innovations as well as the gimmicks and celebrity endorsements successfully utilized by some manufacturers. Value to the customer is the ratio of benefits to price (this is further described in section 4.1). Current manufacturers recognize these market requirements and incorporate various design features that attempt to address these concerns. The cushioning and performance requirements are currently best served by the use of air pockets or gel bags in the heel and midsole area of the shoe. Ventilation is provided through passive means such as vents, holes, porous panels or through design, as for example, in the latest range of athletic sandals.

2.5   Benefits of Breeze Technology

Breeze technology represents a major step forward in satisfying these market requirements through positive displacement ventilation and controlled heel compression and rebound. Breeze's forced ventilation technology provides a measurable and significant reduction in the temperature and the humidity of the environment surrounding the foot. In controlled testing, confirmed by the Australian Institute of Sport (the premier national body for sports research and training), the technology reduced in-shoe temperature by 7.3°F (see Appendix II) and reduced the heat index by 46°F, compared to an unmodified shoe (see Appendix III). A reduction of these magnitudes in shoe temperature and humidity is expected to dramatically reduce foot odor, fungal infections, blistering and muscle fatigue. The user can "feel" the refreshing effect of the ventilation and all test subjects confirmed that the ventilation "felt good," and was in no way intrusive to the activity in which they were engaged.

The benefits provided by controlled heel compression are a measurable reduction in the intensity and duration of shock transmitted to the user. The heel of a shoe becomes increasingly hard as it approaches full compression; the faster the compression, the greater the shock transmitted to the users anatomy. The Breeze technology incorporates an outlet valve which allows air to escape the heel chamber at a predetermined pressure and thus, slows compression and softens impact forces. The rate at which air escapes the chamber can be varied to suit shoe size, user weight, and type of shoe (or user application). Indeed, the use of a valve with variable settings on some models will allow user-adjustment to optimize shoe performance for different activities.

Additional benefits provided to the market by Breeze technology are the possibility of more durable, waterproof and better insulated (yet ventilated) uppers. By making porous upper materials obsolete, the technology will allow manufacturers to use materials that are capable of better supporting, protecting and insulating the foot. Breeze shoes also have the ability to evacuate water that has entered through the neck of the shoe (e.g., from rain or puddles) and to subsequently dry the user's socks and foot. Breeze technology will thus enable the manufacturer to offer a drier, cooler shoe. Indeed, the valve system can be reversed to heat the feet effectively in some circumstances and can be "turned off" if neither cooling nor heating is required.

The market's current expectations have not yet been awakened to these benefits because it has been impossible to deliver these under the current footwear paradigm. When consumers learn that these benefits can be provided they will ultimately demand them across the full range of footwear. Thus the definitive elements of footwear comfort will expand to include dryness, water/moisture evacuation, user-regulated temperature and user-regulated heel compression and rebound characteristics. For consumers that seek style, fashion and fads the manufacturer may incorporate Breeze technology into existing strategies, perhaps even enhancing these possibilities.

Three broad segments define the footwear market: (i) dress; (ii) casual/athletic/outdoor; and (iii) special purpose (including military, police and other "duty" footwear, industrial workboots and specialized sports footwear). Although Breeze technology is ultimately applicable to virtually all shoes, the technology lends itself to immediate application in the athletic/casual footwear segment. Once established there, diffusion throughout the entire footwear market will be a logical and systematic outcome of the further development of the technology and the market's embrace of the new footwear paradigm.

Breeze

Exhibit I: What Breeze Technology Offers the Market

The MARKET WANTS:	The MARKET GETS:	BREEZE OFFERS:
1. COMFORT: • Cushioning • Dry feet • Ventilation - temperature reduction - humidity reduction - odor reduction	• Air or gel bags • Water penetration • Passive ventilation - porous fabrics - holes/vents/sandals - odor cures	• Improved cushioning • Restricted water entry • Positive evacuation of water and humidity • Positive ventilation - space-age fabrics - lower temperature - lower humidity - odor prevention

2. PERFORMANCE:
• Injury avoidance
• Rebound/energy return
• Optimal foot support
	• Structural design
	• Air/gel bags
	• Deteriorating foot support
	   as the shoe ages
		• Retains all benefits
		• Potential improvements
		• Optimal foot support for
		   longer period

3. STYLE/FASHION:
• Design
• Colours
• Gimmicks
• Celebrity endorsements
	• Various	• Retains all benefits and
		   offers additional
		   possibilities

4. VALUE
• Price
 	
• Benefits
	• Increasing price
	
	• Minimal increase in benefits
		• Insignificant increase in
		   price
		• Significant increase in
		   benefit

3. STRATEGIC OPTIONS

Two main strategic options were identified. Breeze might manufacture shoes incorporating the technology or, alternatively, license the technology to one or more current operators in the footwear industry.

3.1   Manufacturing

The manufacturing option would require Breeze to source large amounts of venture capital through equity partners, seeking debt on the open market, or through a joint venture (perhaps with one of the current footwear manufacturers). This venture capital would then be used to undertake the R&D necessary to identify the specific materials and associated manufacturing requirements. The expense of researching, designing and commissioning production processes and tooling would also have to be met. The manufacturing option would require that Breeze enter into a highly competitive arena with the current footwear manufacturers, all keen to retain market share in a mature market. The business and financial risks of this option are substantial.

3.2   Licensing

Licensing, on the other hand, requires relatively little capital up front and would establish Breeze in a strategic alliance, rather than an adversarial relationship, with at least one of the footwear manufacturers. Licensing will accelerate the process by which the technology becomes accepted as the industry standard. It will also allow access to markets that would not otherwise be accessible. In other words, while it is possible to enter the US athletic shoe market via the manufacturing option, Breeze could not simultaneously introduce the technology to the major international markets (no less the other segments of the footwear market). Licensing allows Breeze to simultaneously enhance the competitive position of its licensee while providing immediate net gains to its owners. A licensee would build and stimulate demand, provide brand name recognition for the technology and share the costs of pioneering. A large and financially strong licensee would also vigorously defend against theft of the intellectual property.

In short, it is substantially more promising to license the technology to one or more operators in the industry. At the same time, Breeze is cognizant of the pitfalls of licensing. It creates a direct competitor by giving access to the firm's competitive advantage. It provides short term profits but may adversely effect long term profits. Most importantly, the licensor may be vulnerable to attack from the licensee. In light of these issues, Breeze will position itself defensively to minimize its vulnerability to these threats.

3.3   Licensing Protocols

Various licensing protocols were investigated. There might be a large initial payment followed by relatively modest royalty payments, or the converse. An outright sale of the technology is simply the extreme case (with a large initial payment and zero royalty rate). Royalties might be based on, for example, the annual value of wholesale invoices, a fixed royalty per pair of shoes, or a percentage of gross revenues plus a percentage of any increase of market share accruing to the licensee. It was determined that Breeze would attempt to negotiate a flat fee per period for assignment of the technology, with a royalty rate based on the licensee's wholesale sales at invoice cost (for shoes incorporating the technology) to be applicable beyond some minimum level of sales revenue. The size of the flat fee and the minimum sales revenue target would be negotiated to allow a strong inducement for the licensee to integrate the technology quickly throughout the firm's product line.

Exhibit II indicates the strategic choices made. The preferred strategy is to approach one of the market leaders in the athletic/casual market and seek to license the technology to that party. If success is not achieved with one of the major manufacturers, the backup strategy is to approach several smaller manufacturers and marketers and offer them the opportunity to adopt the technology in an effort to steal market share from the majors. Finally, if no existing manufacturer is willing to license the technology at reasonable rates, Breeze as a strategy of last resort, will enter niche markets as a manufacturer of footwear products with potential expansion later into mainstream lines. If the technology is licensed, Breeze expects to begin manufacturing (of other product innovations) in year three, in any case.

Exhibit II: Market Segments, Strategic Options and Target Markets

Broad Market Segments

Strategic Option	Dress/Fashion	Casual/Athletic	Special Purpose
Manufacture			3
Exclusive License to a Market Leader	Diffusion	1	Diffusion
Licence to several smaller shoe companies		2	

3.4 Target Market

It was necessary to identify manufacturers that may be interested in the Breeze technology. Our preliminary analysis of the footwear market identified the major manufacturers and their respective market positions. As shown in Exhibit III, there are two major players in the US athletic/casual footwear market, followed by a half dozen smaller players. Internationally, Adidas and Reebok are each larger than Nike; Puma also has a relatively large share outside the US market.

182

Exhibit III: Major Athletic Shoe Manufacturers in the US Market

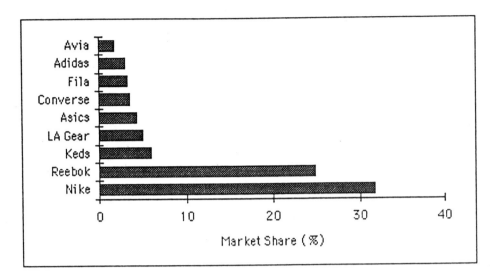

In 1993, the total retail value of athletic/casual shoes in the US market was $11.6 billion (see Appendix VI). Nike, for example, is responsible for nearly $4 billion in sales at retail and over $2 billion at wholesale in the US market alone. Nike are also the leaders in market segment diversification, having the most comprehensive range of products. Nike is seen as a performance brand first and fashion statement second. Reebok (with 28% of the market including their subsidiary Avia), has a fashion/life-style image rather than one of performance. Reebok is currently in transition mode, attempting to become more focused on their marketing with a broader product line within the casual footwear market. Their non-core businesses are for sale and it remains to be seen if their new strategy will bear positive results. Both Nike and Reebok are experiencing a maturing market for athletic/casual shoes and as a result each have diversified into apparel and sports equipment in an attempt to maintain overall growth.

Of the minor brands, Keds is the market leader in the children's footwear segment. They are currently in a turnaround situation and are concentrating on keeping their brand attractive to top retailers. LA Gear is in the middle of a major restructuring. They have traditionally produced fashion-oriented products and are currently repositioning themselves at the lower priced end of the market (below $65). The remaining competitors are aggressively seeking share through product innovation and heavy advertising campaigns. In a June 1993 report on the industry, Shearson Lehman Brothers stated that Nike was the best placed company in the industry to take advantage of any rebound of the depressed economy that was largely responsible for the poor trading conditions. Shearson also stated that Nike products and marketing strategies

-11-

were already well considered and in place, in marked contrast to their competitors.

On the basis of this analysis, and on advice from other key sources in the US, one major US manufacturer has been approached. Discussions with this company are ongoing and several follow-up meetings are planned.

4. MARKETING STRATEGY

Breeze acknowledges a primary and a secondary market for its technology. The company's primary market is the footwear manufacturers and wholesalers. The secondary market is the end-use consumer. The needs of the secondary market were discussed earlier in this report. In meeting secondary market demand, the technology will be pulled through the primary market. Breeze's strategy for marketing its technology to it's primary market is now considered.

Personal selling of the technology to top executives of the target footwear manufacturer is the chosen strategy . Breeze first commissioned the development of prototype shoes to allow independent testing and verifying of O'Dwyer's initial test data (see Appendix C). This verification came from subsequent testing at the Australian Institute of Sport (see Appendix II). Additional prototype shoes were then manufactured in the shoe size of senior executives at the targeted footwear manufacturer. An animated video which explains the technical aspects of the technology was also developed. This was considered the superior method of communicating the physical dynamics of the technology. This video will be used, as necessary, in conjunction with the prototypical footwear, in selling the technology to industry executives. A technical manual was also compiled which provides the test data and specifications. This material is available to the research and development department of the targeted company for in-house evaluation of the technology.

4.1   Pricing Strategy

In acknowledging that both primary and secondary markets exist, two pricing issues arise. In respect of the primary market, the cost to a manufacturer of incorporating the Breeze design into their shoes is restricted to the cost of the royalty (see Exhibit 7) and could well be offset by reductions in manufacturing and material costs. With porous upper materials rendered unnecessary, the manufacturer is free to experiment with new and superior materials and manufacturing methods. These may well be more cost effective than present methods and include, for example, the injection-molding of uppers and sole in a single operation using a synthetic, substitute material.

The retail price to the end consumer is dependent upon the strategy of the shoe manufacturer, who may wish to pursue a premium pricing strategy. This strategy would appear consistent with focus group results which indicate consumer willingness to pay for the additional benefits. This strategy is also supported by the competitor content analysis and discussions with top executives in the athletic shoe industry. If the manufacturer chooses, instead, to pass on their royalty cost (a maximum of 67 cents per pair in year one), then the retail price of a pair of premium shoes would be not expected to rise more than $3.00.

Breeze will negotiate a pricing strategy which includes a commitment or option fee, plus a royalty based on wholesale invoice price and a diffusion incentive structure. Breeze has retained a professional negotiator to join in this phase of the negotiations. The negotiating team will bring to the attention of the potential licensee the magnitude of cross-segment diffusion possibilities the substantial likelihood of increased market share and the inevitable revitalization of their product life cycle curve. The licensee will also enjoy the benefits associated with being identified as a technology leader by consumers.

While negotiations are continuing, the financial projections in this plan are based on conservative estimates of the commitment fee and royalty rates, as detailed in the financial section later in the plan.

5. RESEARCH & DEVELOPMENT

The first phase of Breeze's R&D strategy is to adapt the existing technology (and subsequent developments) to different segments of the footwear market in order to assist the licensee in diffusing the technology across the full range of footwear products.

The first phase is already under way. Breeze has begun the necessary research and development that will be required to maximize the efficiency of the technology in walking and casual shoes. While running requires a softer heel cushion to absorb 2-3 times the runner's weight, walking and casual shoes are more comfortable if the heel cushioning is softer. Thus, R&D efforts are concentrating on reducing the positive bias of the heel (its ability to resist deformation and recover original form after deformation) and increasing the restriction in the exhaust system to provide the necessary deceleration on heel impact.

A logical progression of this line of development is the introduction of a user-adjusted variable restriction on the exhaust port to enable user "interaction" with the product. This development will allow the user to adjust the deceleration characteristics of the footwear heel to suit the user's weight as well as differing activities, for example, rapid deceleration for walking and delayed deceleration for running. A

-13-

Breeze

concurrent development will be the inclusion of a facility to reverse the ventilation system in cold weather to take advantage of the warming effect of reverse airflow and/or the superior insulation of the nonporous upper materials that are permitted by this technology.

Breeze technology will also be adapted to work in a rigid sole boot. This entails an entirely different set of challenges. Breeze is currently investigating the common parameters and characteristics of rigid sole boots that will need to be considered in adapting our technology to this class of footwear. It may require some form of inertial motion mechanism to operate the pumping chamber. This mechanism will be incorporated in the sole of the footwear and operate independently of any external movement or flexing of the footwear. With the successful testing of this adaptation we expect entry into the military, industrial, and hiking/outdoors segments of the market. Directly stemming from the developments of the rigid sole adaptation we expect to introduce our technology to the booted sports equipment segments such as skates, rollerblades and cleated boots.

Funded by the income from the licensing of the footwear technology, Breeze will proceed to develop new technology that will apply to new and diverse products in the sports, leisure and recreation markets. Reliance on one technology, one market, and perhaps one licensee poses certain risks to the company's longer term viability. In view of this, Breeze plans to broaden its technology base beyond that applicable to footwear. Other technologies applicable to the sports, leisure, and recreation industries have been identified and these will, after due process that ensures their viability, be commercialized. This strategy will create a portfolio of investments and offset Breeze's exposure to the footwear market in the medium-to-long term.

6. ORGANIZATIONAL STRUCTURE

Exhibit IV: Ownership Structure of Breeze Technology Inc.

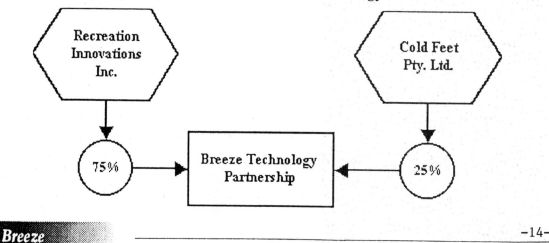

186

Breeze Technology Inc. is based in Delaware. It is jointly owned by Recreation Innovations Inc. (owned by the management team) and Cold Feet Pty. Ltd. owned by J. Mike O'Dwyer, the inventor.

6.1   Executive Experience and Responsibilities

Robert (Bob) Brough is the Chief Executive Officer of Breeze Technology. Bob has a wealth of prior business experience, having been a Managing Director and major shareholder of a diverse range of businesses over the last nine years, including the sale of Petroleum Products at both a retail and wholesale level. Most recently, Bob created a chain of 17 retail video, music, and entertainment hardware stores located in various cities over three States and a five year period. These were sold before he entered the Bachelor of Laws (Hons) program at Bond. After graduating from law Bob commenced his MBA studies. His business experience, legal knowledge, and pro-active leadership are important strategic assets for Breeze. Bob's responsibilities include dealing with legal issues, strategic planning, marketing, and providing the vision and leadership to take the company forward.

Timothy (Tim) Zwemer, an expatriate American, is the Operations Manager of Breeze. His MBA studies have complemented his wide-ranging managerial experience and previous engineering studies. Prior to his MBA studies, Tim was Managing Director, and is still a major shareholder, of a large rural contracting company. His other business experience includes management positions in a company operating in the security and protection industry in Australia. He has also been involved in a multi-store retail fashion house and was associate editor and production manager in the launch of a specialist medical journal in the United States. Tim's experience in management, marketing, and competitive strategy are an important asset to the development and growing of the business. Tim's substantial technical abilities will underpin his major responsibilities which include managing the commercialization and application of current technologies and managing the R&D department of Breeze.

Peter Homan, the Financial Manager, is a qualified chartered accountant (equivalent to a CPA in the US). Since graduating from the University of Queensland with a Bachelor of Commerce in 1986, Peter has worked for two of the "Big Six" accounting firms and is presently employed as a specialist tax manager at Bentleys, a boutique firm based in the State capitol. Currently on a 12 month leave of absence, Peter is in his last semester of MBA studies at Bond University. Peter's professional work in preparing complex budgets and in the preparation of business plans provides a wealth of experience in new venture budgeting, business structuring and forward planning, particularly in relation to taxation and financial law issues.

Exhibit V shows the organization chart for Breeze. The unnamed positions in the third, fourth, and fifth levels will be filled in year three, when Breeze's manufacturing and/or licensing of other technologies is scheduled to begin.

Exhibit V: Organizational Chart for Breeze Technology Inc.

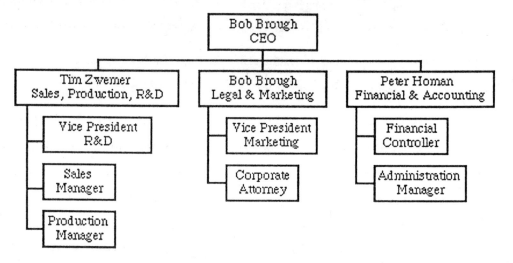

Breeze will set up an office and research facility close to the licensee. A major role of this office will be to manage Breeze's relationship with the licensee and develop products in cooperation with the licensee's R&D department. The initial staff required will be small, including only a secretary/receptionist, an office manager and two engineers in addition to the management team. Additional staff will be required when new product rollouts begin in year 3. These will include:

•A Production Manager to liaise with the contract manufacturer(s) to ensure production meets the high standard of quality demanded and is produced within time and on budget;

•A Marketing Manager, whose role will be to develop and implement the company's niche product marketing, advertising and promotional strategy;

•A Sales Manager, whose role will be to develop a sales program and run a small sales team in the niche markets targeted;

7. RISK REDUCTION STRATEGIES

Breeze is aware of the of risks that may threaten the viability of its operation. The following summarizes the main risk reduction strategies implemented:

• Intellectual property protection via patents, copyrights and design registration (Appendix VII);

• Patent insurance and a patent defence fund developed income;

• Injunction readiness, with patent attorneys ready at a moment's notice;

• License structured to encourage rapid diffusion of the technology;

• Dividend policy to discourage exit of major shareholders;

• Continuing discussions with several inventors to develop a diverse portfolio of technological innovations.

• Continuing discussions with several inventors to develop a diverse portfolio of technological innovations.

8. EXIT & HARVEST STRATEGIES

Breeze's present business strategy does not require external capital at any time within the five year horizon covered by the plan. Because the future product roll-out opportunities require limited capital expenditures, management expects to adopt a high dividend policy, essentially a harvest strategy. Sufficient funds will be retained to fund R&D, to market and sell roll-out products, to build a defence fund for litigation against imitators, and to maintain a contingency fund. Should either O'Dwyer or one of the Breeze managers wish to sell their equity, or should it become necessary to take on external shareholders in order to fund self manufacture (i.e., option 3), the usual range of options exist. These include:

• Initial Public Offering (IPO) - Would allow the shareholders to remain active in management while reducing their holdings over time. It is acknowledged that the timing of the IPO is dependent upon suitable market conditions and will result in a reduced level of privacy and management freedom.

• Private Sale - A sale of the company to a private buyer, most likely the initial licensee looking to backward integrate.

• Management Buy Out - This would allow the founders to select their successor and reduce their shareholdings gradually over time if necessary.

9. FINANCIALS

The following assumptions and facts impact the financial statements:

• All figures are shown in US real dollars;

• A significant proportion of our professional advice on accounting, intellectual property, market research and legal issues was provided *gratis* and thus is not reflected in the financial statements;

–17–

Breeze

189

•The management team has also negotiated legal and other services on a contingency basis, thus reducing the financial risk and cash expenses;

•From year 3, revenues will begin to flow from manufacturing and/or licensing of other products in addition to the royalty stream derived from the Breeze technology;

•Company policy is to avoid investment in substantial fixed assets, preferring to lease or hire such assets to enhance flexibility and conserve cash flow;

•Tax rates vary widely among jurisdictions and Breeze is presently unsure of its domicile for tax purposes. Breeze wishes to be a good corporate citizen but will nonetheless direct efforts to minimize tax payable. An income tax rate of 33% is assumed payable once yearly in December.

9.1 Fund Raising

The initial seed capital for this business was raised by of a contribution of $700 by each of the three shareholders of Recreation Innovations Inc. to fund investigation of the Breeze proposal. These inquiries illuminated the potential of the venture and were followed by further shareholder contributions of $14,000 each. These funds were used for the development and testing of prototypes, legal and other fees to define and protect intellectual property, establishing legal structure and travel costs.

Once the legal structure was established, these funds were converted to share capital in Breeze. To cover further intellectual property and negotiation expenses and to ensure adequate funding reserves for the remainder of the project, Breeze negotiated with a local investor, Gurumbal Pty Ltd, for $70,000 in funding on the following terms:

•A three year $70,000 bond with a coupon rate of 18%.

•Monthly interest payments, or to compound at coupon rate, at our discretion.

•Secured by directors' guarantees of $70,000 and a lien over Director's shares in Breeze.

9.2   Agreement with the Inventor

The technology assignment documentation requires Breeze to commercialize the invention and pay the inventor $1 million within three years and within 30 days of revenues less operating costs, exceeding $1.5 million. If this payment is not made, the original technology will revert to the inventor. Subsequent technical innovations will be retained by Breeze.

9.3   Royalty Income

It is expected that a commitment fee of $2m will be received in May 1994, followed by quarterly payments at the rate of $2.5m per year for the remainder of year 1 and year 2. Royalties will increase as the licensee exceeds the base sales levels which have been established as part of the incentive royalty structure. The royalty structure is based on the licensee's wholesale sales and is designed to induce the rapid diffusion of the technology across a wide range of products i.e., the use of a high minimum payment with a reduced royalty rate as volume increases. While our research determined that license fees for proven technology vary from 5% to 8% of wholesale prices, the financial projections are based on more conservative royalty rates as shown in Exhibit VI. These rates may be exceeded in negotiations with licensees.

Exhibit VI: Incentive Royalty Rate Structure

Sales ($m)	Royalty Rate (%)	Base Fee ($m)
0	0.00	2.5
100	2.00	2.5
200	1.75	4.5
400	1.50	8.0
800	1.25	13.0
5000	1.00	55.0

Exhibit VII shows the sensitivity of annual royalty revenues to the diffusion rate into the licensee's product line. The cost for the licensee per pair of shoes is also detailed.

Exhibit VII: Royalty Sensitivity to Diffusion Rate

Mkt. share (%)	Royalties ($m)	Cost per pair ($)
1%	2.50	0.67
5%	5.25	0.28
10%	9.25	0.25
25%	18.63	0.20

9.4 Cash Balances, Dividends and Owners' Equity

As seen in the financial spreadsheets, Cash Balances remain positive throughout, at least double each year, and exceed $10 million in year 5. Such cash balances are considered necessary as a contingency for legal attack against theft of intellectual property relating to Breeze's technology and to build a fund to take advantage of opportunities that may arise. Dividend payouts are substantial, accumulating to $4.9m over 5 years. Owners' Equity grows from $363,820 in year 1 to $15.3m in year five.

9.5 Ratio Analysis and Sensitivity Analysis

The financial ratios show exceptionally conservative values, as can be seen in the projected financial statements. The ratios show encouraging levels of liquidity and profitability and minimal reliance on leverage. Profits and dividends are highly sensitive to the royalty income, but expenses are almost entirely discretionary and would be reduced in line with royalty incomes falling below anticipated levels. A pessimistic scenario was developed, with assumptions that differ from the projected scenario as shown in Exhibit VIII. The end result is income levels less than one-sixth the projected scenario, but even at this level Breeze is profitable, as shown in Exhibit IX.

Exhibit VIII: Expected and Pessimistic Scenario Assumptions

Assumption	Expected Scenario	Pessimistic Scenario
Upfront Commitment Fee	$2,000,000	$500,000
Minimum Annual Royalty	$2,500,00 Base	Zero Base
Roll out products	Begin Year 3	None
Diffusion Rate by Year 5	15%	5%
Maximum Royalty Rate	2.5%	1.25%

Exhibit IX: Expected Scenario Income, Cash Balances and Dividends

	Year 1 ($)	Year 2 ($)	Year 3 ($)	Year 4 ($)	Year 5 ($)
Income	3,562,500	2,500,000	5,375,000	11,000,000	17,000,000
Expenses	2,399,601	1,587,232	2,571,026	6,037,858	9,236,630
Net Income	1,162,899	912,768	2,803,974	4,962,142	7,763,370
Cash Balance	335,899	648,667	2,557,641	6,019,783	10,733,153
Dividends	900,000	600,000	400,000	1,000,000	2,000,000

Exhibit X: Pessimistic Scenario Income, Cash Balances and Dividends

ITEM	Year 1 ($)	Year 2 ($)	Year 3 ($)	Year 4 ($)	Year 5 ($)
Income	83,000	333,333	1,041,666	1,666,666	2,500,000
Adjusted Expenses	150,000	250,000	1,100,000	400,000	1,200,000
Net Income	(67,000)	83,333	(58,334)	1,266,666	1,300,000
Cash Balance	47,100	130,433	72,099	1,188,765	1,488,765
Dividends	NIL	NIL	NIL	150,000	1,000,000

Note that to generate sufficient income to cover the minimal expenses necessary to maintain the relationship with the licensee, the diffusion rate into the licensee's product line could fall as low as 4% (utilizing the pessimistic royalty rate of 1.25%).

192

9.6 Capital Value

Valuation of rapidly growing companies is always difficult as both the growth and discount rates are critical. Simple price earnings multiples can often undervalue the company especially if there is considerable growth potential, as is the case with Breeze. Assuming Breeze profits continue to grow, on a long term trend, at a conservative 12% per year and using a discount factor of 20%, the value of the company at year five would be $97 million using a variation on the Gordon share valuation model (Present Value of a constant growth annuity). This value equates to a price earnings multiple of approximately 14 which is at the low end of expectations when compared to technology licensing companies such as Orbital Engine Co. Ltd with a PE multiple exceeding 20.

10. SUMMARY

Breeze Technology Inc. has an exciting and profitable future in sports, leisure and recreation industries. Breeze will be well placed financially to commercialize several other sports and leisure related inventions of J. Mike O'Dwyer and other inventors, already identified. Perusal of the following four pages of detailed financial spreadsheets will serve to detail a more complete financial picture. Following these spreadsheets are the Appendices which contain more specific information to support other issues raised in the plan.

BUDGET (Year 1 by month)

	Jan	Feb	Mar	Apr	May	Jun	Jul	Aug	Sep	Oct	Nov	Dec	Year 1
Sales													
Breeze technology	0	0	0	0	2,000,000	0	312,500	0	625,000	0	0	625,000	3,562,500
Roll out products													0
Total Sales	0	0	0	0	2,000,000	0	312,500	0	625,000	0	0	625,000	3,562,500
Cost of Goods Sold													
Contract manufacturing													0
% of Total Sales	0%	0%	0%	0%	0%	0%	0%	0%	0%	0%	0%	0%	0%
Total Cost of Goods Sold	0	0	0	0	0	0	0	0	0	0	0	0	0
Gross Profit	0	0	0	0	2,000,000	0	312,500	0	625,000	0	0	625,000	3,562,500
Gross Margin	0%	0%	0%	0%	100%	0%	100%	0%	100%	0%	0%	100%	100%
Operating Expenses													
Sales, Marketing & Production													
Advertising & Promotion													0
Contract distribution													0
Salaries													0
Trade Shows & Travel			6,000	6,000	10,000	10,000	10,000	5,000	5,000	5,000	5,000	5,000	67,000
Total Sales & Marketing Costs	0	0	6,000	6,000	10,000	10,000	10,000	5,000	5,000	5,000	5,000	5,000	67,000
% of Total Sales	0%	0%	0%	0%	1%	0%	3%	0%	1%	0%	0%	1%	2%
Research & Development													
Salaries & consulting fees							350,000	18,333	18,333	18,333	18,333	18,333	441,667
Acquisition of technology							1,000,000						1,000,000
Equipment hire & Testing													0
R & D Materials													0
Total R & D Costs	0	0	0	0	0	0	1,350,000	18,333	18,333	18,333	18,333	18,333	1,441,667
% of Total Sales	0%	0%	0%	0%	0%	0%	432%	0%	3%	0%	0%	3%	40%
General & Administrative													
Admin Salaries & Superannuation								32,500	32,500	32,500	32,500	32,500	162,500
Equipment Lease								3,000	3,000	3,000	3,000	3,000	15,000
Insurance								150	150	150	150	150	750
Legal & Accounting fees			1,500	75,000				8,333	8,333	8,333	8,333	8,333	118,167
Licenses and Permits								100	100	100	100	100	500
Office Expenses								1,000	1,000	1,000	1,000	1,000	5,000
Office Rental or Lease								2,500	2,500	2,500	2,500	2,500	12,500
Telephone & Utilities		500	500	500	500	1,000	1,500	1,500	2,000	2,500	2,500	2,500	15,500
Total G & A Costs	0	500	2,000	75,500	500	1,000	1,500	49,083	49,583	50,083	50,083	50,083	329,917
% of Total Sales	0%	0%	0%	0%	0%	0%	0%	0%	8%	0%	0%	8%	9%
Total Operating Expenses	0	500	8,000	81,500	10,500	11,000	1,361,500	72,417	72,917	73,417	73,417	73,417	1,838,583
% of Total Sales	0%	0%	0%	0%	1%	0%	436%	0%	12%	0%	0%	12%	52%
Income From Operations	0	(500)	(8,000)	(81,500)	1,989,500	(11,000)	(1,049,000)	(72,417)	552,083	(73,417)	(73,417)	551,583	1,723,917
% of Total Sales	0%	0%	0%	0%	99%	0%	0%	0%	88%	0%	0%	88%	48%
Interest Income		9	7	148	97	5,882	5,857	1,506	581	2,879	2,581	1,657	21,203
Interest / Financing Expense				1,050	1,050	1,050	1,050	1,050	1,050	1,050	1,050	1,050	9,450
Income before Taxes	0	(491)	(7,993)	(82,402)	1,988,547	(6,168)	(1,044,193)	(71,961)	551,614	(71,587)	(71,886)	552,190	1,735,670
Taxes on Income (calculated yearly)	0	0	0	0	0	0	0	0	0	0	0	572,771	572,771
Net Income After Taxes	0	(491)	(7,993)	(82,402)	1,988,547	(6,168)	(1,044,193)	(71,961)	551,614	(71,587)	(71,886)	(20,581)	1,162,899
% of Total Sales	0%	0%	0%	0%	99%	0%	0%	0%	88%	0%	0%	0%	33%

CASH FLOW STATEMENT (Year 1 by month)

	Jan	Feb	Mar	Apr	May	Jun	Jul	Aug	Sep	Oct	Nov	Dec	Year 1
Beginning Cash Balance	0	2,100	1,609	35,615	23,214	1,411,761	1,405,593	361,400	139,439	691,053	619,466	397,580	0
Cash Receipts													
Total Sales	0	0	0	0	2,000,000	0	312,500	0	625,000	0	0	625,000	3,562,500
Interest Income	0	9	7	148	97	5,882	5,857	1,506	581	2,879	2,581	1,657	21,203
Total Cash Receipts	0	9	7	148	2,000,097	5,882	318,357	1,506	625,581	2,879	2,581	626,657	3,583,703
Cash Disbursements													
Salaries & Labor	0	0	0	0	0	0	0	32,500	32,500	32,500	32,500	32,500	162,500
Advertising & Promotion	0	0	0	0	0	0	0	0	0	0	0	0	0
Contract distribution	0	0	0	0	0	0	0	0	0	0	0	0	0
Cost of Goods Sold (non-labor)	0	0	0	0	0	0	0	0	0	0	0	0	0
Other Disbursements	0	500	8,000	81,500	10,500	11,000	1,361,500	34,417	34,917	35,417	35,417	35,417	1,648,583
Interest payments	0	0	0	1,050	1,050	1,050	1,050	1,050	1,050	1,050	1,050	1,050	9,450
Taxes on income	0	0	0	0	0	0	0	0	0	0	0	572,771	572,771
Equipment Lease	0	0	0	0	0	0	0	3,000	3,000	3,000	3,000	3,000	15,000
Office Rental or Lease	0	0	0	0	0	0	0	2,500	2,500	2,500	2,500	2,500	12,500
Total Cash Disbursements	0	500	8,000	82,550	11,550	12,050	1,362,550	73,467	73,967	74,467	74,467	647,238	2,420,804
Net Cash from Operations	0	(491)	(7,993)	(82,402)	1,988,547	(6,168)	(1,044,193)	(71,961)	551,614	(71,587)	(71,886)	(20,581)	1,162,899
Cash dividends					(600,000)			(150,000)			(150,000)		(900,000)
Sale of Stock			3,000										3,000
Proceeds of loan from shareholders	2,100		39,000									(41,100)	0
Proceeds of Investor Loan				70,000									70,000
Net Cash Balance	2,100	1,609	35,615	23,214	1,411,761	1,405,593	361,400	139,439	691,053	619,466	397,580	335,899	335,899

BUDGET (Years 2 and 3 by Quarter)

Sales	Qtr 1	Qtr 2	Qtr 3	Qtr 4	Year 2	Qtr 1	Qtr 2	Qtr 3	Qtr 4	Year 3
Breeze technology	625,000	625,000	625,000	625,000	2,500,000	625,000	625,000	625,000	3,500,000	5,375,000
Roll out products					0	150,000	200,000	400,000	600,000	1,350,000
Total Sales	625,000	625,000	625,000	625,000	2,500,000	775,000	825,000	1,025,000	4,100,000	6,725,000
Cost of Goods Sold										
Contract manufacturing					0	90,000	120,000	240,000	360,000	810,000
% of Total Sales	0%	0%	0%	0%	0%	0%	15%	29%	35%	20%
Total Cost of Goods Sold	0	0	0	0	0	90,000	120,000	240,000	360,000	810,000
Gross Profit	625,000	625,000	625,000	625,000	2,500,000	685,000	705,000	785,000	3,740,000	5,915,000
Gross Margin	100%	100%	100%	100%	100%	88%	85%	77%	91%	88%
Operating Expenses										
Sales, Marketing & Production										
Advertising & Promotion	10,000	10,000	10,000	10,000	40,000	10,000	10,000	10,000	10,000	40,000
Contract distribution	0	0	0	0	0					0
Salaries	0	0	0	0	0	30,000	30,000	30,000	30,000	120,000
Trade Shows & Travel	30,000	30,000	30,000	30,000	120,000	30,000	30,000	30,000	30,000	120,000
Total Sales & Marketing Costs	40,000	40,000	40,000	40,000	160,000	70,000	70,000	70,000	70,000	280,000
% of Total Sales	6%	6%	6%	6%	6%	9%	8%	7%	2%	4%
Research & Development										
Salaries & consulting fees	68,750	68,750	68,750	68,750	275,000	90,000	90,000	90,000	90,000	360,000
Equipment hire & Testing	20,000	20,000	20,000	20,000	80,000	25,000	25,000	25,000	25,000	100,000
R & D Materials	20,000	20,000	20,000	20,000	80,000	40,000	40,000	40,000	40,000	160,000
Total R & D Costs	108,750	108,750	108,750	108,750	435,000	155,000	155,000	155,000	155,000	620,000
% of Total Sales	17%	17%	17%	17%	17%	20%	19%	15%	4%	9%
General & Administrative										
Admin Salaries & Superannuation	97,500	97,500	97,500	97,500	390,000	136,250	136,250	136,250	136,250	545,000
Equipment Lease	9,000	9,000	9,000	9,000	36,000	18,000	18,000	18,000	18,000	72,000
Insurance	450	450	450	450	1,800	900	900	900	900	3,600
Legal & Accounting fees	15,000	15,000	15,000	15,000	60,000	20,000	20,000	20,000	20,000	80,000
Licenses and Permits	300	300	300	300	1,200	600	600	600	600	2,400
Office Expenses	3,000	3,000	3,000	3,000	12,000	6,000	6,000	6,000	6,000	24,000
Office Rental or Lease	7,500	7,500	7,500	7,500	30,000	15,000	15,000	15,000	15,000	60,000
Telephone & Utilities	7,500	7,500	7,500	7,500	30,000	15,000	15,000	15,000	15,000	60,000
Total G & A Costs	140,250	140,250	140,250	140,250	561,000	211,750	211,750	211,750	211,750	847,000
% of Total Sales	22%	22%	22%	22%	22%	27%	26%	21%	5%	13%
Total Operating Expenses	289,000	289,000	289,000	289,000	1,156,000	436,750	436,750	436,750	436,750	1,747,000
% of Total Sales	46%	46%	46%	46%	46%	56%	53%	43%	11%	26%
Income From Operations	336,000	336,000	336,000	336,000	1,344,000	248,250	268,250	348,250	3,303,250	4,168,000
% of Total Sales	54%	54%	54%	54%	54%	32%	33%	34%	81%	62%
Interest Income	4,199	6,537	8,904	11,301	30,941	8,108	4,711	6,834	9,983	29,636
Interest / Financing Expense	3,150	3,150	3,150	3,150	12,600	3,150	3,150	3,150	3,150	12,600
Income before Taxes	337,049	339,387	341,754	344,151	1,362,341	253,208	269,811	351,934	3,310,083	4,185,036
Taxes on Income				449,572	449,572				1,381,062	1,381,062
Net Income After Taxes	337,049	339,387	341,754	(105,421)	912,768	253,208	269,811	351,934	1,929,021	2,803,974
% of Total Sales	54%	54%	55%	0%	37%	33%	33%	34%	47%	42%

CASH FLOW STATEMENT (Year 2 and 3 by Quarter)

	Qtr 1	Qtr 2	Qtr 3	Qtr 4	Year 2	Qtr 1	Qtr 2	Qtr 3	Qtr 4	Year 3
Beginning Cash Balance	335,899	522,948	712,335	904,089	335,899	648,667	376,876	546,687	798,620	648,667
Cash Receipts										
Total Sales	625,000	625,000	625,000	625,000	2,500,000	775,000	825,000	1,025,000	4,100,000	6,725,000
Interest Income	4,199	6,537	8,904	11,301	30,941	8,108	4,711	6,834	9,983	29,636
Total Cash Receipts	965,098	1,154,485	1,346,239	1,540,390	2,866,840	1,431,776	1,206,587	1,578,520	4,908,603	7,403,303
Cash Disbursements										
Salaries & Labor	166,250	166,250	166,250	166,250	665,000	256,250	256,250	256,250	256,250	1,025,000
Advertising & Promotion	10,000	10,000	10,000	10,000	40,000	10,000	10,000	10,000	10,000	40,000
Contract distribution	0	0	0	0	0	0	0	0	0	0
Cost of Goods Sold (non-labor)	0	0	0	0	0	90,000	120,000	240,000	360,000	810,000
Other Disbursements	96,250	96,250	96,250	96,250	385,000	137,500	137,500	137,500	137,500	550,000
Interest / Financing Expense	3,150	3,150	3,150	3,150	12,600	3,150	3,150	3,150	3,150	12,600
Tax Payments	0	0	0	449,572	449,572	0	0	0	1,381,062	1,381,062
Equipment Lease	9,000	9,000	9,000	9,000	36,000	18,000	18,000	18,000	18,000	72,000
Office Rental or Lease	7,500	7,500	7,500	7,500	30,000	15,000	15,000	15,000	15,000	60,000
Net Inc. in Inventory & Debtors						225,000				225,000
Net inc. of Plant & Equipment						200,000				200,000
Total Cash Disbursements	292,150	292,150	292,150	741,722	1,618,172	954,900	559,900	679,900	2,180,962	4,375,662
Net Cash from Operations	672,948	862,335	1,054,089	798,667	1,248,667	476,876	646,687	898,620	2,727,641	3,027,641
Cash dividends	(150,000)	(150,000)	(150,000)	(150,000)	(600,000)	(100,000)	(100,000)	(100,000)	(100,000)	(400,000)
Sale of Stock					0					0
Proceeds of Investor Loan					0				(70,000)	(70,000)
Net Cash Balance	522,948	712,335	904,089	648,667	648,667	376,876	546,687	798,620	2,557,641	2,557,641

Breeze

INCOME STATEMENT (Years 1 - 5)

Sales	Year 1	Year 2	Year 3	Year 4	Year 5
Breeze technology	3,562,500	2,500,000	5,375,000	8,000,000	11,000,000
% of Total Sales	100%	100%	80%	73%	65%
Roll out products	0	0	1,350,000	3,000,000	6,000,000
% of Total Sales	0%	0%	20%	27%	35%
Total Sales	3,562,500	2,500,000	6,725,000	11,000,000	17,000,000
Cost of Goods Sold					
Contract manufacturing	0	0	810,000	1,800,000	3,600,000
% of Total Sales	0%	0%	12%	16%	21%
Total Cost of Goods Sold	0	0	810,000	1,800,000	3,600,000
Gross Profit	3,562,500	2,500,000	5,915,000	9,200,000	13,400,000
Gross Margin	100%	100%	88%	84%	79%
Operating Expenses					
Sales & Marketing	67,000	160,000	280,000	308,000	338,800
% of Total Sales	2%	6%	4%	3%	2%
Research & Development	1,441,667	435,000	620,000	682,000	750,200
% of Total Sales	40%	17%	9%	6%	4%
G & A	329,917	561,000	847,000	931,700	1,024,870
% of Total Sales	9%	22%	13%	8%	6%
Total Operating Expenses	1,838,583	1,156,000	1,747,000	1,921,700	2,113,870
% of Total Sales	52%	46%	26%	17%	12%
Income From Operations	1,723,917	1,344,000	4,168,000	7,278,300	11,286,130
% of Total Sales	48%	54%	62%	66%	66%
Interest Income	21,203	30,941	29,636	127,882	300,989
Interest / Financing Expense	9,450	12,600	12,600		
Income before Taxes	1,735,670	1,362,341	4,185,036	7,406,182	11,587,119
Taxes on Income (calculated yearly)	572,771	449,572	1,381,062	2,444,040	3,823,749
Net Income After Taxes	1,162,899	912,768	2,803,974	4,962,142	7,763,370
% of Total Sales	33%	37%	42%	45%	46%

CASH FLOW STATEMENT (Years 1 - 5)

	Year 1	Year 2	Year 3	Year 4	Year 5
#REF!	0	335,899	648,667	2,557,641	6,019,783
Cash Receipts					
Total Sales	3,562,500	2,500,000	6,725,000	11,000,000	17,000,000
Interest Income	21,203	30,941	29,636	127,882	300,989
Total Cash Receipts	3,583,703	2,530,941	6,754,636	11,127,882	17,300,989
Cash Disbursements					
Cost of Goods Sold	0	0	810,000	1,800,000	3,600,000
Sales & Marketing	67,000	160,000	280,000	308,000	338,800
Research & Development	1,441,667	435,000	620,000	682,000	750,200
G & A	329,917	561,000	847,000	931,700	1,024,870
Interest / Financing Expense	9,450	12,600	12,600	0	0
Taxes on Income (calculated yearly)	572,771	449,572	1,381,062	2,444,040	3,823,749
Net Inc. in Inventory & Debtors			225,000	400,000	850,000
Net Inc. of Plant & Equipment	0	0	200,000	100,000	200,000
Total Cash Disbursements	2,420,804	1,618,172	4,375,662	6,665,740	10,587,619
Cash dividends	(900,000)	(600,000)	(400,000)	(1,000,000)	(2,000,000)
Sale of Stock	3,000	0	0	0	0
Proceeds of Investor Loan	70,000	0	(70,000)	0	0
Net Cash Balance	335,899	648,667	2,557,641	6,019,783	10,733,153

(Yr 1 from monthly Cash Flow; Yrs 2-5 External Values)
(Yr 1 from monthly Cash Flow; Yrs 2-5 External Values)

RATIO ANALYSIS

Ratios	Year 1	Year 2	Year 3	Year 4	Year 5	
Current Ratio	0.00	0.00	9.25	11.43	11.29	Current Assets / Current Liabilities
Quick Ratio (Acid Test)	0.00	0.00	8.79	10.83	10.64	Quick Assets (Cash + Receivables) / Current Liabilities
Return on Total Assets	349.02%	142.66%	87.81%	66.65%	57.58%	Net Income After Taxes / Total Assets (at year end)
Total Assets Turnover	10.61	3.85	2.10	1.48	1.26	Total Sales / Total Assets (at year end)
Total Debt to Total Assets	0.21	0.11	0.10	0.08	0.09	Total Liabilities / Total Assets
Gross Profit Margin	100.00%	100.00%	87.96%	83.64%	78.82%	Gross Profit / Total Sales
Operating Profit Margin	48.39%	53.76%	61.98%	66.17%	66.39%	Income From Operations (Before Interest & Taxes) / Total Sales
Net Profit Margin	32.64%	36.51%	41.69%	45.11%	45.67%	Net Income After Taxes / Total Sales
Return on Sales	32.64%	36.51%	47.40%	53.94%	57.94%	Net Income After Taxes / Gross Profit (Net Sales)
Return on Owners' Equity	437.35%	61.73%	62.55%	56.10%	49.74%	Net Income After Taxes / Total Owners' Equity (at year end)
Total Debt to Owners' Equity	0.26	0.05	0.07	0.07	0.07	Total Liabilities / Total Owners' Equity

BALANCE SHEET

Assets	Year 1	Year 2	Year 3	Year 4	Year 5	
Current Assets						
Cash	335,899	648,667	2,557,641	6,019,783	10,733,153	(From Cash Flow Statements)
Investments	0	0	0	0	0	External Values
Accounts Receivable	0	0	300,000	750,000	1,500,000	External Values
Notes Receivable	0	0	0	0	0	External Values
Inventory	0	0	150,000	375,000	750,000	External Values
Total Current Assets	335,899	648,667	3,007,641	7,144,783	12,983,153	
Plant and Equipment						
Building / Leasehold improvements	0	0	0	0	0	External Values
Plant and Equipment	0	0	200,000	300,000	500,000	External Values
Total Net Property & Equip	0	0	200,000	300,000	500,000	
Other Assets	0	0	0	0	0	External Values
Total Assets	335,899	648,667	3,207,641	7,444,783	13,483,153	
Liabilities & Owner Equity						
Current Liabilities						
Short Term Debt	0	0	0	0	0	External Values
Accounts Payable	0	0	225,000	500,000	1,000,000	External Values
Income Taxes Payable	0	0	0	0	0	External Values
Accrued Liabilities	0	0	100,000	125,000	150,000	External Values
Total Current Liabilities	0	0	325,000	625,000	1,150,000	
Long Term Debt	70,000	70,000	0	0	0	(From Cash Flow Statements)
Total Liabilities	70,000	70,000	325,000	625,000	1,150,000	
Owner/Stockholder Equity						
Common Stock	3,000	3,000	3,000	3,000	3,000	(From Cash Flow Statements)
Retained Earnings	1,162,899	2,075,667	4,879,641	9,841,783	17,605,153	
Less Cash Dividends	(900,000)	(600,000)	(400,000)	(1,000,000)	(2,000,000)	External Values
Total Owners' Equity	265,899	1,478,667	4,482,641	8,844,783	15,608,153	
Total Liabilities & Equity	335,899	1,548,667	4,807,641	9,469,783	16,758,153	

SOURCE & USE OF FUNDS

Source of Funds	Year 1	Year 2	Year 3	Year 4	Year 5	
Net Income After Taxes	1,162,899	912,768	2,803,974	4,962,142	7,763,370	(From Income Statement)
Funds From Operations	1,162,899	912,768	2,803,974	4,962,142	7,763,370	
Sale of Stock	3,000	0	0	0	0	(From Cash Flow Statements)
Increased Long Term Debt	70,000	0	(70,000)	0	0	(From Cash Flow Statements)
Total Source of Funds	1,235,899	912,768	2,733,974	4,962,142	7,763,370	
Use of Funds						
Building / Leasehold improvements	0	0	0	0	0	(From Balance Sheet)
Plant and Equipment	0	0	200,000	100,000	200,000	(From Balance Sheet)
Cash Dividends	900,000	600,000	400,000	1,000,000	2,000,000	(From Balance Sheet)
Increased Working Capital*	335,899	312,768	2,133,974	3,862,142	5,563,370	(From Summary of Changes in Working Capital below)
Total Use of Funds	1,235,899	912,768	2,733,974	4,962,142	7,763,370	
Summary of Changes in Working Capital:						
Cash	335,899	312,768	1,908,974	3,462,142	4,713,370	(Cash derived from Cash Flow Statements; remaining items derived from Balance Sheet)
Investments	0	0	0	0	0	
Accounts Receivable	0	0	300,000	450,000	750,000	
Notes Receivable	0	0	0	0	0	NOTE: Increases in these items appear as
Inventory	0	0	150,000	225,000	375,000	positive values; decreases appear as
Short Term Debt	0	0	0	0	0	negative values.
Accounts Payable	0	0	(225,000)	(275,000)	(275,000)	
Income Taxes Payable	0	0	0	0	0	
Increased Working Capital*	335,899	312,768	2,133,974	3,862,142	5,563,370	

BUDGET ASSUMPTIONS

ROYALTY CALCULATIONS	Low	%	Base
Vertical lookup table 1st column -	0	0.00	2.500
sales of shoes incorporating Breeze	100	2.00	2.500
technology	200	1.75	4.250
	400	1.50	7.250
2nd column - percentage royalty rate	800	1.25	12.250
on portion of sales	5000	1.00	54.250

Once only commitent fee	2,000,000
Annual prepayment of royalty	2,500,000
Interest receivable rate	5.00%
Interest payable rate	18.00%
Contract manufacturing expense	60.00%

	Year 1	Year 2	Year 3	Year 4	Year 5
Estimated sales of shoes incorporating Breeze Technology	20	80	250	400	600
Sales to exceed minimum royalty	100	100	100	100	100

INCOME STATEMENT ANNUAL GROWTH (YEARS 2 - 5)

Operating Expenses	Year 2	Year 3	Year 4	Year 5
Sales & Marketing	1.00	1.00	1.10	1.10
Research & Development	1.00	1.00	1.10	1.10
G & A	1.00	1.00	1.10	1.10

Breeze

12. APPENDICES

APPENDIX I - Focus Group Analysis

    Focus group interviews were commissioned to qualitatively collect information from consumers regarding how they evaluate and select footwear. The focus groups were conducted on site at Bond University. Potential respondents were identified from the university directory and each respondent was called and recruited to participate. The moderator's guide for the focus groups was developed around three major themes: (1) the features or benefits consumers desire when purchasing footwear; (2) the "negatives" involved with purchasing and/or using footwear; and (3) the respondent's "wish list" for footwear (i.e., those features or benefits they would like their footwear to have).

    The focus group protocols were analyzed and the Table that follows outlines the comments made by and discussion between respondents within each theme.

FEATURES / BENEFITS DESIRED	NEGATIVES	WISH LIST
1. Quality	Stinky Feet	Cool Feet
Arch Support	Sweaty Feet	Dry Feet
Good Stitching	Bulky	Can Regulate Temperature
Waterproof	Heavy	Ventilation
Ankle Support	Unattractive	Enhanced Circulation
Good Soles	Break in In	No Maintenance
Durability	Not Waterproof	Waterproof
2. Comfort	Gets Dirty Easy	Gel Sole Conforms to foot
Ankle Support	Air Holes Crack	
Arch Support	Materials Rip and Fail	
Weight	Uncomfortable	
Cushioning	Poor traction	
No Blisters	Expensive	
Heel Comfort	Too Hot	
Traction	Too Warm	
Shock Absorption		
Cool		
Dry		
Waterproof		
3. Performance		
Shock Absorption		
Rebound		
Durability		
Lateral Stability		
Arch Support		
Ankle Support		
4. Style		
Color		
Brands		
Looks		
Fashion		
5. Price		
Low Prices		
Good Value		

APPENDIX II - Competitor Content Analysis

In the process of analyzing the advertising content of the competitors in the personal recreational equipment market, 42 manufacturers were identified using 46 individual advertisements. All of the advertisements were market specific and the attribute identification was determined from the analysis, not in an a-priori manner (See Exhibit 1). In an attempt to condense the original findings and increase their specificity to the footwear market, a second analysis was conducted and several attributes were combined in the following manner. Support and Fit were combined under Support; Performance, Traction, Flexibility, Weight, and Stability and Control were collapsed to form Performance; Breathable/Ventilation, Temperature and Airflow were formed into Ventilation/Temperature; Durability/Ruggedness, Protection and Longer wear were transformed into Durability/Ruggedness; and Dryness and Waterproofing were integrated under Dryness. Comfort, Shock Absorption/Cushioning and Fashion were transferred as separate categories. Additionally the percentage of copy addressing each individual attribute was identified (See Exhibit 2).

Exhibit 1: Personal Recreational Equipment

Attribute	Footwear	Clothing	Equipment
Breathable/Ventilation	12	1	2
Fashion	5	0	0
Temperature	1	2	1
Quality	0	1	0
Environment	2	0	0
Anatomical Fit	9	0	4
Comfort	10	5	2
Support	11	1	0
Stability/Control	5	0	2
Durability/Ruggedness	11	1	0
Water Proofing	6	0	0
Performance	4	0	0
Traction	2	0	0
Dryness	8	1	0
Protection	3	0	0
Shock Absorption / Cushioning	7	0	0
Flexibility	1	0	0
Weight	5	1	0
Air-Flow	2	0	0
Longer Wear	1	0	0
None	3	0	1

Exhibit 2: Recreational Footwear

ATTRIBUTE	FREQUENCY	% of ADVERTISERS
Support	20	43
Performance	17	36
Ventilation / Temperature	15	32
Durability/ Ruggedness	15	32
Dryness	14	30
Comfort	10	21
Shock Absorption / Cushioning	7	15
Fashion	5	11

Australian Sports Commission

Leverrier Crescent, Bruce ACT 2617
PO Box 176, Belconnen ACT 2616
Telephone (06) 252 1111
Facsimile (06) 251 2680
Telex AUSIS AA 62400

25th March, 1994

Dean Shephard
Breeze Inc.

FAX (075) 951160

Dear Dean,

Here are the results of the tests that we ran on your new
shoe design. I understand that you will be leaving for the US
this weekend so in the interest of time I will summarise the
results that we found and send you a more complete report at
a later date.

Just to refresh your memory we tested your "modified" shoe
versus a normal unmodified shoe of the same make and age. We
placed temperature sensors inside the shoe at a position
directly below the first joint of the toes and under the
instep. The subject ran on a treadmill at 12 km/hr for 15
minutes. I would have liked to have used a longer run but one
of the sensors stopped sending data at 19 minutes so we
stopped the test and used the last collection time (15
minutes) as the end time. If necessary I would be happy to
repeat the tests over a longer time and perhaps at different
ambient temperatures.

The results are as follows:

	start	finish	difference
Modified shoe			
toe	80.4 F	91.6 F	11.2 F
instep	89.2 F	98.8 F	9.6 F
sock weight	1.02 oz	1.1 oz	.08 gm
Unmodified shoe			
toe	80.2 F	98.4 F	18.5 F
instep	86.9 F	98.2 F	11.3 F
sock weight	1.0 oz	1.11 oz	.11 oz

The results clearly demonstrate that the modified shoe
significantly reduces the temperature rise inside the shoe
compared to a normal unmodified shoe. The difference between
the shoes, 7.3 F, was quite oustanding. In addition the

subject noted while he was running that the modified shoe "definitely felt cooler".

It is difficult to say based on only one test but based on this test I would agree with you that a shoe with this design would definitely make a difference in perceived comfort to the user, as well as reducing the temperature and perspiration conditions that promote foot odour and conditions such as athlete's foot. Initially I was quite skeptical that we would see such a huge difference in temperature that you initially reported but these results confirm your initial findings. I would imagine that if we had continued the test for a longer time we would have seen an even greater temperature difference.

I regards to the extra cushioning effect I realise that the shoe that you sent down was only a prototype, but knowing the alteration that you are making to the normal shoe I imagine that in a full production shoe there would be an "extra" cushioning effect which would be a further advantage to the user.

As I said above we would be happy to conduct more tests if necessary. Good luck with this innovative new design.

Sincerely,

Peter G. Davis   Ph.D.
Australian Institute of Sport

APPENDIX IV - Inventor's Test Results

A number of tests were conducted by the inventor using shoes modified with the Breeze design features. Each of these tests gave very similar results. The following is indicative of both the test protocol and a typical result.

Protocol:

Right shoe Modified. Left Shoe unmodified. Time: 4:30 pm. Pressure 1024 mb. Humidity 49%. Wind 5 knots. Cloud 5/8. Air temperature 79.3 degrees Fahrenheit. Surface - close cut dry grass.

Method: The athlete rested for 30 minutes to stabilize body temperature prior to putting the shoes on. After jogging commenced, temperatures were recorded every 5 minutes.

Two sensors were used in each shoe. These were located under the bridge of the toes. The heads of the sensors were placed very close together so that the maximum variation between the readings did not exceed 0.3 degrees Fahrenheit.

The Results have been tabulated below (in degrees Fahrenheit).

ELAPSED TIME	MODIFIED SHOE	UNMODIFIED SHOE
At start	89.4	89.6
5 minutes	86.7	90.1
10 minutes	86.4	90.7
15 minutes	86.0	91.2
20 minutes	86.2	91.4
25 minutes	86.0	91.6

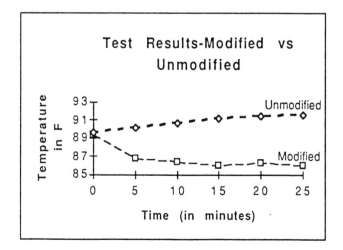

The Heat Index Effect

The heat index is a function of humidity and ambient air temperature. The efficiency of body cooling is directly proportional to the heat index. For example, the heat index shows that for an actual air temperature of 100 degrees Fahrenheit and a relative humidity of 50%, the effect on the human body (i.e. the apparent temperature) would be the same as an air temperature of 120 degrees. The effect is fully detailed in the chart below.

Relative Humidity	Air Temperature										
	70	75	80	85	90	95	100	105	110	115	120
	Apparent Temperature										
30%	67	73	78	84	90	96	104	113	123	135	148
40%	68	74	79	86	93	101	110	123	137	151	
50%	69	75	81	88	96	107	120	135	150		
60%	70	76	82	90	100	114	132	149			
70%	70	77	85	93	106	124	144				
80%	71	78	86	97	113	136					

The effect of the heat index on the apparent temperature inside a shoe is very important as it is often the case that a hot and humid environment is produced. With the apparent temperature in the shoe being a function of the actual temperature and the humidity (which increases with the amount of perspiration produced) abnormally high temperatures result. This in turn increases the amount of perspiration produced which fuels an increasing cycle, increasing the humidity which lifts the apparent temperature and so on. By ventilating the shoe, the Breeze design cools the foot and removes moisture from the shoe, thus significantly reducing the conditions on which the heat index is founded.

Breeze

204

Application to Test Results

From test results, after approximately 20 minutes of activity the temperature around the foot in an unmodified shoe will be close to 95 degrees Fahrenheit, with a relative humidity of around 80%. The apparent temperature will be 136 degrees Fahrenheit and the ability of the foot to cool itself will be substantially impaired. By comparison, the temperature in the modified shoe was approximately 85 degrees Fahrenheit with a relative humidity of 60%. Thus the apparent temperature is reduced to 90 degrees Fahrenheit, a difference of 46 degrees. These results are shown in graphical form below.

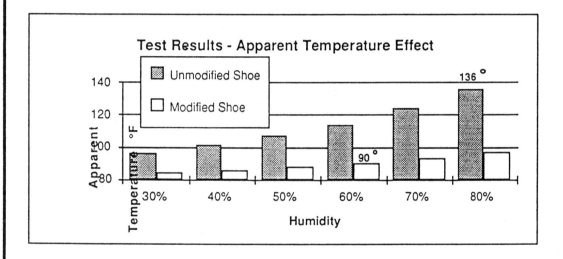

Robert Craig Brough

Year of Birth

1958

Qualifications

- Bachelor of Laws (Hons) (Bond)

- Presently a candidate for an MBA (Bond).

Professional Experience

From 1993 to present:

Chairman of Gulf Entertainment Corporation, an operator of integrated entertainment centres which operate

in Bahrain and other middle eastern States.

From 1986 to 1993

Managing Director of Brough David Holdings Pty Ltd. Owned and operated 17 video and music superstores

located in various towns and cities across 3 States of Australia (from start-up).

From 1985 to 1986

Managing Director of Eastside Petroleum Pty Ltd, a regional wholesaler of Mobil fuel, oil and lubricants.

Also the owner/operator of a Mobil Roadhouse (retail fuel, vehicle repairs and food).

From 1980 to 1985

Police Prosecutor attached to Northern Territory Crown Prosecutions.

From 1977 to 1980

Northern Territory Police Officer.

APPENDIX V -II- Directors' Resumes

Timothy Grant Zwemer

Year of Birth

1958

Qualifications

- Master of Business Administration (Bond).
- Commercial Pilots Licence (Command Instrument Rated)

Professional Experience

From 1993 to present:

Director of Gulf Entertainment Corporation. Based in Bahrain and with US$20 million in equity funding the company is shortly to open the first of a projected 10 entertainment superstores in the Gulf States over the next 3 years.

From 1987 to 1993

Managing Director of Teganal Pty Ltd, a specialist rural contracting company.

From 1986 to 1987

Operations Manager for Maharani Pty Ltd, a specialist motor vessel manufacturer.

From 1986 to present

Chairman of the Board of Security Control Group Pty. Ltd.

From 1984 to 1986

Publisher and Assistant Editor of the US based Journal of Facial Orthopedics and Temporomandibular Arthrology.

From 1978 to 1983

Managing Director of Address Boutiques Pty Ltd, a chain of 5 woman's retail fashion stores.

APPENDIX V -III- Directors' Resumes

Peter Gerard Homan

Year of Birth

1963

Qualifications

• Bachelor of Commerce (University of Queensland)

• Qualified Chartered Accountant (equivalent to US CPA)

• Presently a candidate for an MBA (Bond).

Professional Experience

From 1989 to 1993:

Manager of Bentleys Chartered Accountants, Brisbane. Bentleys is a medium sized firm of approximately 100 people offering a full range of traditional accounting services to a conservative low profile client base. Major areas of expertise included business restructuring, financing and corporate governance.

Presently on 12 month leave of absence to complete the MBA.

From 1988 to 1989

Senior Accountant at Arthur Young, Brisbane (antecedent firm to Ernst and Young) working in Business Services and computer selection.

From 1985 to 1988

Graduate intern at Touche Ross, Brisbane (antecedent firm to KPMG Peat Marwick).

APPENDIX VI - US Market Data

The US athletic shoe market generates nearly $12 billion of annual retail sales as detailed in Exhibit 1. Premium brands such as Nike and Reebok generate average gross margins to retailers of 47% making this segment highly attractive to retailers.

U.S. ATHLETIC SHOE MANUFACTURERS MARKET SHARE AND VOLUME OF SALES BY CATEGORY (in millions of pairs of shoes)						
Brand	Mkt %	Number	Womens	Mens	Girls	Boys
Nike	32	120	52	37	18	13
Reebok	24	89	39	28	13	9
Keds	6	22	10	7	3	2
L.A. Gear	5	19	8	6	3	2
ASICS	4	15	6	5	2	2
Others	29	108	na	na	na	na
TOTAL	100	373	115	83	39	28

The top five manufacturers account for over 70% of the 373 million pairs of shoes sold annually and enjoy gross margins of 38.2% to 40.8% and operating margins of 13.3% to 15.7%. The $11.6 billion in retail sales translates into wholesale sales of in excess of $5 billion. The Exhibits below detail further market information.

The average wholesale shoe price for the top five manufacturers is approximately $30.00 with their market share heavily skewed towards the more expensive end of the market.

U.S. ATHLETIC SHOE MANUFACTURERS MARKET SHARE AND DOLLAR SALES BY CATEGORY ($ millions)					
Brand	Total	Womens	Mens	Girls	Boys
Nike	3,715	1,505	1,613	277	320
Reebok	2,785	1,128	1,209	208	240
Keds	696	282	302	52	60
L.A. Gear	580	235	252	43	50
ASICS	465	188	202	35	40
Others	3276	na	na	na	na
TOTAL	11,607	3,338	3,578	615	710

Breeze

209

APPENDIX VII - Technical Drawings

International Patent Application No. PCT/AU 92/00554

United States Patent Application Serial No. 08/048,661

Australian Provisional Patent Application, PM 4890

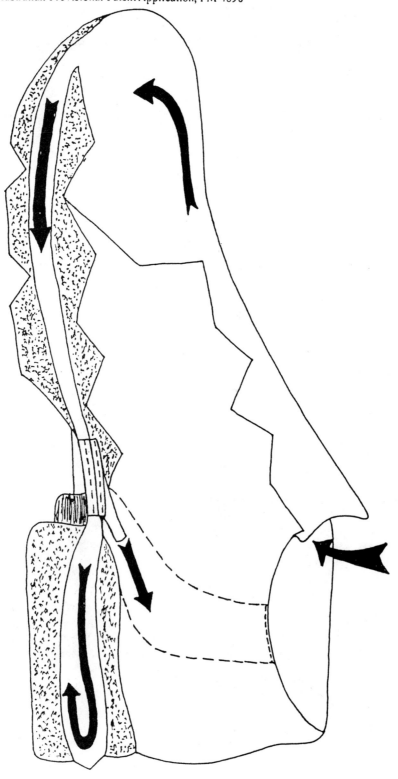

210

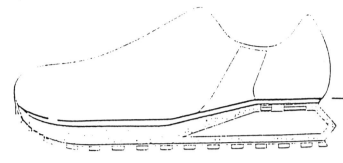

The expanded pumping chamber
holds 4 1/2 cubic inches of air

Similar to the volume of air
contained around the foot

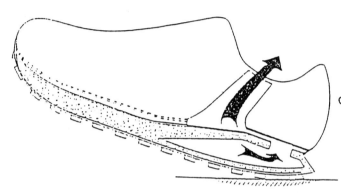

EXHAUST

The pumping chamber
compresses, and the contents
is propelled out through
the exhaust.

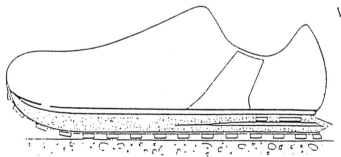

With the exhaust complete

the pumping chamber is

fully compressed

INTAKE

The chamber compresses, and
fills with heated moist air
drawn from around the toes.
Fresh air then enters around
the top of the shoe.

211

Discussion Questions
for
Breeze Technology Incorporated

1. Breeze plans to build a business by licensing its footwear ventilation technology to a major athletic shoe manufacturer and then using the proceeds to extend the technology to other shoe and foot products.

   - What is your assessment of the attractiveness of an athletic shoe with Breeze's ventilation technology? In other words, how good is the idea?

   - What is your assessment of Breeze's strategy to license its technology rather than manufacturer athletic shoe incorporating the technology?

   - What does Breeze have to do well to make money with this idea? In other words, what are the critical success factors?

   - How well has Breeze established the demand for athletic shoes incorporating its ventilation technology?

   - What are the major risks?

2. Breeze has three management team members.

   - How capable is this team of launching the business?

   - Who among the group is most critical to Breeze's success?

   - Are any additional talents or skills needed?

3. Breeze is currently in negotiations with a major athletic shoe manufacturing company.

   - How critical is this alliance to Breeze?

   - What would motivate the athletic shoe manufacturer to sign a licensing agreement with Breeze?

   - How attractive is the licensing structure involving a flat fee per period which Breeze is attempting to negotiate?

4. Breeze's pro forma income statement for year 5 shows revenues of $17,000,000 and net income of $7,763,370.

   - Which assumptions are most critical?

   - Where and when is the $1,000,000 payment to the inventor reported?

   - Assess the balance sheets.

   - Are the financial statements credible?

   - How could the presentation of the financial statements be improved?

5. Breeze is not currently looking for additional investors. However, assume that you were offered the opportunity to purchase the $70,000 bond held by Gurumbal Pty Ltd., that it was convertible into 5% of the common shares outstanding, and that you had sufficient capital to make this investment.

   - What do you see as the major strengths and weaknesses of this investment opportunity?

- What are the major risks?

- How would you get your money out of Breeze?

- Would you invest?

MOOT CORP®
Judge's Evaluation

Company: _____   Judge No: _____

I. Written Business Plan (40%)

Please evaluate the written <u>business plan</u> on the following aspects:
(Using this rating system: 1 = very poor, 2 = poor, 3 = fair, 4 = adequate, 5 = good, 6 = very good, 7 = excellent)

1. **Executive Summary (5%)**
    (Clear, exciting and effective as a stand-alone
    overview of the plan)   1   2   3   4   5   6   7
    Comments/Questions _____
    _____
    _____

2. **Company Overview (5%)**
    (Business purpose, history, genesis of concept,
    current status, overall strategy and objectives)   1   2   3   4   5   6   7
    Comments/Questions _____
    _____
    _____

3. **Products or Services (10%)**
    (Description, features and benefits, pricing, current
    stage of development, proprietary position)   1   2   3   4   5   6   7
    Comments/Questions _____
    _____
    _____

4. **Market and Marketing Strategy (10%)**
    (Description of market, competitive analysis, needs
    identification, market acceptance, unique
    capabilities, sales/promotion)   1   2   3   4   5   6   7
    Comments/Questions _____
    _____
    _____

5. **Operations (15%)**
    (Plan for production / delivery of product or
    services, product cost, margins, operating
    complexity, resources required)   1   2   3   4   5   6   7
    Comments/Questions _____
    _____
    _____

6. **Management (10%)**
    (Backgrounds of key individuals, ability to execute
    strategy, personnel needs, organizational structure,
    role of any non-student executive, which students
    will execute plan)   1   2   3   4   5   6   7
    Comments/Questions _____
    _____
    _____

In rating each of the above, please consider the following questions:
*   Is this area covered in adequate detail?
*   Does the plan show a clear understanding of the elements that should be addressed?
*   Are the assumptions realistic and reasonable?
*   Are the risks identified and the ability to manage those risks conveyed?

(Using this rating system: 1 = very poor, 2 = poor, 3 = fair, 4 = adequate, 5 = good, 6 = very good, 7 = excellent)

7. **Summary Financials (10%)**
Presented in summary form and follow U.S. generally accepted accounting principles.
Consistent with plan and effective in capturing financial performance; Quarterly for first two years, Quarterly/annually for years 3-5.

a. Cash Flow Statement	1	2	3	4	5	6	7
b. Income Statement	1	2	3	4	5	6	7
c. Balance Sheet	1	2	3	4	5	6	7
d. Funds Required/Uses	1	2	3	4	5	6	7
e. Assumptions/Trends/Comparatives	1	2	3	4	5	6	7

Comments/Questions _____
_____
_____

8. **Offering (10%)**
(Proposal/terms to investors—indicate how
much you want, the ROI, and the structure
of the deal; possible exit strategies)   1   2   3   4   5   6   7
Comments/Questions _____
_____
_____

9. **Viability (20%)**
(Market opportunity, distinctive competence,
management understanding, investment
potential)   1   2   3   4   5   6   7
Comments/Questions _____
_____
_____

10. **Brevity and Clarity (5%)**
(Is the plan approximately 25 pages with
minimal redundancy)   1   2   3   4   5   6   7
Comments/Questions _____
_____
_____

Additional Comments

MOOT CORP®
Judge's Evaluation

Company: _____ Judge No: _____

II. Presentation (20%)

(Using this rating system: 1 = very poor, 2 = poor, 3 = fair, 4 = adequate, 5 = good, 6 = very good, 7 = excellent)

1. **Formal Presentation (50%)**
   a. Materials presented in clear, logical and/or
      sequential form.   1   2   3   4   5   6   7
   b. Ability to relate need for the company with
      meaningful examples, and practical applications.   1   2   3   4   5   6   7
   c. Ability to maintain judges' interest.   1   2   3   4   5   6   7
   d. Quality of Visual Aids.   1   2   3   4   5   6   7

2. **Questions and Answers (50%)**
   a. Ability to understand judges' inquiries.   1   2   3   4   5   6   7
   b. Appropriately respond to judges' inquiries
      with substantive answers.   1   2   3   4   5   6   7
   c. Use of time allocated (minimal redundancy).   1   2   3   4   5   6   7
   d. Poise and confidence (think effectively on their
      feet).   1   2   3   4   5   6   7

Strengths of Presentation

Weaknesses of Presentation

217

MOOT CORP®
Judge's Evaluation

Company: _____ Judge No: _____

III. Viability of Company (40%)

	Definitely No						Definitely Yes
1. **Market Opportunity (20%)** (There is a clear market need presented as well as a way to take advantage of that need.)	1	2	3	4	5	6	7
2. **Distinctive Competence (20%)** (The company provides something novel/unique/ special that gives it a competitive advantage in its market.)	1	2	3	4	5	6	7
3. **Management Capability (20%)** (This team can effectively develop this company and handle the risks associated with the venture.)	1	2	3	4	5	6	7
4. **Financial Understanding (20%)** (This team has a solid understanding of the financial requirements of the business.)	1	2	3	4	5	6	7
5. **Investment Potential (20%)** (The business represents a real investment opportunity in which you would consider investing.)	1	2	3	4	5	6	7

Company Strengths

Company Weaknesses

Additional Comments

218

Innovative products for relaxed living.

Business Plan
April 25, 1995

TRUE DIMENSIONS, INC.

3925 West Braker Lane
Austin, TX 78759-5321
(512) 305-0190

The University of Texas at Austin
Gary M. Cadenhead, Ph.D., Faculty Advisor

Mike Hanratty, President
1801 Rio Grande, #207
Austin, TX 78701
(512) 472-5258
346-52-2157

Irene Bond, Director of Marketing
12424 Deer Track
Austin, TX 78727
(512) 335-0773
585-70-3770

Jeff Hoogendam, Financial Consultant
6915 Old Quarry Lane
Austin, TX 78731
(512) 502-0097
463-94-0556

Wes Boyd, Marketing/Sales Consultant
3211 French Place
Austin, TX 78722
(512) 480-0298
275-52-9050

Leslie Frank, External Relations Consultant
4409 Duval Street, #106
Austin, TX 78751
(512) 451-9611
437-39-8106

The Flogiston™ Chair

(flo-JIS-ton)

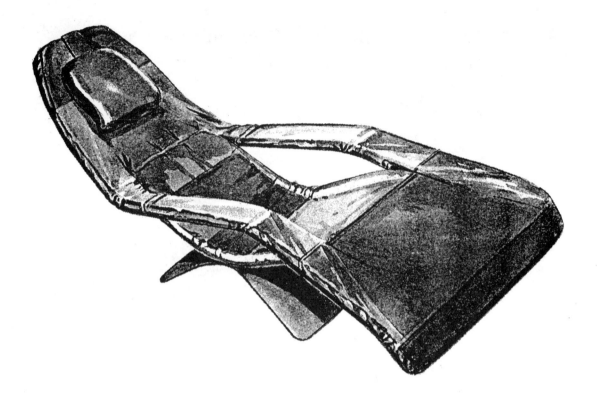

"My husband loves the chair and went so far as to say it was worth waiting for. He's happier, his meditation and disposition are much better, and it is beautiful! I hope millions of people understand how wonderful the chair is."

Hellane Spaivak, Owner of a Flogiston™ Chair

"After a couple of weeks with the chair, I can barely imagine life without one. I try to finish work ten minutes early so I can chill out and arrive home much better prepared to enjoy my family."

Thomas Dolby, Owner of a Flogiston™ Chair

TRUE DIMENSIONS, INC.
EXECUTIVE SUMMARY

THE OPPORTUNITY

True Dimensions, Inc. has an exclusive worldwide license to manufacture and market the Flogiston™ Chair (flow-JIS-ton), a product designed from NASA research on astronaut sleeping patterns in a microgravity environment. The chair comfortably supports the body in a modified version of the neutral body posture experienced in zero gravity. Through this patented posture and a flexible aluminum frame, the body finds its own internal equilibrium and balance, providing deep relaxation of the body and mind.

The Flogiston™ Chair has already received widespread recognition in the virtual reality industry as the optimal stress-free environment for virtual reality experiences. Recent publications featuring the chair and its benefits include periodicals such as *Omni, Wired, NASA Tech Briefs, Machine Design,* and *Mondo-2000*. These publications reach over 1.1 million subscribers annually. The Flogiston™ Chair was also featured in *The Lawnmower Man*, a futuristic movie set in the context of virtual reality adventure. The inventor has already sold 25 chairs, and more than 1100 prospective customers have expressed interest in purchasing the chair when it becomes available. NASA, ARPA, Panasonic, Rockwell, Walt Disney Imagineering, The New York Modern Art Museum, and other organizations have expressed interest in the chair.

True Dimensions will use the Flogiston™ Chair as the foundation for building a cohesive line of complementary, ultra-contemporary furniture with the highest level of comfort. True Dimensions has established operations at the Austin Technology Incubator and is working to fill a backlog of 16 orders.

THE MARKET

The $19 billion furniture industry is characterized by a large number of suppliers, a large number of buyers, fragmented distribution, limited product differentiation, and low barriers to entry for new suppliers. These characteristics would not appear to make an attractive market for a start up furniture manufacturing and marketing company; however, our marketing strategy will position the company in several of the most profitable furniture niche markets which have remained insulated and are continuing to grow. These segments include novelty/specialty products, ultra-contemporary furnishings, home audio/theatre seating, and ergonomic/therapeutic seating. True Dimensions intends to deliver its home furnishings to a customer base willing to pay a premium for innovation, unique design, and a differentiable level of comfort.

Initially, True Dimensions will leverage the large amount of publicity given to the Flogiston™ Chair through direct sales to identified prospective customers and organizations. This 6 to 12 month period of direct sales will allow the company to establish itself financially and enhance the chair's features for additional markets. In the long run, the company will follow market research which supports using value-added resellers to distribute products and educate consumers on product benefits. Four retail marketing channels will be utilized via a phased approach:

- Novelty/specialty retail outlets (i.e. Sharper Image)
- Ultra-contemporary retail stores
- Interior designers and architects
- Home audio/theatre specialty retail stores

Sales representatives from each of these channels were interviewed and shown the prototype of the Flogiston™ Chair. In these meetings, True Dimensions received affirmation of the Flogiston™ Chair's functional features, visual appeal, and suggested retail price.

COMPETITIVE ADVANTAGE

True Dimensions has an unique approach to designing furnishings for the home centered on creating a minimum stress environment for the body. Competitive advantages include the following:

- Exclusive worldwide license of product protected by US Utility Patent #5,141,285
- Unique product design and unparalleled comfort
- Reduced exposure to fixed costs by utilizing outsourced manufacturing
- An experienced and committed management team supported by a qualified Board of Advisors

INITIAL FUNDING

True Dimensions was initially funded with $30,000 invested by its current principals. This funding will support initial direct sales. In August, 1995, True Dimensions will seek $200,000 in exchange for 35% of common stock and a prorata seat on the Board of Directors. By May we expect to establish a manufacturing and marketing track record on a limited scale. The funds are required primarily for working capital needs during the national sales rollout.

Based on proforma projections, fifth year revenues will be $3.6 million, yielding an operating income of $375,000. An investor can expect a 30% five year compounded annual return on their 35% equity.

224

Table of Contents

1. THE COMPANY

True Dimensions, Inc. manufactures and markets ultra-contemporary, ergonomic furnishings. The company coordinates numerous interdependent resources to provide functional and stylish pieces of furniture to meet the market's needs for a differentiable level of comfort and cutting edge design. True Dimensions accomplishes its objectives by forming cooperative partnerships with designers, manufacturers, and resellers to supply customers with its unique products.

True Dimensions' products sacrifice neither comfort nor style in favor of ergonomic design. By placing the body in a minimal stress position, entertainment, computing, and communications devices configure to create an environment conducive to optimal relaxation and productivity.

Founded on January 6, 1995, True Dimensions, Inc. is a Subchapter S Corporation headquartered in Austin, Texas. The company has established primary and secondary outsourcing agreements with manufacturers in Texas. Initial shipment of product is scheduled in April, 1995. As sales grow the company will begin backward integration into a full production facility by year 5.

2. PRODUCTS

2.1 Introductory Product: The Flogiston™ Chair

Studying yoga to learn stress reduction techniques, Brian Park found himself unable to meditate comfortably in the lotus position. Stimulated by a *NASA Tech Briefs* article, Park contacted NASA and requested data on the physics of sleep collected during Skylab Missions. Research in NASA's anthropomorphic and ergonomic studies, combined with his desire to meditate comfortably, led Park to the creation of the Flogiston™ Chair. (See Appendix A, page 23)

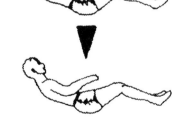

Experimenting in his garage, Park tested and refined his prototype. Encouraged by enthusiastic customer response, Park founded Flogiston Corporation. He filed for, and received US Utility Patent #5,141,285 on the *modified neutral posture* in August, 1992.

The core of the Flogiston™ Chair's technology lies in the patented modified neutral body posture designed to replicate the natural posture the body takes in zero gravity. This posture merges the neutral body posture with the Savasana yoga position. The Savasana yoga position has been used for thousands of years by yogi to achieve liberation of the self through enhanced meditative relaxation. The Flogiston™ Chair's features are designed to simulate this derived posture yielding the same benefits.

NASA recognizes the comfort level of the Flogiston™ Chair and currently utilizes the chair attached to a Personal Motion Platform (PMP) for delivering virtual reality training designed to teach astronauts the physics of dealing with objects in zero gravity. (See Appendix B, pages 24-25).

2.2 Development of Future Products

Product development focuses in the following areas:

- *Product line extensions:* Customized chairs will be designed to adapt the product to the special needs of each market niche, including novelty/specialty items, ultra-contemporary furnishings, home theatre, audiophile seating, and chronic pain/stress relief treatment. For the novelty/specialty market (i.e. Sharper Image), the company is developing and testing "infrasound" technology which generates low frequency vibrations for enhanced therapeutic relaxation.

- *New Products:* True Dimensions is currently developing relationships with several talented artists and furniture designers. The company will call upon their expertise in designing new products. These include Dale Eggert of Wauwatosa, Wisconsin, Jim Wallace and Kevin Merino of Austin, Texas, and Jeff Scott of Santa Monica, California. In addition, new products derived from virtual reality applications will be developed through sponsored research agreements with Flogiston Corporation.

COZY SPOON

Preliminary design of a love seat for the home theatre market.

BAT SEAT

Preliminary design of a love seat to complement the Flogiston Chair.

3. MARKET ANALYSIS

3.1 Market Size

Manufacturing USA estimated the **national upholstered** household furniture market to be $6 billion in 1992. According to the Research and Information Group of Texas Department of Commerce, the **Texas upholstered** household furniture market was $53.3 million in 1992 (SIC Code 2512).

Approximately 8.45 million households, or 13% of the 65+ million US households, are members of the company's target income group, earning over $75,000 per year. The upholstered furniture buying power of these affluent households is $2.0 billion annually. (US Bureau of Census, S&P Industry Surveys, November, 1992).

3.2 Upholstered Furniture Niche Markets

- *Novelty/Specialty Market*
  The novelty/specialty niche delivers new high-tech products to people who are willing to pay a premium for the latest items offering specialized functionality. Sharper Image is pioneering a new segment of products focused on living a healthier life. Like its competitors, Brookstone and Hammacher Schlemmer, Sharper Image sells styles of shiatsu massage recliners ranging from $2,300 to $3,500 retail. These products are designed to offer relaxation and stress reduction.

  The novelty/specialty customer base closely matches the profile of our target customer. The typical customer, 65% of whom are male professionals, is between the ages of 35 and 54. High-tech, high-end merchandise is especially popular. Retail centers located in urban and financial districts provide convenient access to professional men and their families. Families in this market typically have an income of $75,000 or greater and tend to be city dwellers.

- *Ultra-Contemporary Furnishings Market*
  The *ultra-contemporary* furniture market is positioned at the high-end of furnishings in terms of quality, modern style, price, and margins. Ultra-contemporary retail stores are looking for the latest, cutting edge designs to place in their showrooms. Ultra-contemporary upholstered furniture sales represent 6% of the upholstered furniture market ($360 million in annual sales). (HFD Home Furnishings Weekly Newspaper, October, 1994).

  Retailers in this market often require exclusivity for a product in a given geographic region or city. They are able to charge higher prices due to their exclusivity, higher perceived quality, and unique styling. Almost 500 retail outlets serve the US ultra-contemporary furniture market with most upholstered products on their showroom floors turning 4 to 12 times per year.

- *Interior Design Market*
  Interior designers and architects assist affluent homeowners in furnishing a new home or remodeling an existing home, offering the highest level of personalized service. They are entrusted with the responsibility of creating the desired image, specifying products and finishes that meet their sophisticated clients' decorative and functional needs within a defined budget. The design and architect professions are an attractive channel, because they have direct links to affluent customer bases that purchase high-end furnishings. They are considered the industry trend setters.

- *Home Entertainment Market*
  Affluent households spend an increasing portion of their furniture budgets in a single dedicated entertainment and relaxation room. This room often contains a wide screen television, a surround-sound stereo system, and video game or other interactive television technologies. The nucleus of the home is the one area in which every effort is made to create an environment conducive to relaxation.

  Today, most seating used for home entertainment is in the traditional form of sofas, love seats, and recliners. Furniture used in this segment of the market must match the evolution of two separate trends: home furnishings style and home theatre technology. Few seating products have been designed specifically for the evolving home theatre market. Most furniture manufacturers fail to consider this as a viable market, because their products do not meet the functionality required by this market.

3.3 Future Niche Markets

True Dimensions is currently evaluating the long term potential opportunity in three emerging upholstered furniture markets. The company is positioning itself to enter the following niches:

- *Psychotherapy and Chronic Pain Treatment Markets*
  A survey was mailed to selected specialists at the Tulane Pain Clinic in New Orleans, one of the premiere clinics for chronic pain research. Preliminary survey results indicate that the Flogiston™ Chair would be best used for treatment of psychiatric problems. Specialists in psychiatry, occupational therapy, and clinical psychology found the chair to be appropriate for relaxing apprehensive patients, stress management, hypnosis, bio-feedback, and other treatments requiring a stress-free relaxed environment.

  While these results seem promising, a look at overall medical trends shows that the Flogiston™ Chair may be ideally positioned to take advantage of one of the newer medical applications, the treatment of chronic pain. Still relatively new, the treatment of chronic pain takes a holistic approach to treating a combination of both physical and psychological causes of pain. Since the Flogiston™ Chair puts the patient in a position which reduces external forces on the body, it would be ideal for helping doctors isolate the physical and non-physical sources of a patient's pain. Properly marketed, the chair could become the treatment chair of choice for this and other mental health related fields.

- *Office Market*
  The Occupational Safety and Health Administration (OSHA) has drafted a proposed national ergonomic protection standard intended to reduce the occurrences of "cumulative trauma disorders" in the workplace. According to the Bureau of Labor statistics, 280,000 employees filed workers' compensation claims for carpal tunnel syndrome in 1992, resulting in costs of approximately $30 billion. Ergonomists believe the new federal standard will force many employers to replace outdated office equipment and furniture and rethink the way jobs requiring repetitive motions and long periods behind desks are done.

  Industry experts believe the new OSHA regulations will cause a boom in the office furniture and equipment industry and short term price increases. True Dimensions will evaluate how it can participate in the evolution of new workplace furnishings that emphasize comfortable, ergonomically supportive environments over traditional desktops to improve productivity.

- *Virtual Reality Market*
  As virtual reality technologies are being developed for both commercial and entertainment uses, the user environment has become the key factor in differentiating the degree of "reality" experienced by the user. Today, virtual reality theme parks, such as Virtual World®, are appearing across the globe in which "travelers" interact with other travelers in virtual reality adventure games. Walt Disney Imagineering, through its Epcot Innovations Pavilion, is developing virtual reality applications for its guests to enjoy. Disney has contacted the designer with interest in using the

chair for this application. Richard Crane Productions, a theme park developer, has expressed interest in creating an immersive cyberspace facility utilizing the Flogiston™ Chair.

The Geneva Research Group predicts that by 1999 business applications alone will create a $575 million market for these devices. Moreover, they predict this figure to top $1 billion by the year 2000.

3.4 Market Trends

Manufacturing Trends

The US furniture industry is experiencing a period of consolidation to larger, more capital intensive, production facilities. Between 1980 and 1990, the number of furniture manufacturers declined from 5,000 to 2,500. Industry changes include vertical integration between manufacturing and retailing operations to satisfy increasing demand for custom-built furniture, consumer preferences shifting to more comfortable casual furniture, rather than formal furniture, and enhanced manufacturing productivity.

Standardization for mass production by major manufacturers, along with the demise of many smaller manufacturers, *has created new opportunities for the success of start up niche furniture manufacturers*. Examples of young successful furniture manufacturing companies include:

- *Viewpoint*, a $30 million leather upholstery manufacturer, is currently growing at 42% per year.

- *Uniqseat* had sales of $1.5 million in 1994 and is experiencing an annual growth rate of 300%.

- *Body Built Chair*, a manufacturer which focuses on ergonomic office furniture, demonstrated 35% annual growth rate for three years, with more than $20 million sales in 1994.

Demographic Trends

Research shows that relaxation and stress management products have the greatest appeal to affluent baby boomers (ages 35-44). The future direction (sales levels and preferences) of the furniture market will most likely be determined by aging baby boomers. A recent *Cincinnati Enquirer* article, "How Retailers Are Changing To Meet Aging Baby Boomer's Needs," emphasizes that primary concerns of this group, such as comfort and safety, relate to the home and are providing forward thinking firms the opportunity to build businesses which meet these needs. The members of this large consumer segment will likely move to the higher end of the furniture market as they reach their prime earning years and replace worn furniture with lasting pieces.

3.5 Customer Need

"Exhausted: A Nation of the Quick and the Dead," the cover story for the March 6, 1995, edition of *Newsweek* describes a disturbing trend among working Americans. The following quotation best summarizes the article's main theme: "We're fried by work, frazzled by the lack of time. Technology hasn't made our lives better, just busier. No wonder one quarter of us say we're exhausted. We need to chill out before we hit the breaking point." Now more than ever people have a universal need to escape and experience true relaxation of the body, mind, and soul.

When relaxing, the human tendency is to lean back and elevate the feet. Capitalizing on this behavior, the typical product provided by residential mass marketers is a product comparable to the La-Z-Boy™ recliner. Rather than produce innovative and stylistic pieces of furniture, most manufacturers have simply incorporated the reclining motion into two and three-seat sofas. To date, ergonomics has not been a significant consideration in the design of lounge seating.

American National Standards Institute (ANSI) and Human Factors Society (HFS) define standards for ergonomic seating. ANSI HFS 100-1988 forms the cornerstone of the proposed OSHA legislation. The Flogiston™ Chair meets the dimensions for comfort and lumbar support required by this standard.

The Business and Institutional Furniture Manufacturers Association (BIFMA) states that 40 million people now work primarily in home offices. As consumers become familiar with the OSHA standard and the increased level of comfort it provides, HFS predicts that a greater proportion of home furnishings will incorporate ergonomic features.

3.6 Competitive Analysis

Mass Market Manufacturers

Sufficient competition exists in mass production manufacturing due to the large size of this market. Competitors such as Masco, Thomasville, and La-Z-Boy™ dominate this market through low-cost, high volume manufacturing and high degrees of product standardization. True Dimensions will not compete directly with mass market producers, as we will approach the higher margin/lower volume niche markets.

Novelty/Specialty

Currently only two manufacturers offer competitive products to the novelty/specialty market. The marketing strategy of a young company in Florida, Somatron, most closely resembles that of True Dimensions, with an added focus on audio components and medical applications. Japanese giant Panasonic sells $5 to $7 million wholesale in shiatsu massage chairs annually into this market segment. All of these products retail between $2,300 and $3,500.

Ultra-contemporary Furnishings

Leaders in this segment produce $25 to $75 million in revenues. Primarily European, this group of competitors includes Desede, Urbana, Weiman's, Jaymar, Westnofa, and Thayer Coggin. A number of small design firms compete in the most expensive and exclusive end of this market segment. Many of these smaller $1 to $5 million companies are located in Southeast Florida and in several California design centers.

Home Audio/Theatre

To date, this industry has focused on the sale of consumer electronic components and entertainment centers designed to house these products. At this time, only Thayer Coggin has developed an upholstered product line designed specifically for the home theatre. It is important to note that some crossover already exists between the novelty/specialty and home audio/theatre segments. Examples of this include NAD stereo components featured in the Sharper Image catalogue and Panasonic massage chairs with built-in speakers. For Stereo 2000, located in the Houston Galleria, the Panasonic chair is one of the best selling items.

4. PRODUCT TECHNOLOGY & OPERATIONS

4.1 Flogiston™ Technology

The core of Flogiston™ technology is the patented modified neutral body posture which allows the body to relax in its natural position. This posture minimizes internal and external physical stress so that all muscular forces are in balance and the body is in biomechanical equilibrium. The Flogiston™ Chair's high-tensile strength aircraft aluminum hull flexes in response to the body's movements. The chair's inherent responsiveness provides the occupant with a floating sensation, much like the feeling experienced in zero gravity. Ergonomically designed, the frame also provides correct lumbar support.

The Flogiston™ Chair's features break traditional industry paradigms. For example, a common myth is "more cushion means more comfort." By incorporating high density, temperature-sensitive softening memory foam, the Flogiston™ Chair conforms to each person's body for a customized fit. Also, it is common for most furniture to have a narrow footspace, even though the body relaxes best with the feet placed in a wider stance. The chair features a wider footspace to satisfy this natural drive. These unique features combine to provide a minimal stress environment, allowing the Flogiston™ Chair's occupant to escape and experience the most natural flow of peace and deep relaxation.

4.2 Manufacturing Operations

True Dimensions is currently outsourcing all phases of production. This strategy has eliminated the need for extensive fixed assets while maintaining flexibility in design and production. It allows the company to focus attention on sales, marketing, and product development to establish initial market acceptance. True Dimensions has streamlined the production in two primary phases:

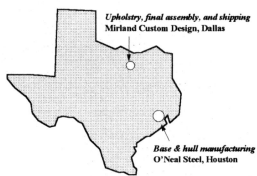

Operations Strategy

Upholstry, final assembly, and shipping
Mirland Custom Design, Dallas

Base & hull manufacturing
O'Neal Steel, Houston

- *Hull construction* -- Sheet aluminum is laser cut, formed, and a black epoxy finish is applied to create the chair frame. Initial hull production orders will be in quantities of 20 to 50. O'Neal Steel in Houston, Texas, is the current aluminum hull supplier.

- *Upholstery construction* -- Dense, high memory polypropylene foam is cut and trimmed. Fabric or leather is cut and stitched. The chair is completely assembled, packaged, and sidemarked according to the customer's shipping instructions. Mirland Custom Design of Dallas, Texas, currently handles upholstery and final assembly.

Production scheduling, order entry, shipping releases, and invoicing will all be handled by True Dimensions. Current product cost breakdown is as follows:

Task	Current Vendor	Cost	Lead Time
Aluminum fabrication	O'Neal Steel	$220	2-3 weeks
Upholstery & assembly	Mirland Custom Design	$370	1-4 weeks
Hardware & packaging	Miscellaneous	$ 57	2 weeks
Total		**$647**	**4 - 6 weeks**

Production Insourcing Transition:

When sales reach approximately $60,000 a month, it becomes economically viable to manufacture the products in-house. We will realize several advantages:

- Increased operating leverage and reduced variable costs
- Greater control and flexibility in manufacturing
- Quality inspections will be easier.

The initial production facility will be approximately 5,000 square feet and will focus primarily on upholstery and final assembly. Initial fixed machinery costs will be approximately $20,000.

5. CUSTOMER INTERVIEW RESULTS

Twenty-two Flogiston™ Chair owners who purchased the chair directly from the inventor were interviewed to determine their reason for purchase and level of satisfaction with the chair. Highlights from the telephone interviews are as follows:

- Uses for the chair included meditation, stress relief, escape, yoga, back-ache relief, artistic piece, developing virtual reality entertainment technologies, and personal computer user environment research.

- The chair's style/design was described as "elegant," "eclectic," "modern," "futuristic," "graceful," "ultra-contemporary," and "streamlined."

- The chair's comfort features were described as "fabulous," "perfectly relaxing," "like floating in water," "responsive," "it moves with your body," "balanced," "even weight distribution," and "it is like having a Ferrari in your living room!"

6. MARKETING STRATEGY

6.1 Overview

Key success factors to marketing and selling the Flogiston™ Chair in most channels are:

- Buyers and consumers must be able to experience the benefits of the chair during the purchase decision process.

- Resellers must perceive the chair as a high quality, unique piece of ultra-contemporary furniture worth the suggested retail price.

- True Dimensions must educate resellers in the inherently unique benefits of the Flogiston™ posture manifested in the chair's design and features.

- True Dimensions must capitalize on the role NASA research played in the development of the Flogiston™ Chair in its communications to resellers and end-users.

Given the prescribed criteria for success, the Flogiston™ Chair and subsequent products must be sold to end-users by reputable value-added resellers. It is critical to generate awareness and trial by placing the chair in showrooms. In these showrooms, the consumer requires information and assistance in making his or her purchasing decision. True Dimensions must educate its channel partners on the Flogiston™ Chair's features and benefits and enable them to perform the majority of the promotional functions.

No significant channel conflict exists among the different value added resellers which will sell the Flogiston™ Chair. In interviews with representatives from reselling organizations, the company learned that each channel views its customer base as having different fundamental needs. For example, ultra-contemporary retail outlets believe style and uniqueness of design drive the purchase decision for their customers. However, novelty/specialty outlets such as the Sharper Image feel that their customers purchase primarily for their unique functionality and high-tech appeal. By developing customized products designed to meet the needs of each reseller market, True Dimensions has an opportunity to pursue a multi-channel marketing strategy.

6.2 Marketing Strategies by Distribution Channels

True Dimensions has selected a variety of distribution channels to reach the end-user. The company will customize its marketing communications to different channels. This strategy will allow True Dimensions to build a dealer network in each channel. The Flogiston™ Chair will be sold through direct sales in the first year, then using the following retail channels: Novelty/specialty retail stores, ultra-contemporary retail outlets, interior designers, architects, and home audio/theatre retail channels.

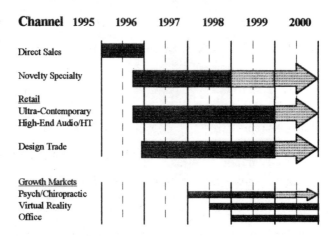

Sales Rollout Strategy

| Channel | 1995 | 1996 | 1997 | 1998 | 1999 | 2000 |

True Dimensions   **Page** 10

236

6.2 Marketing Strategies by Distribution Channels

Direct Sales Strategy

The Flogiston™ Chair has received a tremendous amount of publicity from which True Dimensions is currently leveraging in its direct sales. Although the Flogiston™ Chair has been seen by 1.1 million people in *Omni Magazine*, *NASA Tech Briefs*, and *Wired Magazine*, it has only been produced on a limited basis by the designer of the chair. Anticipating future production, he has created and maintained a database of 1100+ interested customers identified through trade shows and responses to articles and advertisements in various publications. Given the company's need for an immediate source of working capital, it is using this database to generate direct sales.

True Dimensions has recently launched a direct mail campaign targeting the identified prospective customers from the database. The company has developed a brochure and order form that has been mailed to these people. A special introductory discount and a thirty day money-back guarantee trial period will enhance the buying incentive. The company is following up with these prospective customers to determine their interest in purchasing the chair and to gather additional leads.

The designer currently receives inquiries for the Flogiston™ Chair over the Internet. Mosaic home pages and electronic bulletin board advertisements will be used to enable Internet users and virtual reality aficionados to locate product and order information. In addition, utilization of list servers such as *Fringeware Review* will increase electronic exposure for the chair. The company will continue to seek coverage in virtual reality publications, high end audio magazines, interior design journals, and popular press.

Direct sales is the most significant channel for generating revenues during 1995, producing sales of 81 units. True Dimensions projects 2.5% of the existing database of 1100 prospective customers to purchase chairs, resulting in 28 unit sales. The additional sales will result from individual contacts, trade shows, and ongoing publicity. Direct sales will be phased out as a primary channel after the first year, concurrent with the development of reseller channels.

Novelty/Specialty Strategy

The novelty/specialty market represents the potential early "home run" for True Dimensions and Flogiston™ Chair sales. Given its customer base profile and the high-tech product mix found in retail stores, the upscale novelty/specialty channel appears to be an excellent match for the Flogiston™ Chair. The quality, functionality, uniqueness of the chair (especially when connected with NASA and virtual reality), and suggested retail price ensure a "good fit" according to Diane Cantera, a representative from

Brookstone. The company will target Sharper Image as its first distributor in the novelty/specialty. Once the chair is accepted, Sharper Image will perform the majority of the marketing functions and flows. A key advantage of reselling products through Sharper Image and other novelty/specialty stores is gaining national distribution immediately upon acceptance of product. Through product education and personal use in their own homes, Sharper Image's salespeople become intimately familiar with each product's unique features and benefits in order to optimally sell to consumers. Sharper Image stores are referred to as "exploratoriums," meaning that everything can be used and touched by the customer on the showroom floor. This atmosphere will allow customers to try the Flogiston™ Chair and immediately feel the differentiable relaxation level provided.

True Dimensions will offer Sharper Image a technologically enhanced version of the Flogiston™ Chair for distribution. Working in conjunction with The University of Texas Electrical Engineering Department, the company is developing and testing simplified versions of "infrasound" technology which were originally developed for virtual reality applications. In this system a simple electromechanical device transmits therapeutic vibrations through the chair to provide the occupant augmented relaxation. True Dimensions is evaluating other emerging technologies that would meet evolving market needs. For example, the chair may also feature mounting points for remote controls, keyboards, and mouse pads for PC use at home. True Dimensions is preparing a marketing presentation for Sharper Image in October, 1995 and developing entry plans for other novelty/specialty outlets such as Brookstone and Hammacher Schlemmer.

The potential viability of this reseller channel is reinforced by Panasonic's annual wholesale revenues of $5 to 7 million. Although acceptance by these novelty/specialty retail firms would quickly give True Dimensions high sales levels with fewer company marketing and sales resources expended, it is probable that sales levels would taper off in congruence with the product's life cycle. Because placing a product in one of these retail outlets is typically a "one-shot" attempt, we are being conservative and not including novelty/specialty sales in the company's detailed financial projections. Instead we have performed a sensitivity analysis (See: Appendix D, Page 37) showing sales and income comparisons without novelty/specialty sales and with novelty/specialty sales (shown as "best case" scenario). If novelty/specialty sales do not materialize we will re-focus marketing efforts on the following channels.

Ultra-Contemporary Retailer Strategy

Ultra-contemporary stores target a customer segment which is also ideal for the Flogiston™ Chair. The consumer's purchase decision in this market is primarily driven by uniqueness of design and premium quality. True Dimensions has visited numerous ultra-contemporary retail stores throughout Texas and five other states. Upon viewing a photograph of the prototype, showroom personnel confirmed that the Flogiston™ Chair has the visual appeal their customers look for. Examples of ultra-contemporary retailers in Texas are Cantoni in Houston and Dallas and Austin's Trendz. Palazzetti has locations in 10 major metropolitan areas across the US.

Due to the unique nature of their offerings, these retailers often desire an exclusive agreement among ultra-contemporary retail outlets to protect their image as well as their margins. Competing for market share, Cantoni and Palazzetti tout the exclusivity of their respective product lines. True Dimensions will engage in exclusive agreements with reputable ultra-contemporary retailers to support their marketing efforts in their competitive territories.

In its early years, True Dimensions will sell products directly to ultra-contemporary retailers. The company will establish a relationship with the store's buyer, deliver a presentation and product demonstration, negotiate terms, take orders, ship product, and ensure each store has adequate stock to maintain a chair on the showroom floor at all times. To maximize return on investment for both parties, the company will provide sales support through demonstration kits and sales training materials. True Dimensions will employ a direct salesforce. By year 5, True Dimensions will employ 7 regional salespeople as shown in the Personnel Requirement Assumptions (page 30). The company will initially focus its selling efforts on ultra-contemporary retailers in the southwestern and southern regions, as they are convenient to Austin and are experiencing the highest growth (23% vs. 9% national average) in retail furniture sales.

Regional market centers are a focal point for marketing to furniture resellers in the US. True Dimensions will use regional market centers to introduce and expose its products to ultra-contemporary dealers. Dealers come to market centers to view and buy products manufactured by exhibitors at wholesale. In October, 1994, the company attended the International Home Furnishings National Market, the pre-eminent furniture industry trade show, in High Point, North Carolina. This market center exhibits home furnishings from more than 1,900 manufacturers representing all 50 states as well as 75 countries. At this show, over twenty independent ultra-contemporary sales representatives saw a photograph of the prototype, and they confirmed that the chair's unique style would have visual appeal to consumers in their market niche. True Dimensions has leased floor space to display the Flogiston™ Chair at the Dallas Home Furnishings Show in June, 1995. The company also plans to attend the San Francisco Home Furnishings Show in July, 1995 and the International Home Furnishings National Market in October, 1995. True

Dimensions will target other major market centers serving extensive regional markets which are located in Atlanta, Chicago, Seattle, and Tupelo, Mississippi.

In the event that novelty/specialty sales do not fully materialize, sales to ultra-contemporary retailers represent 63% of the company's total projected revenues by 1999. Scheduled product introductions build a product line consisting of 7 models by year 5 (Detailed in Appendix D, page 31). After 1999, sales will level off as nationwide distribution is accomplished. Product introductions and deletions continue in accordance with customer demand. Individual dealer sales are projected at 5 units per location in 1996. As the number of models increases, the projection tapers to sales of 2.4 units per retail outlet times number of models in product line by 1999.

Interior Designers and Architects Strategy

True Dimensions will capitalize on the interior designers' and architects' customer networks to reach targeted end-users living in major markets and small to mid-sized markets not large enough to support a high-end retail outlet. In the trade, it is essential to place the chair in reputable ultra-contemporary showrooms during national and regional market shows for these resellers to evaluate. From interviews, interior designers expressed a preference for acquiring furnishings through these showrooms because it is more reliable than dealing directly with manufacturers. True Dimensions will implement creative programs at these market shows to prompt trial and encourage referrals.

The company will also use the American Society of Interior Designers (ASID) database of 20,000+ names to build a network of designers focusing on high-end, contemporary clients. A recent ASID report states that over 50% of its registered interior designers are interested in seeing new residential furniture products. In addition, advertising in industry publications such as *Interior Design, Interiors, Architectural Review,* and *Architectural Digest* will be used to encourage purchasing the chair in 1996.

Interior designers and architects are expected to generate revenues equivalent to 15% of the volume sold by ultra-contemporary retailers.

Home Audio/Theatre Retail Outlets Strategy

True Dimensions will target upscale dealers of consumer electronics specializing in high performance branded technologies such as Lucasfilm Home THX® Systems, Linn, NAD, and Magnepan. These specialists provide full custom design and installation of home audio/theatre systems to affluent households. Lounge seating is an integral part of the home theatre mock-ups that provide the experiential element needed to close the sale. Like ultra-contemporary retail, these stores are "high touch, high customization" outlets for their customers.

Creston Funk, owner of Concert Sound, San Antonio's exclusive Linn dealership, ordered 3 chairs. One was earmarked for his home listening pleasure, the others are for the store's theatre mock-up. Funk's goal is to provide his customers with lounge seating that is as unique as the entertainment systems he designs.

True Dimensions views this channel as a first-mover opportunity, as most contemporary furniture manufacturers concentrate primarily on the traditional retail outlets. Displaying and selling the Flogiston™ Chair provides these audio electronics outlets with an incremental profit opportunity not typically utilized in this trade. Recently, True Dimensions has been contacted by several audio stores and currently is filling orders for 5 more chairs.

The sales processes for home audio/theatre and novelty/specialty retail outlets are similar. However, True Dimensions will take a specialized approach in educating and selling the salespeople (mostly audiophiles and technologically inclined people) on the differentiable benefits of the chair in the context of home audio/theatre environment. The company will accomplish this with sales materials and end-user seminars. In addition, True Dimensions will attend a few targeted consumer electronics trade shows to exhibit the Flogiston™ Chair and subsequent products.

An enhanced version of the Flogiston™ Chair introduced in 1996 for home audio/theatre will result in rapid sales growth. True Dimensions plans to have the listening chair installed in 100 retail outlets by the end of 1997.

Future Channels Strategy

As previously mentioned, True Dimensions is evaluating the opportunity and making plans to position itself to market the Flogiston™ Chair in three potential emerging markets in 1997:

- Psychotherapy and chronic pain treatment
- Office (OSHA compliance)
- Virtual reality

Revenues from these channels are not currently figured into the financial section of this business plan due to the long term developmental nature of each. In time, they will each provide strategic opportunities for the company to pursue.

6.3 Promotion Strategy

In 1995, press releases and product reviews will be the primary means of advertising. The company recently sent out a public relations packet to numerous community, business, furniture, and technical publications. In upcoming years, True Dimensions will advertise in industry specific trade publications which encompass the channels previously discussed. The company will develop creative promotions at national and regional market shows and consumer electronics trade shows as a means to prompt trial of the Flogiston™ Chair. True Dimensions is seeking additional public relations opportunities for the Flogiston™ Chair such as placement in modern museums of art, design competitions, and miscellaneous appearances. For example, the chair was showcased on *The New Price Is Right* television game show in December, 1994.

6.4 Pricing Strategy

Upholstered furniture customers can be divided into three separate segments:

Unique Piece Purchaser: Affluent consumers interested in acquiring leading edge designs of premium quality, relatively price insensitive.

Value Purchaser: Motivated to strike a balance between quality, price, and design.

Discount Purchaser: Price is the primary concern in making a purchasing decision.

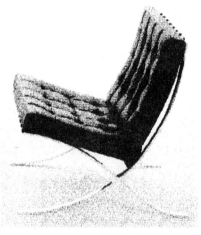

KNOLL STUDIOS, INC.
Barcelona Chair

Designer: Mies van der Rohe

Frame: 1" bar stock steel.
Finish: Polished nickel over copper.
Cushion: 8 way hand tied springs.
Upholstery: Premium top grain leather.

Suggested Retail: $6500

True Dimensions will target the unique piece purchaser segment in selling the Flogiston™ Chair. The Flogiston™ Chair must be competitively priced in this price segment. True Dimensions will employ a manufacturer's suggested list price of $2,800 to minimize any suggestion of conflict between channels. Normally, furniture retails at or just below manufacturers list price. Sale prices are often 75% of list price.

The Upholstered Furniture Customer

Retail Prices

$8,000

Unique Piece Purchaser
- Price insensitive
- Quality is top priority
- Ultra-contemporary tastes

← **$2,800 Flogiston Price**

$2,000

Value Purchaser

$750

Discount Purchaser

1) The target consumer has relatively low price sensitivity as he or she is shopping for differentiable quality and uniqueness of product.

2) The company has established a patented posture, a unique chair design, past sales, and current orders.

3) $2800 retail price has been affirmed by representatives from the reseller trades as an appropriate price given the Flogiston™ Chair's features.

4) The company has yet to establish brand equity or designer reputation in various resellers' industries.

True Dimensions is evaluating alternate materials and construction techniques which would allow the company to offer a lower priced Flogiston™ Chair to the value purchaser customer segment. In addition, the company is considering the option of selling a higher-end, higher priced version of the Flogiston™ Chair with the strategy of offering a full-line of chair options for the consumer, which historically increases the sales of the standard version.

True Dimensions is also researching potential competitors to determine annual volume and profitability. The company will use this information to further evaluate its price positioning relative to competition. Price ranges for specific chairs are illustrated on the next page.

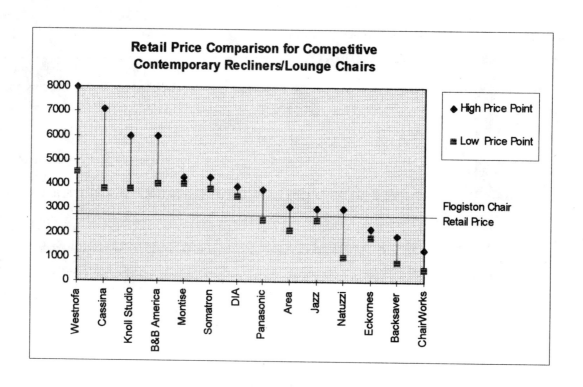

Retail Price Comparison for Competitive Contemporary Recliners/Lounge Chairs

7. ORGANIZATIONAL STRUCTURE

7.1 Relationship with Flogiston Corporation

On January 6, 1995, True Dimensions entered into a licensing agreement with Flogiston Corporation for exclusive worldwide rights to the Flogiston™ Chair. Flogiston Corporation's principal, Brian Park, is also the designer of the chair. True Dimensions will continue to develop new products with Flogiston Corporation through sponsored research agreements. Park's current projects include work as a general contractor for NASA in the development of motion based platforms used for extra-vehicular activity (EVA) training. Park is also working on various experiential virtual reality theme park projects that integrate light, sound, motion, and infrasound, with the Flogiston™ Chair. Brian Park is a 5% stakeholder of True Dimensions and holds a seat on the Board of Directors.

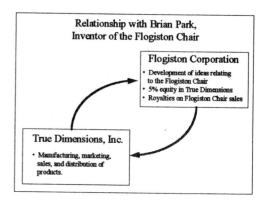

True Dimensions

Page 18

7.2 Patents, Licenses, and Royalty Agreements

Flogiston Corporation will receive a 5% royalty on net sales for 2 years, a 4% royalty charge for 2 years, a 3% royalty for 11 years, and a 1.5% royalty thereafter. Other furniture designers will be hired to develop future products. They will earn either a flat fee or a similar 3% to 5% of sales.

7.3 Company Management

On January 6, 1995, the management team launched True Dimensions, Inc. as a manufacturing and marketing entity featuring the Flogiston™ Chair as its initial offering. The team possesses relevant work experience in finance, manufacturing, and marketing. One member of the team has twelve years of experience in the furniture industry. Another member has eight years of industrial marketing and sales experience. Beyond June, 1995, two team members will remain full-time with True Dimensions and the remaining three will perform consulting and sales services on a part-time basis.

- **Michael Hanratty, President**
  Mike has a mechanical engineering degree and eight years of prior managerial experience that includes commercializing NASA technology, manufacturing quality assurance, and industrial product marketing and sales. Mike directs the company's overall business strategy and is responsible for True Dimensions's production, logistics, product design, and quality specification standards. (See Appendix C, pages 26-27).

- **Irene Bond, Director of Marketing**
  Irene has twelve years experience in the furniture industry including sales of multiple furniture lines and management of three furniture start-up companies. She has ten years experience managing a direct sales force. She currently works for the Austin Technology Incubator on NASA technology commercialization. Irene is the company's contemporary furnishings industry specialist maintaining important industry contacts.

Company Consultants

- **Jeff Hoogendam, Financial Consultant**
  Jeff has three years of prior business consulting experience in the following areas: new venture development, information systems integration, and strategic marketing. Jeff oversees financial planning and legal concerns.

- **Wes Boyd, Marketing/Sales Consultant**
  As a former high school teacher and coach, Wes created and directed a successful start-up outdoor adventure and sports camp. He has experience in launching new consumer packaged products for Procter & Gamble. Wes manages True Dimensions's channel development, promotion strategy, and direct sales efforts.

- **Leslie Frank, External Relations Consultant**
  Leslie has two years of consulting experience with a big six accounting and management consulting firm. Her focus is on the corporate image and external relations development of True Dimensions.

True Dimensions   ***Page** 19*

245

7.4 Board of Advisors

The following Board of Advisors has assisted the company in its formation and are committed to continued involvement in True Dimensions' success.

Jim Wallace: IBD, Bommarito Group
-Architecture and design firm

Bowen Loftin: NASA, University of Houston
-Director of virtual reality training

E. Lee Walker: Community Investment Corporation
-Entrepreneur, Professor of Management at the University of Texas Graduate School of Business

Francine Fox: Stress Management Group
-Owner and President, has successfully marketed her products through Sharper Image

Mary Anne Sikes: ASID, IFDA
-Interior designer

Rebecca Stinson: JG Systems
-Furniture manufacturer's representative and former retailer

James Cole: formerly with ARTEDI (ultra-contemporary furniture manufacturer)
-Independent sales representative, former product manager

7.5 Company Structure and Ownership

True Dimensions is registered in the State of Texas as a Subchapter S Corporation with 1,000,000 shares authorized. Ownership before any offering is as follows: Brian Park- 5000 shares, Jeff Hoogendam- 40,000 shares, Michael Hanratty- 40,000 shares, and 15,000 are held over in treasury stock for future employee stock incentives.

8. RISK ANALYSIS AND RESPONSE

8.1 Patent and Trademark Infringement

True Dimensions has exclusive rights to US Patent #5,141,285, a utility patent with claims on the "modified neutral body posture" that the Flogiston™ Chair adopts. The company will register for international trademarks for the company name and the name of the chair in 1995. The trademark will be True Dimensions's primary source of protection against infringement. True Dimensions will build brand equity in the company name and its products using marketing programs aimed at communicating the chair's unique history and association with NASA, the patented Flogiston™ posture, and differentiable features. Internationally, the company will rely exclusively on the trademark, as the patent provides limited overseas protection.

8.2 Price Competition

Product differentiation through innovative unique designs allow manufacturers in the ultra-contemporary market to maintain high margins. True Dimensions will continue to develop new products and reduce prices as each product matures.

8.3 Cost/Quality Tradeoff

True Dimensions has selected its current vendors based on their reputation for quality work and the recommendation of industry advisors. The company is establishing required quality specifications for its outsourcing suppliers and will monitor their output.

The current production cost has created a need for True Dimensions to evaluate production and design alternatives. Any future material changes will take into consideration the value of aluminum's inherent responsiveness and uniqueness in design. As demand increases, other significant cost reductions will be realized through volume discounts on leather upholstery, and production insourcing.

8.4 Production Scheduling

To hedge against potential supplier problems in meeting demand lead times, the company has evaluated and chosen competent manufacturing partners which are in position to meet the company's growth needs. True Dimensions recognizes that conditions may change requiring the company to take a more self reliant approach. True Dimensions currently owns all tooling held by contracted vendors specifically used for the production of the company's products, and is prepared to shift from one vendor to another should it become necessary.

9. FINANCIAL INFORMATION

9.1 Initial Capitalization

True Dimensions is currently funded with $30,000 invested by its principals. This funding will support initial direct sales. In August, 1995, True Dimensions will seek $200,000 in exchange for 35% of the common stock and a pro-rata seat on the Board of Directors. We desire an equity infusion in order to permit accelerated growth. The funds are required primarily for working capital needs during the national sales rollout. An investor can expect a 31% five year compounded annual return on their 35% equity stake.

9.2 Financial Projections

Financial projections are detailed in Appendix D. The following chart shows the net income and sales for True Dimensions over the next 5 years.

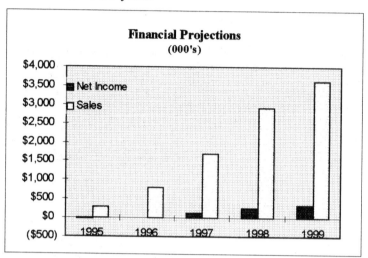

9.3 Harvest Strategy and Valuation

At the end of year 5, True Dimensions expects sales at roughly $3.6 million, and net income at $358,000. Using the discounted cash flow model shown in Appendix D (page 38), True Dimensions' terminal value in year 5 is expected to be $2.1 million. This assumes a conservative 2% growth rate after we have established national distribution in year 5. Should the inventor or management wish to sell their equity, or should it become necessary to raise capital for in-house manufacturing, the company will evaluate a range of exit scenarios.

- Sale to industry - This would include the sale of True Dimensions to another furniture manufacturer interested in product line diversification.

- Management buyout - This option would allow management to choose successors of the company and reduce their holdings in the company over time.

- Dividend payout - Return capital to investors through a series of dividend payments.

STYLE

FROM OUTER SPACE TO YOU:
Turning NASA research into a comfy chair

By Nina L. Diamond

It may look strange, but Brian Park's Flogiston Chair promises unparalleled comfort for reading, meditation, or just sitting around—plus, it's got NASA's seal of approval.

When Brian V. Park set out to build himself a reclining chair so he could meditate in comfort, he had no idea it might end up being used by astronauts to simulate microgravity. But it's actually rather fitting that Park's sleek "Flogiston Chair" should find its way to NASA, because it was NASA research that inspired him in the first place.

The first chair to duplicate the neutral body posture, the natural position a body assumes in weightless space, Park's chair minimizes internal and external physical stress so that "all the muscular forces are in balance; the body is in biomechanical equilibrium," he says. Back in 1980, Park, then an oil-industry design engineer, just wanted to achieve nirvana without getting wet. "I thought that sitting stiffly in the lotus position wasn't exactly optimum," he laughs. "You end up focusing on the pain in your legs instead of meditating." Floating in water—used by NASA for microgravity training—seemed the only way at the time to keep the body stress free.

Then, flipping through an issue of *NASA Tech Briefs*, he noticed drawings of the neutral body posture. That was the "Aha!" he'd been looking for. While designing his chair, Park took advantage of the voluminous NASA research available to the public, reviewing Skylab studies on body posture, consulting with engineers at the Johnson Space Center, and incorporating ideas from NASA's *Anthropomorphic Source Book*, an exhaustive three-volume study of the human body's size, shape, and motion characteristics used by the designers of the astronauts' workstations.

In 1981, Park built his prototype chair with a plywood frame "and sat in it for eight years won-

dering what it was for." His original design evolved into a final state that includes long-memory foam, similar to the foam used in the space shuttle's seats, covered by fabric or leather. The chair can be in a fixed position, rockable, or suspended from the ceiling; comes in two standard sizes; and can also be custom fit. It's tapered, wider at the feet than the head, and "makes you perpendicular to gravity," he explains. "Your behind and your back are at 30 degrees up, your shoulders are at normal rest, your elbows are bent, and your knees are level with your chest."

Sounds odd, but Park reminds us that "when you lie in this chair, you're in a posture the body loves to be in. Everyone has a neutral posture, but we can only experience it floating in water and partially when we're on our side in a semifetal position. After a few minutes in a completely neutral posture, you lose awareness of the body because it's in balance. The pressure is evenly distributed and there are no hard contact points."

Park received a utility patent on the Flogiston Chair in late 1992 and formed his Austin, Texas-based Flogiston Corporation

to market it for office and home. Every *body* at a desk or computer can benefit, he says, because the chair counteracts physical and mental stress and helps to increase concentration. He also sees it as a comfy place to read, watch TV, and, of course, meditate; in the not-so-distant future, it will form the perfect base for virtual-reality adventures. The chair will be on the market shortly—prices will start at just under $1,000 for the standard model.

Once Park finished his design, NASA began to look at the chair not only as a nifty spinoff of their research, but as a piece of comfy hardware that could come full circle. Mounted on the astronauts' training platform, it could provide the ideal recliner for simulations. Wearing goggles, the astronauts "will use virtual reality and feel like they're in microgravity in a miniature flight chamber," says Park. That's a major improvement, because "up until now, the only way to simulate that was to float in water tanks."

NASA hopes to begin using the Flogiston Chair in astronaut training in late summer 1994—Park is busy modifying it for them, adding a special base so it can move around. R. Bowen Loftin, principal investigator for Advanced Training Technologies at Johnson Space Center, says the chair "has the potential to add a large dimension of *reality* to the virtual-reality experience," adding that, with the new base, "we can simulate the behavior of the body in motion in space."

Park's space-age designs have led him out of oil and into an entirely new career. Working with Oceaneering Space Systems, a NASA subcontractor, Park is also designing the space station refrigerator and galley.

We just hope he still has time to meditate ∞

U N I V E R S I T Y *of* H O U S T O N

Department of Computer Science   Houston, TX 77204-3475   713/743-3350

November 22, 1994

Ms. Irene Bond
True Dimensions, Inc.
8920 Business Park Drive
Austin, TX 78759

Dear Ms. Bond:

I understand that your company is considering licensing the rights to market the Flogiston Chair, conceived and developed by Mr. Brian Park. I am familiar with the chair and excited about its potential applications; thus, I am pleased to write in support of your company's plans to market this unique product.

For almost ten years I have served as the NASA/Johnson Space Center Principal Investigator for Advanced Training Technologies. In this capacity I have explored, developed, and delivered a number of advanced training systems to NASA, other government agencies and the private sector. During the past four years much of my attention has been directed at the use of virtual environment technology (also known as "virtual reality" technology) in support of NASA's training requirements. I became aware of the Flogiston Chair at the beginning of this phase of my work and have both encouraged Mr. Park and NASA's interest in the chair.

The Flogiston Chair was conceived by Mr. Park when he encountered reports of data on human posture in space, acquired during the SkyLab missions of the 1970's. In particular, Mr. Park was interested in the true "equilibrium" posture of the human body—the posture naturally assumed by the body while sleeping in microgravity. It occurred to Mr. Park that this posture represented an ideal one for enabling states of tranquillity, that is, states in which the mind could "forget" its attachment to the body. He proceeded to construct a chair that conformed to a modified "neutral buoyancy" posture and patented his invention. He has been marketing the chair, on his own, as a means of achieving deep relaxation and supporting rest and meditation. Having spent time in a number of Flogiston Chairs, I can personally attest to their efficacy in aiding relaxation.

My professional interest in the chair focuses on its potential for aiding astronauts in training for intra- and extravehicular activities. I have hypothesized that the Flogiston

Chair, coupled with an appropriate motion base and visual environment, can be effective in enabling astronauts to experience some of the physical (objective) and subjective sensations of microgravity and, in particular, interaction with objects (bulkheads, payloads, and other astronauts) in space. To this end, NASA has awarded Mr. Park a Phase I Small Business Innovative Research contract and is seriously considering a Phase II award at this time. At the conclusion of Phase I, my laboratory received delivery of the first Personal Motion Platform—a marriage of the Flogiston Chair and a high-performance, three-degree-of-freedom motion base. We have already begun to integrate this device into virtual environments that support the replication of typical space operations and will soon begin formal experiments to determine the Personal Motion Platform's "value added" in astronaut training.

I am convinced that the Flogiston Chair is a unique and remarkable device, one that has great potential in the nation's space program and in the lives of individuals in the private sector. I look forward to your company's aggressively marketing the chair and bringing Mr. Park the recognition and success that his creativity deserves.

Please call upon me if I can provide additional information about our use of the Flogiston Chair.

Sincerely yours,

R. Bowen Loftin, Ph.D.
Professor of Computer Science and Director,
Virtual Environment Technology Laboratory
University of Houston

Professor of Physics
University of Houston-Downtown

Appendix C
Management Resumes

Michael Hanratty, President

Education
MBA, Operations and Entrepreneurship, University of Texas at Austin, 1995
BS, Mechanical Engineering, Marquette University, 1985
Experience
9/93 -- 9/94   *Project Coordinator, NASA Technology Commercialization Center*
   Managed commercialization of NASA technology.
11/89 -- 8/93   *Technical Services Manager, Briggs & Stratton Corporation*
   Coordinated quality assurance and technical support for division with $200 million in sales. Restructured pricing
   plan to improve profitability of after-market sales.
Activities & Awards
UT Associate Dean's Policy Advisory Council
UT Entrepreneur Society, Special Projects

Irene Bond, Director of Marketing

Education
MSLIS, Competitive Intelligence, University of Texas at Austin, 1995
BS, Elementary and Special Education, New Mexico State University, 1977
Experience
9/93 --   *Project Coordinator, Austin Technology Incubator*
   Managed commercialization of NASA technology.
1/92 -- 7/92   *Account Executive, NASA Business Interiors*
   Senior sales representative for contract interiors firm under new ownership. Instructed staff in conceptual sales
   techniques, specifications and space planning of systems furniture.
12/84 -- 12/90   *Vice President, Veristar Incorporated*
   Work entailed specifying systems furniture configurations and purchases, tracking work and purchase orders,
   furniture installation and reconfiguration planning, inventory control, refurbishing, and management of crew.
Activities & Awards
Special Libraries Association
Phi Kappa Phi

Jeff Hoogendam, Financial Consultant

Education
MBA, Finance and Entrepreneurship, University of Texas at Austin, 1995
BS, Mechanical Engineering, Texas A&M University, 1990
Experience
1/94 -- 8/94   *Business Associate, Excel Business Incubator*
   Created a successful nationwide distribution system for a local manufacturing company in three months. Evaluated
   and screened new business opportunities for entrance into the incubator.
9/90 -- 6/93   *Senior Business Systems Consultant, Andersen Consulting*
   Streamlined information systems for two major companies in the energy industry. Each client's savings exceeded
   $350,000 per year. Managed over 40 firm and client personnel.
Activities & Awards
Kauffman Fellows Award
UT Entrepreneur Society, Vice-President
Texas Business Hall of Fame Nominee, 1994

True Dimensions   *Page* 26

Appendix C
Management Resumes

Wes Boyd, Marketing/Sales Consultant

Education
MBA, Marketing, University of Texas at Austin, 1995
BA, Economics, Washington and Lee University, 1990

Experience
6/94 -- 8/94   *Assistant Brand Manager, Procter & Gamble*
 Led multi-functional team in the national launch of a new product.
8/90 -- 7/93   *Founder and Director of "Beyond Darlington," The Darlington School*
 Created and implemented programs and marketing plan for a sports and outdoor adventure camp for teenagers.

Activities & Awards
Marketing Network Job Shops, Director
UT Sports Marketing MBA Task Force, Chairman
Senior Gift Campaign, Director
UT Associate Dean's Policy Advisory Council

Leslie Frank, External Relations Consultant

Education
MBA, Marketing and Management, University of Texas at Austin, 1995
BS, Marketing, Louisiana State University, 1991

Experience
6/94 -- 8/94   *Health Care Consultant, Arthur Andersen & Co.*
 Conducted a comprehensive market analysis and organizational change assessment for physician and community hospital integration.
7/91 -- 8/93   *Staff Analyst, Deloitte & Touche*
 Reduced inpatient Medicaid billing workable inventory 73% in six months. Supervised a hospital billing team consisting of five members and was responsible for staff productivity.

Activities & Awards
UT Graduate Business Council, President
Texas Ambassador
Eyes on Texas, Corporate Relations Committee, Co-Chair
Deloitte & Touche Consulting Challenge, Champion
Marketing Challenge, Finalist

Appendix D
Proforma Financial Statements

Appendix D
Financial Assumptions

- **Revenue and Sales Rationale**

  Utilizing press releases, product reviews and Park's 1100+ database of interested customers, True Dimensions will pursue direct sales primarily during the first six months of 1995 (5% conversion rate assumed). As direct sales diminish, True Dimensions will begin the national rollout. Each product placed in a retail customer's showroom will turn an estimated 5 times per year.

- **Sales & Marketing Expenses**

  True Dimensions plans to attend the following 3 trade shows in 1995: NEOCON in Chicago, Illinois, Dallas Home Furnishings Show in Dallas, Texas, and the International Home Furnishings Association Market in High Point, North Carolina. Total travel and trade show expenses for 1995 are $25,075, of which $7,575 is for the trade shows. The remaining balance will be used for salespeople and travel for the California rollout. Advertising expenses are expected to increase the month prior to and the month of each trade show. The total for advertising is expected to be $3,750.

- **Working Capital**

  Several assumptions are used to determine working capital levels: A/R turnover, inventory turnover, and next months' cost of goods sold. Compared to industry averages, accounts payable is low in the early years due to the assumption that supplier terms will not be readily available and purchases will largely be prepaid. Similarly, inventory is higher than industry averages as the unique manufacturing techniques required to produce the chair will result in a longer learning curve for suppliers. Attractive A/R terms from the direct channels (50% down payment) will likely be offset by credit terms extended to the retail channels.

- **Cost of Goods Sold**

  Costs for Flogiston™ Chair manufacturing were initially high ($750 per chair) due to the inefficiencies in the original process. True Dimensions expects to reduce costs to $675 per chair by 1996 by consolidation of operations and redesigning the product for production in quantities. Manufacturing costs are expected to decline as product refinements are incorporated and suppliers gain expertise.

- **Royalties**

  True Dimensions will pay a 5% royalty to Flogiston Corporation for the exclusive license for 2 years. The royalty rate decreases to 4% for 2 years, then to 3% for 11 years, and 1.5% thereafter. The company will establish similar royalty payment programs with new designers to develop other new complementary products. As the company matures, design costs on new product development will shift from variable to fixed costs in order to decrease long term total design expenses.

- **Salaries, Payroll Taxes, and Benefits**

  No salaries will be taken by *management* until June, 1995. One salesperson will be hired in each new sales region in conjunction with the scheduled retail rollout. Office staff will be hired for order entry and processing.

True Dimensions   *Page* 28

- **Fixed Assets**

  Fixed assets represent production tooling, molds, jigs, and fixtures required. Although this production tooling is used by our suppliers, it will be the property of True Dimensions. The company is investing in flexible tooling that could be easily transferred to True Dimensions's facilities in the event that insourcing becomes viable at a later date. These assets are depreciated over 5 years.

- **Research & Development**

  True Dimensions's development efforts will be focused on producing prototypes and refining the designs of new product introductions. Although the company will still license designs paying royalties, additional expenses will be incurred.

- **Miscellaneous Expenses**

  Product liability insurance is required for ultra-contemporary, home audio/theatre, and novelty/specialty channels. Legal fees in January, 1995, were required for completing the licensing agreement. Thereafter, legal fees are required for new product license agreements, supplier contracts etc. Federal income tax expenses are estimated at 36%.

Appendix D

True Dimensions
Financial Statement Assumptions

Assumptions	1995	1996	1997	1998	1999	Notes
A R Turnover Ratio	8	9	11	12	12	
A R Turnover Days	46	41	33	30	30	
Next Months COGS %	95%	80%	80%	80%	80%	Percentage paid up front to vendors.
A/P Turnover Ratio	1.2	1.2	1.1	1.0	1.0	Calculated based on Next Months COGS %.
Inventory Turnover Ratio	8	8	10	11	12	Average inventory of 45 days in year 1.
Inventory Turnover Days	46	46	37	33	30	
Royalty (% of sales)	5%	5%	4%	4%	3%	Based on license agreement with inventor.
Salary, Payroll Taxes, & Benefits	$163,750	$327,500	$611,250	$991,250	$1,138,750	See Personnel Requirement Assumptions.
Office Expense	2,000	15,000	17,000	20,000	22,000	Technology Incubator office in year 1.
Sales Growth	n/a	200%	131%	80%	33%	Calculated based on Unit Sales Projections
Cash Balance as % of Sales	3%	3%	2%	1.5%	1.5%	Robert Morris & Associates.

Inventory Turnover = COGS/Average Inventory
A R Turnover = Gross Sales/Average accounts receivable
A/P Turnover = Purchases / Average accounts payable

True Dimensions
Pricing Assumptions
(Unit pricing based upon average of entire product line.)

	1995	1996	1997	1998	1999	Notes
Suggested Retail Price	$2,800	$2,650	$2,500	$2,450	$2,350	
Direct						
Selling Price	$1,680	$2,200	$2,500	$2,450	$2,350	Discount price in years 1and 2, therafter charge
Customer Margin	n/a	n/a	n/a	n/a	n/a	suggested retail prices to direct customers.
Gross Margin	61%	70%	74%	73%	72%	
Home Audio/Theatre						
Selling Price	$1,680	$1,590	$1,500	$1,470	$1,410	
Customer Margin	40%	40%	40%	40%	40%	Margins based on home audio/entertainment industry
Gross Margin	61%	59%	57%	56%	54%	research.
Ultra-Contemporary Retail						
Selling Price	$1,288	$1,219	$1,150	$1,127	$1,081	
Customer Margin	54%	54%	54%	54%	54%	Margins based on ultra-contemporary industry data.
Gross Margin	50%	47%	43%	42%	40%	
Novelty/Specialty						
Selling Price	$1,876	$1,776	$1,675	$1,642	$1,575	
Customer Margin	33%	33%	33%	33%	33%	Estimated margins based on financial statements
Gross Margin	65%	63%	61%	60%	59%	and other related information. Products sold to
Interior Designers/Architects						this market will be technologically advanced versions.
Selling Price	$1,680	$1,590	$1,500	$1,470	$1,410	
Customer Margin	40%	40%	40%	40%	40%	Margins based on designer industry research.
Gross Margin	61%	59%	57%	56%	54%	
Unit COGS	$650	$650	$600	$600	$550	COGS decrease during years 1 and 2 as production techniques are refined. Costs are then held constant.

True Dimensions
Personnel Requirement Assumptions

	1995*	1996	1997	1998	1999	
Managers	1	2	3	4	4	
Salary per manager	$25,000	$35,000	$50,000	$60,000	$70,000	
Salespersons	2	3	5	7	7	
Compensation per salesperson **	$38,000	$42,000	$48,000	$54,000	$58,000	
Office/clerical	1	2	3	5	6	
Salary per administrator	$30,000	$33,000	$33,000	$35,000	$37,500	
Total Payroll	$131,000	$262,000	$489,000	$793,000	$911,000	
With payroll taxes and benefits	$163,750	$327,500	$611,250	$991,250	$1,138,750	Payroll taxes and insurance estimated at 25% of payroll.

* Note: 1995 salaries are annual rates, but are paid for only 7 months. Actual expense for this period is $54,687.

Appendix D

True Dimensions
Annual Unit Sales Projections

	1995	1996	1997	1998	1999
Direct Sales					
Units	81	0	0	0	0
Direct Sales	$136,080	$0	$0	$0	$0
Home Audio/Theatre Sales					
Units	48	201	364	521	471
Home Audio/Theatre Sales	$80,640	$336,840	$611,520	$875,280	$790,978
Ultra-Contemporary Retail Sales					
Year End Retail Outlets	21	44	79	116	155
Distinct Product Models	1	2	4	6	7
Units sold	38	238	707	1,416	2,201
Ultra-Comtemporary Retail Sales	$48,944	$290,366	$812,544	$1,595,325	$2,378,838
Interior Designers/Architects					
Units	13	101	176	310	324
Interior Designers/Architects	$21,840	$160,654	$264,000	$455,700	$456,840
Novelty/Specialty					
Units	0	0	0	0	0
Novelty/Specialty Sales	$0	$0	$0	$0	$0
Total Unit Sales	180	540	1,247	2,247	2,995
Total Sales $	$287,504	$787,859	$1,688,064	$2,926,305	$3,626,655

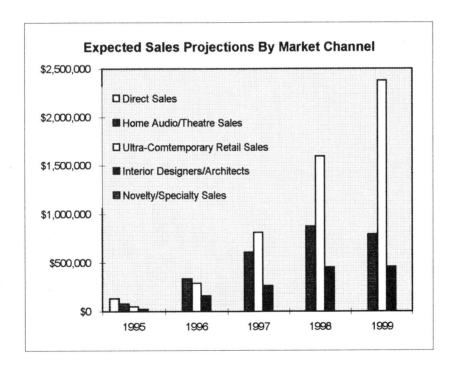

Appendix D

True Dimensions
Annual Income Statements

	1995	1996	1997	1998	1999
Revenue					
Sales	287,504	787,859	1,709,064	2,926,305	3,626,655
Less Royalty	14,375	39,393	68,363	117,052	108,800
Cost of Goods Sold	117,000	350,831	819,364	1,460,258	1,947,017
Gross Profit	156,129	397,635	821,337	1,348,995	1,570,839
Operating Expenses					
Sales & Marketing					
Advertising	4,850	7,000	13,000	16,000	20,500
Travel and Trade Shows	25,075	75,500	125,000	175,000	176,000
Trade Shows	7,500	14,000	16,000	16,000	16,000
Sales Materials	2,600	5,500	9,920	14,400	19,200
Direct Mail	5,000	0	0	0	0
General & Administrative					
Salary, Taxes, & Benefits	95,521	262,000	489,000	793,000	911,000
Office Expense	2,000	15,000	17,000	20,000	22,000
Product Liability Insurance	6,000	6,000	8,000	12,000	16,000
Legal Fees	9,000	7,000	10,000	12,000	15,000
Product Development					
R&D	21,000	50,000	100,000	100,000	100,000
Independent Testing	3,000	5,000	5,000	7,000	10,000
Depreciation	1,417	667	6,667	9,333	10,000
Total Operating Expenses	182,963	447,667	799,587	1,174,733	1,315,700
Operating Income	(26,834)	5,635	133,417	290,595	375,139
Interest Expense	0	0	0	0	0
Income before Taxes	(26,834)	5,635	133,417	290,595	375,139
State Franchise Tax (4.5%)	0	2,053	6,533	13,077	16,881
Net Income	(26,834)	3,582	126,885	277,518	358,258

True Dimensions
Annual Balance Sheet

	1995	1996	1997	1998	1999
Assets					
Current Assets					
Cash	14,177	89,994	141,075	145,327	177,120
Marketable Securities	112,942	106,918	54,828	379,021	622,895
Accounts Receivable	59,069	111,104	213,751	269,124	328,000
Inventory	26,300	55,744	142,662	213,252	268,531
Total Current Assets	212,488	363,760	552,316	1,006,725	1,396,546
Fixed Assets	10,000	10,000	100,000	150,000	150,000
Accumulated Depreciation	(1,417)	(2,083)	(8,750)	(20,583)	(28,083)
Total Assets	221,071	371,677	643,566	1,136,142	1,518,463
Liabilities					
Current Liabilities					
Accounts Payable	15,936	151,288	281,673	451,670	561,230
Royalties Payable	1,969	12,499	23,513	24,221	29,520
Taxes Payable	0	1,142	4,747	2,209	5,192
Notes Payable	0	0	0	0	0
Total Current Liabilities	17,905	164,928	309,933	478,101	595,942
Long Term Debt	0	0	0	0	0
Total Liabilities	17,905	164,928	309,933	478,101	595,942
Owners Equity					
Common Stock	230,000	230,000	230,000	230,000	230,000
Retained Earnings	(26,834)	(23,251)	103,634	428,041	692,521
Total Net Worth	203,166	206,749	333,634	658,041	922,521
Liabilities and Shareholder's Equity	221,071	371,677	643,566	1,136,142	1,518,463

Appendix D

True Dimensions
Quarterly and Annual Income Statements

	1996				1997				1998	1999
	1Q	2Q	3Q	4Q	1Q	2Q	3Q	4Q	Annual	Annual
Revenue										
Revenue	115,221	202,249	220,406	249,984	334,875	372,375	414,000	587,814	2,926,305	3,626,655
Less Royalty	5,761	10,112	11,020	12,499	13,395	14,895	16,560	23,513	117,052	108,800
Cost of Goods Sold	50,323	90,786	98,235	111,488	159,250	177,450	197,340	285,324	1,460,258	1,947,017
Gross Profit	59,137	101,351	111,151	125,997	162,230	180,030	200,100	278,977	1,348,995	1,570,839
Operating Expenses										
Sales & Marketing										
Advertising	1,500	1,500	2,000	2,000	3,000	3,000	3,500	3,500	16,000	20,500
Travel and Trade Shows	15,000	17,500	20,000	23,000	26,000	30,000	34,000	35,000	175,000	176,000
Trade Shows	3,500	3,500	3,500	3,500	4,000	4,000	4,000	4,000	16,000	16,000
Sales Materials	1,375	1,375	1,375	1,375	2,480	2,480	2,480	2,480	14,400	19,200
Direct Mail	0	0	0	0	0	0	0	0	0	0
General & Administrative										
Salary, Taxes, & Bennefits	65,500	65,500	65,500	65,500	122,250	122,250	122,250	122,250	793,000	911,000
Office Expense	3,750	3,750	3,750	3,750	4,250	4,250	4,250	4,250	20,000	22,000
Product Liability Insurance	1,500	1,500	1,500	1,500	2,000	2,000	2,000	2,000	12,000	16,000
Legal Fees	7,000	0	0	0	10,000	0	0	0	12,000	15,000
Product Development										
R&D	50,000	0	0	0	100,000	0	0	0	100,000	100,000
Independent Testing	5,000	0	0	0	5,000	0	0	0	7,000	10,000
Depreciation	167	167	167	167	1,667	1,667	1,667	1,667	9,333	10,000
Total Operating Expenses	154,292	94,792	97,792	100,792	280,647	169,647	174,147	175,147	1,174,733	1,315,700
Operating Income	(39,988)	6,726	13,526	25,372	(11,750)	12,050	27,620	105,497	290,595	375,139
Interest Expense	0	0	0	0	0	0	0	0	0	0
Income before Taxes	(39,988)	6,726	13,526	25,372	(11,750)	12,050	27,620	105,497	290,595	375,139
State Franchise Tax (4.5%)	0	303	609	1,142	0	542	1,243	4,747	13,077	16,881
Period Net Income	(39,988)	6,423	12,917	24,230	(11,750)	11,508	26,377	100,750	277,518	358,258

Appendix D

True Dimensions
Quarterly and Annual Statements of Cash Flows

	1996				1997				1998	1999
	1Q	2Q	3Q	4Q	1Q	2Q	3Q	4Q	Annual	Annual
Cash Flow from Operations										
Net Income	(39,988)	6,423	12,917	24,230	(11,750)	11,508	26,377	100,750	277,518	358,258
Provision for deferred taxes	0	0	0	0	0	0	0	0	0	0
Additions:										
Depreciation	167	167	167	167	1,667	1,667	1,667	1,667	9,333	10,000
Increase in accts payable	86,246	7,077	12,591	45,374	17,290	18,896	83,585	10,615	123,506	156,052
Increase in Royalties Payable	5,761	4,351	908	1,479	896	1,500	3,165	8,618	15,312	(253)
Increase in taxes payable	0	303	306	533	(1,142)	542	701	3,504	867	(422)
Increase in notes payable	0	0	0	0	0	0	0	0	0	0
Subtractions:										
Increase in accts receivable	51,209	38,679	8,070	13,146	10,669	13,636	15,136	63,205	70,372	43,877
Increase in inventory	25,162	20,231	3,724	6,627	23,881	9,100	9,945	43,992	72,423	53,446
Net Cash from (used by) Operations	(24,185)	(40,590)	15,094	52,010	(27,589)	11,376	90,413	17,957	283,741	426,311
Cash Flow from Investing Activities:										
Start-up Costs	0	0	0	0	0	0	0	0	0	0
Capital expenditures	0	0	0	0	(90,000)	0	0	0	(40,000)	(10,000)
Net Cash from (used by) Investing	0	0	0	0	(90,000)	0	0	0	(40,000)	(10,000)
Cash Flow from Financing Activities:										
Long Term Debt	0	0	0	0	8,547	9,504	0	0	0	0
Distributions to Investor	0	0	0	0	0	0	0	0	0	0
Common stock sold	0	0	0	0	0	0	0	0	0	0
Net Cash from (used by) Financing	0	0	0	0	0	0	0	0	0	0
Net Increase (decrease) in Cash	(24,185)	(40,590)	15,094	52,010	(117,589)	11,376	90,413	17,957	243,741	416,311
Beginning Cash Balance	130,515	106,330	65,741	80,835	132,845	15,256	26,631	117,044	827,052	2,041,511
Ending Cash Balance:	106,330	65,741	80,835	132,845	15,256	26,631	117,044	135,001	1,070,793	2,457,822

Appendix D

True Dimensions
Monthly Income Statement

1995	Jan	Feb	Mar	Apr	May	Jun	Jul	Aug	Sep	Oct	Nov	Dec	Fiscal Year 1995
Revenue													
Revenue	0	0	0	25,200	24,875	25,906	28,291	33,062	35,773	37,834	37,184	39,379	287,504
Less Royalty	0	0	0	1,260	1,244	1,295	1,415	1,653	1,789	1,892	1,859	1,969	14,375
Cost of Goods Sold	0	0	0	9,750	9,685	10,205	11,310	13,520	14,690	15,730	15,600	16,510	117,000
Gross Profit	0	0	0	14,190	13,946	14,405	15,567	17,889	19,294	20,212	19,725	20,900	156,129
Operating Expenses													
Sales & Marketing													
Advertising	300	300	300	300	400	400	250	400	400	400	1,000	400	4,850
Travel	0	0	0	0	4,000	4,475	4,000	4,000	4,000	3,100	1,000	500	25,075
Trade Shows	0	0	0	0	0	2,000	0	0	0	4,000	0	1,500	7,500
Sales Materials	0	0	0	1,000	200	200	200	200	200	200	200	200	2,600
Direct Mail	0	2,000	1,000	300	300	200	200	200	200	200	200	200	5,000
General & Administrative													
Salary, Taxes, & Benefits	0	0	0	0	0	13,646	13,646	13,646	13,646	13,646	13,646	13,646	95,521
Office Expense	167	167	167	167	167	167	167	167	167	167	167	167	2,000
Product Liability Insurance	0	1,500	1,500	0	0	1,500	0	0	1,500	0	0	1,500	6,000
Legal & Accounting Fees	4,000	0	0	2,000	0	2,000	0	0	1,000	0	0	0	9,000
Product Development													
R&D	1,000	1,000	1,000	2,000	2,000	2,000	2,000	2,000	2,000	2,000	2,000	2,000	21,000
Independant Testing	3,000	0	0	0	0	0	0	0	0	0	0	0	3,000
Depreciation	83	83	83	83	83	83	83	167	167	167	167	167	1,417
Total Operating Expenses	8,550	3,550	4,050	5,850	7,150	26,671	20,546	20,779	23,279	23,879	18,379	20,279	182,963
Operating Income	(8,550)	(3,550)	(4,050)	8,340	6,796	(12,266)	(4,979)	(2,890)	(3,985)	(3,667)	1,346	621	(26,834)
Interest Expense	0	0	0	0	0	0	0	0	0	0	0	0	0
Income before Taxes	(8,550)	(3,550)	(4,050)	8,340	6,796	(12,266)	(4,979)	(2,890)	(3,985)	(3,667)	1,346	621	(26,834)
State Franchise Tax (4.5%)	0	0	0	0	0	0	0	0	0	0	0	0	575
Period Net Income	(8,550)	(3,550)	(4,050)	8,340	6,796	(12,266)	(4,979)	(2,890)	(3,985)	(3,667)	1,346	621	(27,409)

Rollout Plan (Sales Assumptions)
Direct Sales
Retail Sales
Design Trade

Direct Sales
Southwest Region - Ultra Contemporary
Design Trade

263

Appendix D

True Dimensions
Monthly Statements of Cash Flows

1995	Jan	Feb	Mar	Apr	May	Jun	Jul	Aug	Sep	Oct	Nov	Dec	Fiscal Year 1995
Cash Flow from Operations													
Net Income	(8,550)	(3,550)	(4,050)	8,340	6,796	(12,266)	(4,979)	(2,890)	(3,985)	(3,667)	1,346	621	(26,834)
Provision for deferred taxes	0	0	0	0	0	0	0	0	0	0	0	0	0
Additions:													
Depreciation	83	83	83	83	83	83	83	167	167	167	167	167	1,417
Increase in accts payable	0	0	9,263	(62)	494	1,050	2,100	1,112	988	(124)	865	251	15,936
Increase in royalties payable	0	0	0	1,260	(16)	52	119	239	136	103	(32)	110	1,969
Increase in taxes payable	0	0	0	0	0	0	0	0	0	0	0	0	0
Increase in notes payable	0	0	0	0	0	0	0	0	0	0	0	0	0
Subtractions:													
Increase in accts receivable	0	0	0	37,800	(487)	1,546	3,578	7,157	4,066	3,091	(974)	3,293	59,069
Increase in inventory	0	4,875	9,718	195	1,073	2,210	2,795	1,690	975	325	1,193	1,252	26,300
Net Cash from (used by) Operations	(8,467)	(8,342)	(4,422)	(28,373)	6,772	(14,837)	(9,050)	(10,220)	(7,735)	(6,937)	2,126	(3,397)	(92,881)
Cash Flow from Investing Activities:													
Start-up Costs	0	0	0	0	0	0	0	0	0	0	0	0	0
Capital expenditures	(5,000)	0	0	0	0	0	0	(5,000)	0	0	0	0	(10,000)
Net Cash from Investing	(5,000)	0	0	0	0	0	0	(5,000)	0	0	0	0	(10,000)
Cash Flow from Financing Activities:													
Long Term Debt	166	167	166	29,770	(1,606)	14,329	10,076	17,271	(70,341)	0	0	0	0
Distributions to Investors	0	0	0	0	0	0	0	0	0	0	0	0	0
Common stock sold	30,000	0	0	0	0	0	0	0	200,000	0	0	0	230,000
Net Cash from (used by) Financing	30,166	167	166	29,770	(1,606)	14,329	10,076	17,271	129,659	0	0	0	230,000
Net Increase (decrease) in Cash	16,700	(8,174)	(4,255)	1,397	5,167	(507)	1,025	2,051	121,924	(6,937)	2,126	(3,397)	127,119
Beginning Cash Balance	0	16,700	8,525	4,270	5,667	10,833	10,326	11,351	13,402	135,326	128,389	130,515	0
Ending Cash Balance:	16,700	8,525	4,270	5,667	10,833	10,326	11,351	13,402	135,326	128,389	130,515	127,119	127,119

Appendix D
Sensitivity Analysis

This sensitivity analysis compares the sales and revenue projections for two different scenarios:

1) Expected Case: No sales into the novelty specialty channel forces us to focus on other channels.

2) Best Case: Acceptance into novelty/specialty market focuses marketing efforts into generating sales at Sharper Image and Brookstone. In this scenario we will utilize the novelty/specialty channel to launch the business while developing other channels for long term growth.

It is clear that the novelty/specialty market represents the best opportunity to launch a small start up company. We will make every effort to gain acceptance in this market. However, we still have a strong contingency plan if sales do not materialize in this market niche.

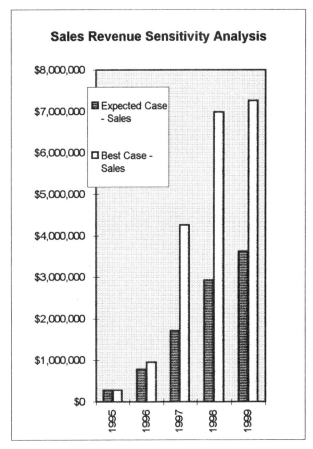

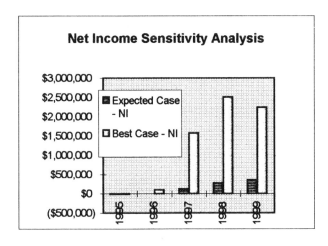

Appendix D

	1995	1996	1997	1998	1999	1993 Industry Data*		
						All Companies	3-5 MM Sales	5-10 MM Sales
	54.3	50.5	48.1	46.1	43.3	24.5	23.4	26.8
	-9.3	0.7	7.8	9.9	10.3	2.9	2.7	5.5
Curr..	11.9	2.2	1.8	2.1	2.3	1.7	1.6	2.4
Quick Ratio	4.1	1.2	1.1	0.9	0.8	0.8	0.6	0.8
Days in Receivables	45.6	40.6	33.2	30.4	30.4	34.0	31.0	31.0
Days in Inventory	45.6	45.6	36.5	33.2	30.4	51.4	48.7	58.9
Net Sales/Working Capital	1.5	4.0	7.1	5.5	4.5	12.1	15.6	7.9
Operating Profit/Net Worth	-0.1	0.0	0.4	0.4	0.4	17.4	25.8	27.1
Operating Profit/Total Assets	-0.1	0.0	0.2	0.3	0.2	6.2	8.0	8.0
Net Sales/Total Assets	1.3	2.1	2.7	2.6	2.4	2.9	3.6	3.0
% Officer Compensation / Sales	0.3	0.3	0.3	0.3	0.3	3.9	n/a	n/a

* Robert Morris and Associates, 1993. Based on SIC code 2512, Upholstered Furniture Manufacturing.

True Dimensions
Valuation

Our valuation will discount the proforma free cash flows at an estimated WACC for the company.

WACC = Ke   Since no long term debt is being issued.

Ke = Rf + b(risk premium) + (Small Company Stock Premium)

Rf = 8.78%	25 Year T Bill rate as of 11/18/94.
BL = .98 and D/E = .1705	SIC 2511-2599, "Valuation & Performance Monitor 9/94"
Small Co. Premium = 4.11%	Calculated from the 1951 to 1993 historic difference in small co.
	and large co. returns as published in Ibbitson Associates' 'SBII 1994 Yearbook'.
Risk Premium= 7.07%	Also calculated based on 1951 to 1993 figures from the 'SBII 1994 Yearbook'.

Now unlevering b = bL / (1 + D/E) = .98 / (1 + .1705) = .8372

B(risk premium) = .8372 * 7.07% = 5.92%. Thus,

Ke = Rf + b(risk premium) + (Small Company Stock Premium)
Ke = 8.78% + 5.92% + 4.11% = 18.81%

Free Cash Flows Estimates

	1995	1996	1997	1998	1999		
EBIT	(26,834)	5,635	133,417	290,595	375,139		
+ Depreciation	1,417	667	6,667	9,333	10,000		
- Capex	(10,000)	0	(90,000)	(40,000)	(10,000)		
- Change in Working Capital	(81,641)	(10,273)	(95,642)	37,953	(28,107)		
Free Cash Flow	(117,058)	(3,971)	(45,557)	297,881	347,033	2,064,441	Gordon Growth Terminal Value
							(Assumes a 2% growth rate)

NPV, When Discouned at	$758,829
Liquidity Discount Factor	0.7
Net Corporate Valuation	$531,180

IRR on $200,000 = 30%

Discussion Questions
for
True Dimensions, Inc.

1. True Dimensions plan to build a business by manufacturing and marketing the Flogiston™ Chair, a product designed from NASA research on astronauts' sleeping patterns in a microgravity environment.

   • What is your assessment of the market opportunity afforded by the Flogiston™ Chair? In other words, how good is the idea?

   • What needs are met by the Flogiston™ Chair?

   • What evidence has the team presented that consumers will pay $2,800 for the Flogiston™ Chair?

   • What does the management team have to do well to build a profitable venture beginning with the Flogiston™ Chair? In other words, what are the critical success factors?

   • What are the major risks?

2. The True Dimensions team is composed of two members who will work full-time launching the venture and three who have accepted jobs with other businesses and will only be available for consultation.

   • Do Mike and Irene have the skills and experience to launch the venture successfully?

   • Are there additional skills which they need to hire prior to launching? If yes, specify the needed skills. If no, explain why not.

   • Evaluate the Board of Advisors. What role could it play for Mike and Irene?

3. The marketing strategy section of the business plans targets four market segments:

   a. Novelty/specialty retailers such as Sharper Image and Brookstone;

   b. Ultra-contemporary furniture retailers;

   c. Interior designers and architects; and

   d. Home audio/theater retailers.

   • What is your assessment of the marketing strategy of targeting these four segments? In which segment do you expect the Flogiston™ Chair to sell the best? What resistance do you expect in each of the segments?

   • Would you target any other segment initially? If yes, identify the segment and explain why.

   • Evaluate True Dimensions' pricing strategy.

4. The management team decided to outsource manufacturing.

   • What are the advantages and disadvantages of outsourcing manufacturing?

   • Do you agree with the planned strategy of bringing manufacturing in-house when sales reach $60,000 per month? Explain.

5. True Dimensions' financial statements and assumptions are presented in Appendix D.

   • $2,150 is the difference between the suggested retailed price of $2,800 and projected costs of $650? Where does this difference appear on the income statement?

- Evaluate True Dimensions' gross profit and gross profit percentage.

- Where do federal income taxes appear in the financial statements?

- What do you conclude from the comparisons with industry data from Robert Morris and Associates?

- Evaluate the team's decision to treat sales to the novelty/specialty market as a "best case" scenario.

6. True Dimensions is seeking $200,000 in exchange for 35% of the common stock.

- What is the implicit valuation of the company? Do you consider this valuation fair?

- Do you think $200,000 will be sufficient to launch the venture? What are the most critical assumptions?

- Could the management team "boot-strap" the launching of True Dimensions? What would be the major risks?

- Evaluate the harvest strategies.

- Would you invest?

MOOT CORP®
Judge's Evaluation

Company: _____   Judge No: _____

I. Written Business Plan (ﾍJ%)

Please evaluate the written <u>business plan</u> on the following aspects:

(Using this rating system: 1 = very poor, 2 = poor, 3 = fair, 4 = adequate, 5 = good, 6 = very good, 7 = excellent)

1. **Executive Summary (5%)**
   (Clear, exciting and effective as a stand-alone
   overview of the plan)   1   2   3   4   5   6   7
   Comments/Questions _____
   _____
   _____

2. **Company Overview (5%)**
   (Business purpose, history, genesis of concept,
   current status, overall strategy and objectives)   1   2   3   4   5   6   7
   Comments/Questions _____
   _____
   _____

3. **Products or Services (10%)**
   (Description, features and benefits, pricing, current
   stage of development, proprietary position)   1   2   3   4   5   6   7
   Comments/Questions _____
   _____
   _____

4. **Market and Marketing Strategy (10%)**
   (Description of market, competitive analysis, needs
   identification, market acceptance, unique
   capabilities, sales/promotion)   1   2   3   4   5   6   7
   Comments/Questions _____
   _____
   _____

5. **Operations (15%)**
   (Plan for production / delivery of product or
   services, product cost, margins, operating
   complexity, resources required)   1   2   3   4   5   6   7
   Comments/Questions _____
   _____
   _____

6. **Management (10%)**
   (Backgrounds of key individuals, ability to execute
   strategy, personnel needs, organizational structure,
   role of any non-student executive, which students
   will execute plan)   1   2   3   4   5   6   7
   Comments/Questions _____
   _____
   _____

In rating each of the above, please consider the following questions:
- Is this area covered in adequate detail?
- Does the plan show a clear understanding of the elements that should be addressed?
- Are the assumptions realistic and reasonable?
- Are the risks identified and the ability to manage those risks conveyed?

Company: _____ Judge No: _____

(Using this rating system: 1 = very poor, 2 = poor, 3 = fair, 4 = adequate, 5 = good, 6 = very good, 7 = excellent)

7. **Summary Financials (10%)**
Presented in summary form and follow U.S. generally accepted accounting principles.
Consistent with plan and effective in capturing financial performance; Quarterly for first two years, Quarterly/annually for years 3-5.

a. Cash Flow Statement	1	2	3	4	5	6	7
b. Income Statement	1	2	3	4	5	6	7
c. Balance Sheet	1	2	3	4	5	6	7
d. Funds Required/Uses	1	2	3	4	5	6	7
e. Assumptions/Trends/Comparatives	1	2	3	4	5	6	7

Comments/Questions _____
_____
_____

8. **Offering (10%)**
(Proposal/terms to investors—indicate how
much you want, the ROI, and the structure
of the deal; possible exit strategies)   1   2   3   4   5   6   7
Comments/Questions _____
_____
_____

9. **Viability (20%)**
(Market opportunity, distinctive competence,
management understanding, investment
potential)   1   2   3   4   5   6   7
Comments/Questions _____
_____
_____

10. **Brevity and Clarity (5%)**
(Is the plan approximately 25 pages with
minimal redundancy)   1   2   3   4   5   6   7
Comments/Questions _____
_____
_____

Additional Comments

MOOT CORP®
Judge's Evaluation

Company: _____ Judge No: _____

II. Presentation (20%)

(Using this rating system: 1 = very poor, 2 = poor, 3 = fair, 4 = adequate, 5 = good, 6 = very good, 7 = excellent)

1. **Formal Presentation (50%)**
   a. Materials presented in clear, logical and/or sequential form.   1   2   3   4   5   6   7
   b. Ability to relate need for the company with meaningful examples, and practical applications.   1   2   3   4   5   6   7
   c. Ability to maintain judges' interest.   1   2   3   4   5   6   7
   d. Quality of Visual Aids.   1   2   3   4   5   6   7

2. **Questions and Answers (50%)**
   a. Ability to understand judges' inquiries.   1   2   3   4   5   6   7
   b. Appropriately respond to judges' inquiries with substantive answers.   1   2   3   4   5   6   7
   c. Use of time allocated (minimal redundancy).   1   2   3   4   5   6   7
   d. Poise and confidence (think effectively on their feet).   1   2   3   4   5   6   7

Strengths of Presentation

Weaknesses of Presentation

MOOT CORP®
Judge's Evaluation

Company: _____ Judge No: _____

III. Viability of Company (40%)

		Definitely No				Definitely Yes	

1. **Market Opportunity (20%)**
   (There is a clear market need presented as well as
   a way to take advantage of that need.)   1 2 3 4 5 6 7

2. **Distinctive Competence (20%)**
   (The company provides something novel/unique/
   special that gives it a competitive advantage in its
   market.)   1 2 3 4 5 6 7

3. **Management Capability (20%)**
   (This team can effectively develop this company
   and handle the risks associated with the venture.)   1 2 3 4 5 6 7

4. **Financial Understanding (20%)**
   (This team has a solid understanding of the financial
   requirements of the business.)   1 2 3 4 5 6 7

5. **Investment Potential (20%)**
   (The business represents a real investment
   opportunity in which you would consider investing.)   1 2 3 4 5 6 7

Company Strengths

Company Weaknesses

Additional Comments

272

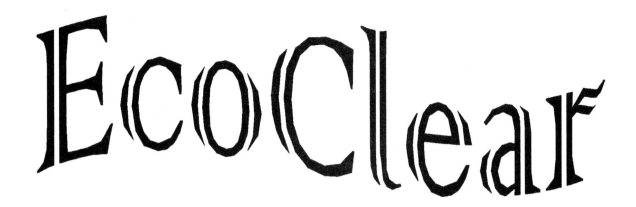

Water Filtration System

Business Plan

Presented by

Andrew Maxwell

Kim Goriss

Prue Kellahan

Representing

BOND UNIVERSITY
Gold Coast, Australia

Unilever

with thanks to our sponsors

QANTAS

Executive Summary

EcoClear Inc. has been established to globalize an innovative self-cleaning water filtration technology, which is applicable to a wide range of markets. Our launch product is a self-cleaning filter for domestic swimming pools. Sales of this product in Australia already exceed 3000 units, ordered by pool builders in the past month. This plan concerns the introduction of that product into the US market and seeks funding for working capital and continued R&D activity.

The strategic competitive advantages of EcoClear Inc. are its performance and cost advantages. The *EcoClear* filter saves substantial maintenance time, water, pool chemicals and electricity, while consistently filtering to a higher level of water clarity. *EcoClear's* simple design, smaller size and low-pressure operation also allows a substantial cost advantage in production. These performance and cost advantages are sustainable in the short to medium term as a result of the web of intellectual property protection built around the technology. The sustainable competitive advantages will be increased over the medium to longer term by reputation building and the fruits of our R&D program.

EcoClear Inc.'s management team of Andrew Maxwell, Kim Goriss and Prue Kellahan represent a strong blend of complementary skills and business experience. In addition to their MBAs, Andrew and Prue have (or soon will have) completed their Masters of Accounting degrees. Prue also has a Bachelor of Laws to her credit, and is presently completing the requirements necessary to be admitted to the Bar. Andrew, the CEO, launched his first business at age 17 and has since started a long list of successful entrepreneurial ventures in Australia and internationally. Kim, the CFO, has substantial start up and corporate business experience internationally. Prue, Legal Liaison, has many years experience within her family business. All three have worked together successfully as a team throughout their MBA program.

Our strategic plan is to seek a license agreement with a major pool filter manufacturer and to achieve penetration of the North American market via that licensee's distribution system. Royalty income from this arrangement will allow EcoClear Inc. to fund ongoing R&D for the diffusion of the technology into other pool markets and other industry applications, e.g. irrigation, aquaculture, brewing and air conditioning. In these subsequent markets, EcoClear Inc. will decide to issue licenses or enter as a manufacturer, as reason dictates.

Royalty income is expected to begin in 1997, growing to $5.3 million in 2001, based on conservative assumptions regarding market penetration and industry growth assumptions. Net Profit after tax is projected to grow to $2.38 million in 2001. Although R&D expenses for the development of extensions into other filtration markets are included in the cash flow analysis, no revenues are included from these other markets - they are part of the 'blue sky' potential.

The NPV of the enterprise is $4.5 million after discounting the cashflows at 40%. The Internal Rate of Return (IRR) is 112%. The value of the company (assuming P/E = 10) is projected to be $23.8 million in 2001.

EcoClear Inc. is seeking a new equity partner with $300,000 and commercial knowledge of the North American swimming pool industry. This capital is required to fund the initial period of negative cashflow while the management of EcoClear Inc. seeks all necessary approvals for the North American market; negotiates an agreement with a manufacturer; and continues to develop the technology.

EcoClear Inc. offers the investor a 33% equity share in the business. The investor can expect to receive payback (from dividend income alone) in 3.1 years and would hold an equity value of nearly $8 million in 2001. The projected NPV to the investor of the dividend stream and the exit value of the equity (discounted at 40%) is $1.4 million and the IRR is 101%.

EcoClear Inc. is an exciting and potentially very rewarding investment opportunity, and the management team looks forward to discussions with you, after you have read this Business Plan.

TABLE OF CONTENTS

The Product

The Marketing Plan

The Operational Plan

The Financial Plan

Appendices

The Company

The Business and its Principal Activities

EcoClear Inc.'s mission is to profitably supply environmentally friendly water filtration systems. The launch product is an innovative self-cleaning swimming pool filter and our lead international market is the US, following the successful testing and launch of the product in Australia. The immediate goals are to secure a licensing agreement with a major American pool industry manufacturer, gain funding for initial working capital, and continue R&D activities to apply the technology to other industries and guarantee the long term success of the company.

The Product

The pool industry has long felt the need for a better filtration technology. Pools are typically filtered by Diatomaceous Earth (DE), sand, or cartridge filters. These filters waste time, energy, water and chemicals in the cleaning (or back washing) function, and offer varying levels of filtration effectiveness. (For background information on pool filtration, refer to Appendix A).

EcoClear is a self-backwashing filter that is more economical, environmentally friendly, and consistently filters to a finer level than existing pool filtration products. It is the invention of an Australian engineer with considerable experience in both the pool and plastic industries.

EcoClear works on the principle of increasing water pressure (caused by the normal congestion of the filter screen) triggering an automatic reversal of water flow back through the filter screen, carrying the sediment away to waste. The resultant drop in water pressure immediately causes a latch mechanism to reset the filter to the filtration mode, and the filter cycle begins again. This self-cleaning process is virtually instantaneous, happens once every 1-4 hours when the pump is running (depending on water condition), and sends only about half a gallon of water to waste each time it cycles. (Schematic diagrams illustrating this process are shown in Appendix B).

EcoClear's Benefits

EcoClear Inc. has identified 10 benefits of the product relative to the criteria that the pool industry and their customers use in their purchase decisions.

- **Saves Production Costs** due to its simple design, substantially smaller size and low pressure operation, allowing lower prices and higher margins;
- **Maintains Water Quality** at a given micron level, whereas other filters become increasingly less effective until they are cleaned;
- **Saves Water** by wasting 85% less water than DE or sand filters, and 66% less than cartridge filters;
- **Saves Pool Chemicals** as waste water contains those chemicals;
- **Saves Electricity** by operating at 2-10 lbs/in^2 compared with the 40-80 lbs/in^2 needed to force water through the other filters;
- **Saves Time** by eliminating the manual cleaning chore of other filters;
- **Reduces Financial Risk** by eliminating the uncertainty of when to backwash the filter and thus avoids unexpected costs resulting from algae infestation;
- **Reduces Health Risk** as it eliminates the use of DE, a known carcinogen;
- **Saves Installation Costs** because it comes with a protective housing; and
- **Saves Poolside Space** due to its compact size.

Product Comparison

The following table indicates that *EcoClear* outperforms the other filter types not only overall, but on every purchase decision criteria.

Decision Criteria	Filter Types			
	Cartridge	Sand	DE	*EcoClear*
Production Cost/Price	7	6	4	9
Water Clarity	5	4	8	9
Water Conservation	6	4	4	9
Chemical Saving	6	4	2	9
Electricity Saving	5	5	5	9
Time Saving	4	8	4	8
Financial risk	4	6	4	8
Health Risk	8	10	0	10
Space Savings	6	5	6	9
Ongoing Costs	5	7	5	8
Total Scores	56	59	42	88

(*Rating Scale: 10 = best possible solution, 0= worst solution)

The Product

**The
Marketing
Plan**

The
Operational
Plan

The
Financial
Plan

Appendices

Marketing Plan

Trend Analysis

These trends indicate that *EcoClear* is being launched at an opportune time.

Social Trends

- Increasing focus on the home environment known as 'cocooning';
- Increasing migration to the 'sun belt' where pools are more frequently found;
- Increasing perception of physical or health risk in using public pools;
- Increasing interest in health and fitness and the use of hydrotherapy; and
- Increasing value of recreation time particularly for dual-income families.

Economic Trends

- Increasing cost consciousness among consumers and pool builders;
- Increasing impact by 'Baby Boomers' on leisure and associated industries; and
- Increasing trend towards professional maintenance of domestic pools;

Technological Trends

- Increasing preference for cartridge filters at the expense of sand and DE filters. Cartridge filters are expected to grow by 15-25% annually; and
- Marginal improvements in filtration material (cellulose in cartridge filters and zeolite for sand filters).

Political, Legal and Regulatory

- Increasing awareness of the environment and natural resource conservation;
- Increasing restrictions by regulatory authorities on the manufacture of items that are wasteful of water and electricity; and
- Increasing restrictions on the use and disposal of DE.

Present Market Situation

Market Overview

The US domestic pool market can be divided into three major product segments: 1) above-ground pools; 2) in-ground pools; and 3) spas/hot tubs. Although the commercial pool market is significant, it will not be considered in this plan as the product requires modification to best satisfy that market's demand. These modifications will be made as part of ongoing R&D, and it is expected that a suitable product will be ready for this market during the third or fourth year of operation. The revenue from commercial pools, or from any other market application of the technology, will not be considered in this plan, but will instead be treated as part of the 'blue sky' potential. Thus, this plan limits its focus to domestic pools and spas of 35,000 gallons and less.

Pool filter purchasers can be divided into two separate categories. The 'first-time' pool purchaser is typically guided by the pool builder or pool designer, as they usually have minimal experience with pool filters. The 'replacement' filter purchaser is more informed in their filter purchase decision, though typically requires updated information from pool service providers or retailers on technology and product developments.

Market Size

In 1995 there were 9.7 million domestic pools and spas in the US. New pool and spa construction in 1995 totalled 883,000 units, a 9% increase. Filter sales are seasonal with the majority of sales occurring between April and September. New pool and spa purchases are sensitive to macroeconomic cycles, but since these cycles are difficult to predict, this plan conservatively assumes that pool and spa construction will increase at the trend growth rate of 5%. Replacement of existing filters occurs on average every 7.5 years for pools and every 10 years for spas. This accounted for a further 1,066,000 unit sales in 1995. Thus total pool and spa filter sales were 1.899 million units in 1995 (which represents $450 million at wholesale) and are forecast to grow to 3.115 million units in 2001.

The estimated 1996 breakdown of sales by filter types is as follows:

Filter Type	% Market Share (1995)	Number of Units Sold (1996 est.)	US$ Retail Sales (1996 est)
DE	40%	818,000	$427,800,000
Sand	37%	757,000	$355,600,000
Cartridge	23%	470,000	$202,100,000
Total	100%	2,045,000	$985,500,000

Major Filter Manufacturers in the North American Market

There are over 30 manufacturers of pool filter products in the US, five of whom hold approximately 80% of the market. The industry is price competitive with regular discounting of list prices by up to 50%.

The following table compares direct production costs, deep discount prices, expected prices and manufacturers' dollar margins.

Comparative Cost and Pricing Data

Filter Type	Direct Cost to Produce	Deep Discount Sale Price (Wholesale)	Expected Sale Price (Wholesale)	Deep Discount Margin per unit	Expected Case Margin per unit
Sand	$165	$210	$245	$45	$80
DE	$200	$255	$285	$55	$85
Cartridge	$130	$165	$200	$35	$70
EcoClear	*$65*	*$165*	*$200*	*$100*	*$135*

(The cost assumptions in this table assume a base model 24" sand filter or it's equivalent in the other filter types. These are direct costs only and do not include indirect manufacturing or marketing costs. For a break down of *EcoClear's* direct costs see Appendix C).

Sustainable Competitive Advantages

Water clarity and price are the major criteria in the pool filter purchase decision. The diagram below demonstrates the potential positioning of *EcoClear* in these two dimensions relative to the other filter types. (There is a range of water quality and price for sand and cartridge filters). As can be seen, *EcoClear* can be positioned above the existing value frontier which will facilitate its market penetration.

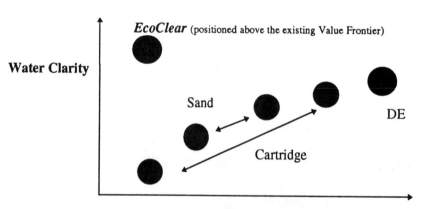

When a new product enters a market with such a pronounced value advantage, competitor retaliation should be expected. In this case however, competitor retaliation is constrained as *EcoClear* has a substantial manufacturing cost advantage and its quality advantage is legally protected. Other sustainable competitive advantages include *EcoClear's* saving of water, chemicals, maintenance time, electricity, installation cost and poolside space.

Strategic Options

The strategic options have been reduced to three, which are shown in the following table along with the perceived advantages and disadvantages of each option.

Strategic Option	Advantages	Disadvantages
1. EcoClear Inc. manufactures and distributes in the US.	• Greater long term profits; • Control of Quality; • Control of Marketing and Distribution.	• High level of business risk; • High level of financial risk; • More capital required; • Reduced short term profits; • Reduced resources for R&D; • No manufacturing expertise; • No access to distribution.
2. EcoClear Inc. sub-contracts the manufacture in conjunction with a retail chain (e.g. Leslie's Poolmart).	• Greater long term profits; • Control of Quality; • Leverages retailers industry knowledge and market strength; • Immediate brand awareness; • Reduced financial risk.	• High business risk; • Reduced short term profits; • Reduced resources for R&D; • Manufacturing is not a primary skill of either party; • Restricts distribution options; • Restricted market access.
3. EcoClear Inc. licenses the technology to a major manufacturer in the pool industry.	• Lower financial risk; • Lower business risk; • Leverages existing manufacturing experience; • Immediate brand acceptance; • No indirect manufacture and distribution costs; • New technology acceptance; • Distribution channel access; • Provides ease of entry to international markets; • Ease of market entry for future roll out products; • Protection of intellectual property from competitor; • Focus on R&D.	• Intellectual property infringement by licensee; • Access to trade secrets; • Reduced long term profits; • Loss of Marketing and Distribution control; • Success is linked to the fortunes of the licensee company and its management.

Based on this analysis, EcoClear Inc. will negotiate an exclusive licensing agreement that will foster a long term strategic alliance with a major pool industry manufacturer.

Mutual Benefits of a Strategic Alliance

Benefits to EcoClear Inc.	Benefits to the Licensee
• Decreased financial risk while building capital for future growth; • Reputation & brand equity of the major manufacturer provides credibility for *EcoClear;* • Access to distribution channels, manufacturing and marketing expertise; • Resources to protect *EcoClear's* intellectual property.	• Exclusive rights to an innovative filtration technology; • Increased market share from both competitors and a greater proportion of overall market growth; • Rejuvenate their product offering while rival products remain static; • First right of refusal on further international licenses; • Access to ongoing innovative R&D.

Target Market

All five of the major manufacturers produce each of the three types of pool filter. No manufacturer dominates a particular filter market and each has a national distribution system. 90% of filter products are manufactured in the US with the "Made in USA" label being highly valued by consumers.

Hayward Pool Products is the market leader with annual sales in excess of $200 million. Sales are generated almost entirely from pool products in the US with exports to Canada and Europe representing less than 8% of total sales. The company has 1500 employees and 80% of its stock is owned by the existing directors who have controlled the company since 1964. The Chairman has outright control with 66% of the stock. Hayward's market share has come under considerable threat in recent times by aggressive moves from American Products and Sta-rite.

Pac-Fab has sales in excess of $90 million, generated entirely from pool products in the US and exports to Canada and Europe. They have 450 employees and are 100% owned by Essef Corporation which gained control in 1971. Pac-Fab relies more heavily on sand filters and thus its market share is being undermined by the trend towards cartridge filters, but they have maintained market share via a number of competitor acquisitions.

Sta-rite has a similar filter market share to Pac-Fab. Its total sales exceed $270 million from a wider range of pool products and electrical pumps, with exports accounting for 30% of sales. They have 1700 employees and are 100% owned by Wicor Inc., which has sales in excess of $850 million. Sta-rite is expanding its market share with a strategy of price competition, product bundling, competitor acquisitions and some innovation in pool filtration.

American Products has sales in excess of $40 million generated entirely from pool products, with 12% of sales to Canada and Europe. In 1995 they became a wholly owned subsidiary of General Aquatics, a major pool builder with sales of $90 million. American Products has rapidly gained market share in recent years, particularly in the 'sun belt' region.

Jacuzzi has sales in excess of $270 million and is a wholly owned subsidiary of US Industries, who in turn have sales of $2 billion. This group has experienced difficulties in recent years with few profitable subsidiaries.

The following graph outlines the market share position for each of the "Big Five" manufacturers.

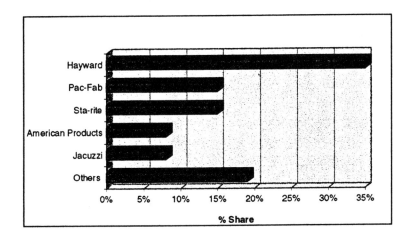

Marketing Strategy

EcoClear's primary market consists of pool filter manufacturers. Pool builders, wholesalers, retail stores and the end consumer are *EcoClear's* secondary market. By exceeding the expectations of the secondary market, *EcoClear* will generate 'pull' through the distribution channel.

Telephone contact has been made with senior executives from each of the companies in the target market. Initial interest has been positive and meetings have been arranged and will be conducted in May. Once a confidentiality agreement has been signed, a video presentation will be made and a product presentation and demonstration will occur for each of the manufacturers. At some point we would expect a preferred candidate to emerge. Before further technical details would be revealed, a 'heads of agreement' would be signed outlining the future licensing agreement. This process is expected to be completed by November 1996, with a view to launching the product in time for the 1997 summer season.

License Agreement

The following are a suggested basis for an exclusive license agreement.

- The royalty will be based on a fixed dollar amount per unit sold within the industry standard of 8% - 15% of expected wholesale price;

- There will be a minimum royalty payment based on an agreed level of expected sales;

- EcoClear Inc. will provide and retain ownership of the production dies;

- The licensee will market the filter under the *EcoClear* brand name;

- An anti-shelving clause including manufacture commencement date and penalties for non-performance;

- Duration of license and termination conditions;

- Licensee will ensure that the product meets the requirements and specifications of all applicable standards;

- Licensee will indemnify EcoClear Inc. against any claims relating to the sale, manufacture or commercial utilisation of the product;

- EcoClear Inc. will appoint the licensee as agent and attorney to protect the intellectual property in the North American market;

- EcoClear Inc. will own any improvements made to the technology by the licensee; and

- EcoClear Inc. will grant access to product upgrades emanating from its R&D program.

Marketing Objectives and Sales Forecasts

Marketing and pricing strategies for the secondary market will be set by the licensee. For the purpose of this plan we have conservatively assumed a $200 wholesale price in the expected scenario and therefore a $20 royalty payment per unit. At a wholesale price of $200, EcoClear Inc. expects to attain, over the first five years, a 10% share of the pool filter market for domestic pools. EcoClear's market share is expected to achieve this market penetration following typical diffusion patterns. The following table indicates the sales forecast figures based on the above marketing assumptions.

Total Sales	1997	1998	1999	2000	2001
Unit Sales	5,062	42,900	121,452	219,696	266,412
Dollar Sales	$101,240	$858,000	$2,429,040	$4,393,920	$5,328,240

The Product

The Marketing Plan

The Operational Plan

The Financial Plan

Appendices

Operational Plan

Company Structure and Ownership

EcoClear Inc. was established as a joint venture between New Endeavour Pty. Ltd. and ABF Pty. Ltd. to launch *EcoClear* into the US market. The management team has since secured two investors and the expanded ownership structure is set out below. EcoClear Inc. is a Delaware company currently registered as Scanex Inc. (the name is in the process of being changed). Lloyd Beck, former CEO of General Motors (Australia) has been appointed as independent Chairman of the Board.

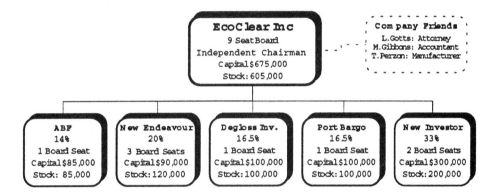

ABF Pty. Ltd. consists of the product's inventor and three investors who have launched *EcoClear* on the Australian market. ABF have assigned the North American rights of the product to EcoClear Inc. and invested $85,000 for a 14% equity share and $1 royalty per unit sold from year two. An option arrangement has been established for the rights to other markets after consideration of the management groups' initial performance in the US.

New Endeavour Pty. Ltd. is owned equally by the management team. This team has worked closely with ABF since mid 1995 as consultants in the product's initial development and marketing research. The management team has a complementary mix of business expertise, new venture initiation experience and a proven ability to raise capital. New Endeavour Pty. Ltd. has a management contract with EcoClear Inc. that guarantees control, provided the worst case financial scenario is attained or exceeded.

Degloss Investments, a Hong Kong based business group has invested $100,000. *Port Bargo Pty. Ltd.,* a group of Australian professionals wishing to invest in new venture opportunities, have invested $100,000. In addition to this they have agreed to provide a line of credit up to $100,000 as a standby facility to finance the worst case scenario. The interest rate would be equivalent to the Australian government 90-day bill rate plus a risk premium of 8%. The management team has underwritten this potential source of funds with personal guarantees.

A New Investor is sought, preferably with expertise in the US pool industry, to contribute $300,000. Details and the expected yield for this investment are on page 25 of the plan.

Key Management Personnel

The management team of EcoClear Inc. for the first year, is detailed in the organisational chart below. The organisational chart for year two and beyond can be found in Appendix D along with detailed resumes of the management team.

EcoClear Inc. Organisational Chart (Year 1).

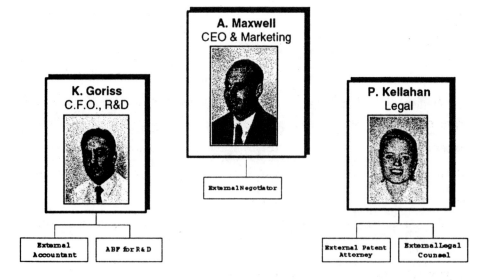

Andrew Maxwell. As Chief Executive Officer, Andrew's responsibilities include overall strategy, marketing and the development of strong relationships with key stakeholders. Andrew will relocate to the US in July 1996. He has prior new venture start up experience in international markets. As National Marketing manager (Retail Business) with Shell Australia, he was an integral part of a team that launched 60 Circle K convenience stores nationally. He has worked as a business development manager in Papua New Guinea dealing with US mining companies. More recently Andrew started Cambodia's only national brewery and established the largest food and liquor wholesaler in that country. Andrew has worked as a Government advisor to assist entrepreneurs start and grow their business.

Kim Goriss is the V.P. Finance and is initially responsible for overseeing R&D in Australia. Kim will relocate to the US in January 1998. Currently Kim is consulting to the State Department of Public Works and Housing as a financial analyst within the Financial Policy and Management Division. Kim has had extensive experience in international markets including the Middle East, India, Singapore, P.N.G., China, Taiwan and Australia. His roles as project manager in the oil exploration industry provided extensive experience in financial planning. Due to the technical nature of this work, Kim is well qualified to oversee R&D operations having been responsible for up to 30 technicians, geophysicists and other technical staff.

Prue Kellahan is the V.P. Legal Liaison. Prue's responsibilities are to coordinate dealings with the external patent attorney and general legal counsel. Prue has an impressive combination of academic qualifications and business experience. She has a law degree, Masters of Accounting and Master of Business Administration and is currently completing a program that will allow her to be admitted to the Bar. This is supplemented by experience in her family's construction company. Kel Constructions is a developer of hotels and resorts in the North of Australia and has swimming pool construction experience. Prue has been responsible for the development and oversight of the legal and accounting departments in this company during her time at university and has an ongoing role.

Action Plan

The following table outlines the management team's action plan.

Action	Commencement Date	Expected Completion
Product Test Program (Aust.)	June 95	Completed
Production Dies Cast	March 96	Completed
Initial Investors Signed	February 96	Completed
Relocation Preparation	May 96	May 96
NSF Approval	May 96	July 96
Manufacturer Meetings	May 96	Ongoing
US Patent Application	June 96	December 97
Promotional Material	June 96	June 96
CEO relocates to US	July 96	July 96
U.L. Approval	July 96	October 96
US Onsite Testing	July 96	Ongoing
Pool Consultant Report	August 96	August 96
Engineer's Report	August 96	September 96
Market Research Report	August 96	August 96
Draft Agreement	April 96	November 96
Product Manufacture	March 97	Ongoing

Technology and R&D

Key Future Research & Development Activities

For the first two years R&D services will be supplied by ABF's technical team in Australia, at ABF's expense in 1997, and thereafter at EcoClear Inc.'s expense. R&D efforts for this period will be monitored by Kim Goriss. From 1998 the R&D function will be located permanently in the US. (Refer to Appendix E for the R&D schedule). The key R&D targets are:

Inline Debris Mulcher: Positioned prior to the filter pump, this would eliminate the need for a skimmer basket and provide better flow rates.

Commercial Pool Market: The original product requires a capacity increase to ensure it's suitability to this market.

Other Industry Uses: *EcoClear's* water filtration technology has potential uses in a number of major markets, including filtration in aquaculture, irrigation, air-conditioning and brewing. The individual market requirements need to be further researched and prototype products produced. Initial interest has been shown in the areas of agriculture and aquaculture, and these areas will be targeted first.

Key Success Factors

1. Secure a licensing agreement with a major manufacturer of pool products;

2. Maintain protection of the company's intellectual property; and

3. Maintain a harmonious and productive working relationship amongst the management team, shareholders and licensee.

Risk Reduction Strategies

EcoClear Inc. recognises the risks associated with this new venture and has chosen to implement the following strategies as a means of risk reduction.

Risk #1: Failure to secure a license agreement in a timely manner.

- Indepth analysis of the target market;
- Relationship with target market initiated and meetings arranged;
- Personal selling of the opportunity by US based CEO;
- Use of professional negotiator and expert legal counsel;
- Line of credit established to finance any license agreement delays.

Risk #2: Infringement of Intellectual Property.

- Inventor has logged the process prior to, and following, the inventive step;
- Indepth independent search of prior art;
- Confidentiality agreements required;
- Exclusive licensing agreement specifically covering trade secrets and knowhow involved with the products' design;
- Licensee obliged to prosecute patent infringements;
- Patent protection via the Patent Cooperation Treaty and national application in the US and selected other countries;
- US Patent Attorney to prosecute any infringement by the licensee;
- Patent Insurance, (defence and indemnity) with total cover of $1,000,000;
- A Patent Protection Trust Fund will be established from cashflow;
- Trademark and Business Name registration in progress.

Risk #3: Disharmony between the management, shareholders and licensee.

- Proven working relationship amongst members of the management team;
- CEO has a long standing relationship with Degloss and Port Bargo;
- All parties bound to a 'no-exit' agreement for three years;
- License agreement with significant benefits accruing to both parties;
- Shareholders' agreement to protect the interests of minority shareholders;
- Management performance contract.

Other Risk Reduction Strategies

The financial viability of EcoClear Inc. rests on a conservative assessment of the US pool market and does not include potential revenues from new roll out products in the future. Market penetration has been estimated on the US market only, and does not include opportunities in Canada, Mexico, South America or other markets.

Operating costs will be kept to a minimum with a flat organisational structure and strict budgetary controls. Salary and benefits in the initial years will be below market rates. The transfer of R&D to the US in year two reduces the reliance on ABF for continued product development. As other applications for the product are brought to market the dependence on the pool market will be reduced.

Harvest and Exit Strategies

Harvest strategies available to the management team are salaries, dividends and capital gain. Management salaries will be below market value initially and will be increased to reflect performance in subsequent years. Dividends will be declared in year two and beyond, at the rate of 50% of net profit. Investors harvest via dividends and receive capital gains on exit. Individual investors may sell down their shareholding after year three.

Four exit strategies have been identified and are listed in order of preference.

The shareholding will be valued and offered to the remaining shareholders in proportion to their existing holdings;

Equity may be sold to an external party upon majority approval;

Sale of the entire business; or

Initial Public Offering.

Financial Plan

Assumptions

- All figures are in real dollars;
- All costs incurred during the initial six-month period of negative cashflows have been shown as January 1997 expenses;
- Expenses for new R&D efforts are included in the Financial Statements. However, revenue for these efforts are not included;
- Straight line growth has been assumed for the filter markets;
- Market penetration is calculated as a five year cumulative normal distribution. The average diffusion rate for each year was used to calculate sales revenue;
- Royalty payments from EcoClear Inc. to ABF ($1 per unit) are paid from year two onwards;
- Royalty payments are received quarterly in arrears;
- Dividend payments are 50% of Net Profits After Tax.

Summary Financial Results (Expected Scenario)

Years	1997	1998	1999	2000	2001
Sales ($)	101,240	858,000	2,429,040	4,393,920	5,328,240
EBIT ($)	(492,427)	199,090	1,398,463	2,820,320	3,457,077
NPAT ($)	(313,756)	164,449	975,622	1,940,704	2,380,977
Cash Balance ($)	51,660	207,330	1,414,649	3,312,691	4,856,680

The Internal Rate of Return (IRR) calculated from the projected profit streams and the end of year 5 valuation of the company (P/E = 10) is 112%. The Net Present Value (NPV) discounted at 40% is $4.5 million.

Key Performance Indicators

	1997	1998	1999	2000	2001
NPAT as % of Sales	-310	19	40	44	45
NPAT as % of Total Assets	-172	43	57	52	45
NPAT as % of Paid Capital	-46	24	145	288	353
NPAT as % Shareholder's Funds	-172	55	106	103	78

Proforma Financial Statements

The following tables show the forecast Profit and Loss statements, Cash Flows and Balance Sheets for the first five years of operation under the 'Expected Scenario'.

The Product

The
Marketing
Plan

The
Operational
Plan

The
Financial
Plan

Appendices

EcoClear Inc.

Profit & Loss Statement (Expected Scenario)

	Jan	Feb	Mar	Apr	May	June	July	Aug	Sept	Oct	Nov	Dec	1997	1998	1999	2000	2001
												31-Dec-97					
									Year Ending								
GROSS PROFIT FROM TRADING ACCOUNT																	
Fee Income	0	0	42,500	0	0	42,500	0	0	10,120	0	0	6,050	101,240	856,000	2,429,040	4,393,920	5,328,240
Other Operating Income	0	0	0	0	0	0	0	0	0	0	0	0	0	0	0	0	0
Total Operating Income	0	0	42,500	0	0	42,500	0	0	10,120	0	0	6,050	101,240	856,000	2,429,040	4,393,920	5,328,240
EXPENSES																	
Direct Costs - Services Entity	0	0	0	0	0	0	0	0	0	0	0	0	66,000	188,235	234,251	309,605	392,338
Research & Development Expense	54,500	3,500	3,500	6,000	3,500	3,500	3,500	6,000	3,500	3,500	3,500	3,500	245,000	270,120	458,283	765,134	869,274
Administration Costs	116,042	23,292	8,292	17,042	8,292	8,292	14,542	10,792	8,292	14,542	8,292	8,292	229,500	178,585	276,043	475,832	557,553
Selling & Distribution Costs	100,033	9,583	9,583	24,583	9,583	9,583	9,583	9,583	9,583	9,583	9,583	9,583					
Interest Expense	0	0	0	0	0	0	0	0	0	0	0	0	0	0	0	0	0
Lease Expense	0	0	0	0	0	0	0	0	0	0	0	0	0	0	0	0	0
Depreciation	0	1,833	1,833	1,833	1,833	1,833	1,833	1,833	1,833	1,833	1,833	1,833	20,167	22,000	22,000	22,000	22,000
Movement in Provisions	0	0	0	0	0	0	0	0	0	0	0	0	0	0	0	0	0
Other Operating Costs	0	0	0	0	0	0	0	0	0	0	0	0	0	0	0	0	0
OPERATING PROFIT BEFORE TAX	(270,625)	(35,208)	19,212	(49,458)	(23,208)	19,312	(29,458)	(28,208)	(13,058)	(29,458)	(23,208)	(17,128)	(452,427)	199,060	1,388,453	2,820,320	3,457,077
Non - Operating Income	0	0	0	0	0	0	0	0	0	0	0	0	0	0	0	0	0
Non - Operating Costs	0	0	0	0	0	0	0	0	0	0	0	0	0	0	0	0	0
Income Tax Expense	(101,299)	(13,166)	5,795	(17,311)	(8,236)	5,795	(10,299)	(10,299)	(4,897)	(10,299)	(8,236)	(6,230)	(178,671)	34,641	422,642	878,616	1,078,100
Dividends	0	0	0	0	0	0	0	0	0	0	0	0	0	82,225	487,811	970,352	1,190,469
Extraordinary Profit	0	0	0	0	0	0	0	0	0	0	0	0	0	0	0	0	0
Amortisation of Intangibles	0	0	0	0	0	0	0	0	0	0	0	0	0	0	0	0	0
Transfer to Reserve	0	0	0	0	0	0	0	0	0	0	0	0	0	0	0	0	0
RETAINED EARNINGS	(178,356)	(25,022)	13,516	(32,147)	(14,972)	13,516	(19,160)	(17,910)	(8,162)	(19,160)	(14,972)	(10,898)	(313,755)	82,225	487,811	970,352	1,190,469

302

EcoClear Inc.

Projected Cashflow (Expected Scenario)

	\ Year Ending 31-Dec-97 \																
	Jan	Feb	Mar	Apr	May	Jun	Jul	Aug	Sept	Oct	Nov	Dec	1997	1998	1999	2000	2001
CASH-INFLOWS																	
Cash Sales	675,000	0	0	0	0	0	0	0	0	0	0	0	675,000	0	0	0	0
Capital Subscriptions	0	0	0	0	0	0	0	0	0	0	0	0	0	0	0	0	0
Loan Drawdowns - Secured	0	0	0	0	0	0	0	0	0	0	0	0	0	0	0	0	0
– Unsecured	0	0	0	0	0	0	0	0	0	0	0	0	0	0	0	0	0
Proceeds from Asset Sales	0	0	0	0	0	0	0	0	0	0	0	0	0	0	0	0	0
Fee Income Services Entity	0	0	0	0	0	0	0	0	0	0	0	0	0	0	0	0	0
Other Operating Income	0	0	0	42,520	0	0	42,520	0	0	10,120	0	0	95,160	792,580	2,296,120	4,220,160	5,250,360
Non-Operating Income	0	0	0	0	0	0	0	0	0	0	0	0	0	0	0	0	0
Receipts from Debtors	0	0	0	0	0	0	0	0	0	0	0	0	0	0	0	0	0
	675,000	0	0	42,520	0	0	42,520	0	0	10,120	0	0	770,160	792,580	2,296,120	4,220,160	5,250,360
CASH-OUTFLOWS																	
Payments to creditors	0	0	0	0	0	0	0	0	0	0	0	0	0	0	0	0	0
Cash Purchase/Additions	0	0	0	0	0	0	0	0	0	0	0	0	0	0	0	0	0
Capital Expenditure	110,000	0	0	0	0	0	0	0	0	0	0	0	110,000	0	0	0	0
Direct Costs Services Entity	0	0	0	0	0	0	0	0	0	0	0	0	0	0	234,251	309,635	382,338
Other Operating & Non-Operating Costs	0	0	0	0	0	0	0	0	0	0	0	0	0	0	0	457,811	970,562
Tax Payment	0	0	0	0	0	0	0	0	0	0	0	0	0	0	0	0	0
Dividend Payments	0	0	0	0	0	0	0	0	0	0	0	0	0	0	0	0	0
Research & Development Expenses	54,500	3,500	3,500	6,000	3,500	3,500	3,500	6,000	3,500	3,500	3,500	3,500	98,000	188,235	82,225	282,727	866,878
Administration and Selling Expenses	225,125	32,875	17,875	41,625	17,875	17,875	24,125	20,375	17,875	24,125	17,875	17,875	475,500	448,675	774,328	1,241,985	1,459,827
Loan Repayments - Secured	0	0	0	0	0	0	0	0	0	0	0	0	0	0	0	0	0
– Unsecured	0	0	0	0	0	0	0	0	0	0	0	0	0	0	0	0	0
Interest Payments	0	0	0	0	0	0	0	0	0	0	0	0	0	0	0	0	0
Increase in Other Assets (incl. Investments)	35,000	0	0	0	0	0	0	0	0	0	0	0	35,000	0	0	0	0
Lease Payments	0	0	0	0	0	0	0	0	0	0	0	0	0	0	0	0	0
Reduction in Other Payables	0	0	0	0	0	0	0	0	0	0	0	0	0	0	0	0	0
	424,625	35,375	21,375	47,625	21,375	21,375	27,625	26,375	21,375	27,625	21,375	21,375	718,500	609,910	1,090,801	2,332,138	3,706,591
NET CASH-FLOW	250,375	(35,375)	(21,375)	(5,105)	(21,375)	(21,375)	14,895	(26,375)	(21,375)	(17,505)	(21,375)	(21,375)	51,660	155,670	1,207,319	1,898,042	1,543,999
CLOSING OVERDRAFT OR CASH	250,375	214,000	192,625	187,520	166,145	144,770	159,665	133,290	111,915	94,410	73,035	51,660	51,660	207,330	1,414,649	3,312,691	4,856,690

EcoClear Inc.

Balance Sheet (Expected Scenario)

1997

	Jan	Feb	Mar	Apr	May	Jun	Jul	Aug	Sep	Oct	Nov	Dec	1997	1998	1999	2000	2001
CURRENT ASSETS																	
Cash and Deposits	250,375	214,000	182,825	187,520	168,145	144,770	158,895	133,290	111,915	94,410	73,035	51,660	51,660	207,330	1,414,849	3,312,691	4,856,680
Debtors	0	0	42,520	0	0	42,520	0	0	10,120	0	0	6,080	6,080	71,500	202,420	365,160	444,020
Stock	0	0	0	0	0	0	0	0	0	0	0	0	0	0	0	0	0
Accrued Interest Receivable	0	0	0	0	0	0	0	0	0	0	0	0	0	0	0	0	0
Other	0	0	0	0	0	0	0	0	0	0	0	0	0	0	0	0	0
TOTAL CURRENT ASSETS	250,375	214,000	225,145	187,520	168,145	187,290	158,895	133,290	122,035	94,410	73,035	57,740	57,740	278,830	1,617,069	3,678,851	5,300,700
NON CURRENT ASSETS																	
Investment	0	0	0	0	0	0	0	0	0	0	0	0	0	0	0	0	0
Land and Buildings	110,000	108,167	106,333	104,500	102,667	100,833	99,000	97,167	95,333	93,500	91,667	89,833	89,833	67,833	45,833	23,833	1,833
Leased Assets	0	0	0	0	0	0	0	0	0	0	0	0	0	0	0	0	0
Plant and Equipment	35,000	35,000	35,000	35,000	35,000	35,000	35,000	35,000	35,000	35,000	35,000	35,000	35,000	35,000	35,000	35,000	35,000
Other	0	0	0	0	0	0	0	0	0	0	0	0	0	0	0	0	0
TOTAL NON-CURRENT ASSETS	145,000	143,167	141,333	139,500	137,667	135,833	134,000	132,167	130,333	128,500	126,667	124,833	124,833	102,833	80,833	58,833	36,833
TOTAL ASSETS	395,375	357,167	378,478	327,020	305,812	323,123	293,895	265,457	252,368	222,910	199,702	182,573	182,573	381,663	1,697,902	3,737,684	5,337,534
CURRENT LIABILITIES																	
Bank Overdraft - Secured	0	0	0	0	0	0	0	0	0	0	0	0	0	0	0	0	0
Loans - Secured	0	0	0	0	0	0	0	0	0	0	0	0	0	0	0	0	0
- Unsecured	0	0	0	0	0	0	0	0	0	0	0	0	0	0	0	0	0
Creditors	0	0	0	0	0	0	0	0	0	0	0	0	0	0	0	0	0
Finance Lease Obligations	0	0	0	0	0	0	0	0	0	0	0	0	0	0	0	0	0
Provisions - Tax	0	0	0	0	0	0	0	0	0	0	0	0	0	82,225	292,727	886,876	1,083,360
- Dividend	0	0	0	0	0	0	0	0	0	0	0	0	0	0	487,811	970,352	1,190,489
- Employee Benefits	0	0	0	0	0	0	0	0	0	0	0	0	0	0	0	0	0
- Other	0	0	0	0	0	0	0	0	0	0	0	0	0	0	0	0	0
Accrued Interest Payable	0	0	0	0	0	0	0	0	0	0	0	0	0	0	0	0	0
Other Current Liabilities	0	0	0	0	0	0	0	0	0	0	0	0	0	0	0	0	0
TOTAL CURRENT LIABILITIES	0	0	0	0	0	0	0	0	0	0	0	0	0	82,225	780,538	1,857,228	2,273,849
NON CURRENT LIABILITIES																	
Loans - Secured	0	0	0	0	0	0	0	0	0	0	0	0	0	0	0	0	0
- Unsecured	0	0	0	0	0	0	0	0	0	0	0	0	0	0	0	0	0
Provisions	0	0	0	0	0	0	0	0	0	0	0	0	0	0	0	0	0
Future Tax Liability	0	0	0	0	0	0	0	0	0	0	0	0	0	0	0	0	0
Finance Lease Obligations	0	0	0	0	0	0	0	0	0	0	0	0	0	0	0	0	0
Other	0	0	0	0	0	0	0	0	0	0	0	0	0	0	0	0	0
TOTAL NON - CURRENT LIABILITIES	0	0	0	0	0	0	0	0	0	0	0	0	0	0	0	0	0
TOTAL LIABILITIES	0	0	0	0	0	0	0	0	0	0	0	0	0	82,225	780,538	1,857,228	2,273,849
NET ASSETS	365,575	357,167	378,478	327,020	303,812	323,123	293,895	265,457	252,368	222,910	199,702	182,573	182,573	299,439	917,365	1,880,457	3,063,685
SHAREHOLDERS FUNDS																	
Ordinary Capital	675,000	675,000	675,000	675,000	675,000	675,000	675,000	675,000	675,000	675,000	675,000	675,000	675,000	675,000	675,000	675,000	675,000
Preference Capital	0	0	0	0	0	0	0	0	0	0	0	0	0	0	0	0	0
Reserves - Revenue	(173,356)	(203,378)	(189,862)	(222,009)	(228,981)	(223,495)	(242,376)	(260,534)	(288,728)	(287,885)	(302,857)	(313,756)	(313,756)	(231,531)	256,280	1,228,632	2,417,120
- Asset Revaluation																	
- Other Capital																	
Retained Earnings	498,844	471,922	485,138	452,991	438,019	451,535	432,376	414,466	408,274	367,115	372,143	361,244	361,244	443,469	931,280	1,901,632	3,062,120
add : Minority Interest	0	0	0	0	0	0	0	0	0	0	0	0	0	0	0	0	0
less : Intangibles	101,289	114,455	108,890	125,971	134,207	128,412	135,711	149,009	153,906	164,205	172,441	178,671	178,671	144,030	13,915	21,175	28,435
SHAREHOLDERS EQUITY	365,575	357,167	378,478	327,020	303,812	323,123	293,895	265,457	252,368	222,910	199,702	182,573	182,573	299,439	917,365	1,880,457	3,063,685

Sources and Uses of Funds

As detailed earlier in the plan, EcoClear Inc. has already raised $375,000 capital and is now seeking an additional $300,000 from a new investor. These funds will be used in the following manner.

SALES AND MARKETING	1996 (6 mos)	1997	1998	1999	2000	2001
Salaries	20000	40000	46435	88581	215757	226488
Trade Shows	0	15000	21450	36436	65909	79924
Travel	6500	12000	12000	15000	25000	50000
Promotional Material	5000	10000	17160	24290	21970	26641
Manuals	10000	8000	12870	14574	15379	14653
Marketing Research Cons	8000	0	0	0	0	0
Promotion and Entertainment	50000	45000	68640	97162	131818	159847
TOTAL	99500	130000	178555	276043	475832	557553

ADMIN COSTS	1996 (6 mos)	1997	1998	1999	2000	2001
Relocation	5000	0	10000	0	0	0
Home Office Set-Up	6000	0	0	0	0	0
Home Office Servicing	1000	3000	7290	9073	13985	16321
Rent	10000	20000	24290	32145	41970	46641
Casual Wages	2500	2500	4290	6073	10985	13321
Utilities	5000	10000	12145	16073	20985	23321
Vehicle Lease	6000	12000	20580	36290	55939	65282
Royalty Payments to ABF	0	0	42900	121452	219696	266412
Retainer and Salaries	6000	12000	46435	88581	105909	119924
Freight & Insurance	5000	0	5000	5000	5000	5000
Travel	5000	5000	12870	36436	65909	79924
US Patent Cost	10000	10000	0	0	0	0
Patent Insurance	6250	18750	20000	20000	20000	20000
Patent Protection Trust	0	15000	25740	72871	131818	159847
Legal	40000	30000	38580	54290	73939	83282
TOTAL	107750	138250	270120	498283	766133	899274

R & D	1996 (6 mos)	1997	1998	1999	2000	2001
R&D Performance Contract	0	30000	0	0	0	0
NSF Approval	6000	0	6000	6000	6000	6000
UL Approval	10000	0	0	0	0	0
Beta Testing	7500	0	0	0	0	0
Salaries	6000	12000	46435	88581	105909	119924
Pool Consultants	5000	0	0	0	0	0
Engineer's Report	10000	0	0	0	0	0
Travel	5000	5000	0	0	0	0
Prototypes (20 x)	1500	0	0	0	0	0
Other R&D Expenses	0	0	42900	60726	87878	106565
Set-Up Costs	0	0	50000	0	0	0
R&D Operating Costs	0	0	42900	78944	109848	159847
TOTAL	51000	47000	188235	234251	309635	392336

Sensitivity Analysis

Years	Changed Aspect			
	Decrease in Revenue of 10%	Increase in Admin Costs of 10%	Increase in Marketing Costs of 10%	Increase in R&D Costs of 10%
	Retained Earnings as a result of changes in the above			
1997	(320,539)	(330,238)	(329,132)	(318,705)
1998	64,074	73,176	76,243	77,472
1999	430,599	471,118	478,563	481,896
2000	864,551	944,687	954,412	962,534
2001	1,061,836	1,160,363	1,171,811	1,180,582
	Ending Cash Balances as a result of changes in the above			
1997	42,144	27,060	28,710	41,860
1998	152,447	155,718	166,525	178,707
1999	1,224,862	1,322,258	1,352,221	1,367,353
2000	2,957,829	3,193,854	3,234,502	3,266,111
2001	4,337,628	4,698,864	4,754,379	4,794,012

Break Even Analysis

Years	1997	1998	1999	2000	2001
Yearly Unit Sales	29,683	24,427	17,916	18,103	19,742
Yearly $ Sales	593,667	488,550	358,311	362,069	394,833
% of Revenue	586%	57%	15%	8%	7%
% of Market Share	0.013%	0.010%	0.006%	0.006%	0.006%

Worst Case Scenario Summary

Assumptions

The 'Worst Case Scenario' assumes the following minimum royalty payments.

Year	1997	1998	1999	2000	2001
Units	0	27,000	36,500	44,000	55,000
Royalty	$0	$540,000	$730,000	$880,000	$1,100,000

- The 'Worst Case Scenario' requires only $50,000 of the $100,000 standby line of credit, leaving an additional buffer of $50,000;
- R&D expenses are reduced; and
- Royalties to ABF are not paid.

The 'Worst Case Scenario' outcomes are summarized in the table below, and detailed Profit & Loss, Cashflow Statement and Balance Sheets are shown in Appendix F.

Years	1997	1998	1999	2000	2001
EBIT	(593,667)	33,700	272,820	390,520	532,225
NPAT	(382,592)	41,297	193,573	277,950	375,978
Cash Balance	5,833	8,200	207,163	508,105	905,022

The Deal

EcoClear Inc. is seeking, in an Investor:

- $300,000 equity capital;
- Pool industry experience (preferable); and
- Harmonious relationship (personality fit).

The Investor will receive from EcoClear Inc.:

- 33% equity (200,000 shares);
- Two seats on the Board, which has an independent Chairperson;
- Shareholder agreement that protects all stockholders;
- The shareholders' agreement requires unanimous consent for annual budgets, dividend policy, acquisition of debt and dilution of shareholding. Dispute resolution is through an agreed third party arbitrator, if required;
- Performance contract with management team;
- In the event that the management fails to exceed the 'worst case scenario' financials the management contract lapses. The future of the management team will then be decided by the board;
- Five year exit value of equity approaching $8 million (assuming P/E = 10).
- NPV to the investor of dividend stream and exit value (discounted at 40%) is $1.4 million, with an internal rate of return of 101%;
- Payback from dividends alone in 3.1 years (see table below).

Entities	Share of Equity	1997 $	1998 $	1999 $	2000 $	2001 $
			Dividend Streams			
ABF	14%	0	11,552	68,535	136,330	167,259
New Endeavour	20%	0	16,309	96,756	192,467	236,130
Degloss	16.5%	0	13,591	80,630	160,389	196,775
Port Bargo	16.5%	0	13,591	80,630	160,389	196,775
New Investor	33%	0	27,182	161,260	320,778	393,550
Total	100%	0	82,225	487,811	970,352	1,190,489

Conclusion

The *EcoClear* water filtration technology is truly innovative. It satisfies long felt needs in the US pool filtration industry. It also offers promising applications in other industries and geographical markets. The management team trusts you will agree that EcoClear Inc. represents an exciting and lucrative investment. The management team look forward to discussing this opportunity with you in greater detail.

The Product

The
Marketing
Plan

The
Operational
Plan

The
Financial
Plan

Appendices

Appendix A: Background on Pool Filtration

Water Filtration

The most immediate indicator of filter efficiency is the clarity of a pool's water. Poor water clarity is usually the result of allowing too much time to elapse before cleaning or backwashing. The length of a filter cycle will vary depending on such diverse factors as swimmer load, how long the pump runs each day, how much debris enters the pool and the capacity of the pumps filter relative to the size of the pool. When the filter medium is clean, water flows through it with relative ease. As the medium loads with dirt, more and more energy is required to make the water pass through the filter, resulting in ever-increasing pressure. This pressure increase is recorded on a gauge, which is the main device used to signal the need to backwash the filter. Pool owners use various methods to track any pressure increase that comes as a result of dirt build up on the filter media. Some mark the gauge with a grease pencil, others keep records on the pressure via log sheets. Still others rely mainly on memory of the last filter backwash and perhaps the majority wait until a noticeable change in the clarity of water has occurred. For an average backyard pool, the filter cycle ranges from one to six weeks. There are three basic types of filter for pool filtration:

Sand Filters

Sand as a form of water filtration dates back to Roman times. In the early part of this century, all swimming pool filters used layers of sand and gravel as filter media. These filters work on the principle known as depth filtration, where dirt is collected throughout the bed of sand as water is passed through it. This filter is cleaned by backwashing the filter - that is, reversing the flow through the filter tank. The reversal of flow causes the bed of sand to rise, releasing the compressed grains to tumble against one another, and thereby shake off dirt that now flows with the water to waste. The typical volume of water wasted per backwash for a sand filter is approximately 295 gallons. Sand filters are the least effective type of water filtration system.

Diatomaceous Earth (DE) Filter

DE filters were first introduced by Hollywood to ensure the water clarity in Ester Williams' films. In these systems, pulverised fossil remains of ancient plankton-like creatures (diatoms) serve as the filtration medium. DE is a fine white powder that cakes under pressure onto nylon-mesh like grids within the filter tank. When water is drawn through DE caked grids, particles are trapped within microscopic spaces between the grains of DE. Backwashing separates the filter cake from the filter's grids, releasing the dirt and debris into the reversed water flow and out to waste. When normal flow is resumed, a slurry of DE powder and water is re-introduced to the system which then coats the grids and allows the filter process to continue. Built up DE needs to be cleared out and replaced periodically. Thus, the filter tank is disassembled, the grids removed and the DE hosed off. After the grids are checked for damage and repaired as necessary, they are reassembled and placed back in the filter tank. Fresh DE is then added to the filter to re-cake the filter media. DE has been a recent target of regulatory authorities due to the health risk involved in handling DE powder, and the damage it causes the environment on disposal. Like sand filters, DE filters require in excess of 295 gallons of water at each backwash cycle. DE filters are rated as the most effective in quality of water filtration, however due to the more intricate filter system, are the most expensive pool filter to purchase on the market.

Cartridge Filter

The newest method of pool and spa filtration (developed in the 50s), cartridge filters, consist of removable filter elements made of porous fabric materials that trap particles. These filters are not backwashed but are either replaced, or can be hosed down and re-used. The filter cycle for cartridge filters is similar to that of sand and DE filters. The cleaning techniques vary by product; some require water to be applied at high pressure, while others require soaking in a light acid wash. With either cleaning method in excess of 100 gallons of water are wasted. Recent developments have seen improvements in the filtering efficiency of cartridge filters.

Appendix B: *EcoClear* Schematic Diagrams

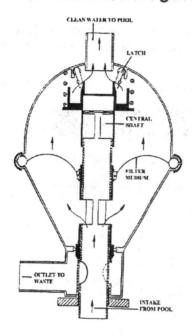

Filtration Mode

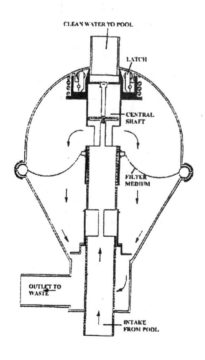

Backwash Mode

Appendix C: *EcoClear's* Direct Production Costs

These figures are based on a production of 5000 units. Although some economies of scale would be expected as volume increases, this saving would be minimal.

EcoClear Direct Manufacture Cost

Item	Cost $US
Manufactured Plastic	$17.16
2 x Screw Adapters	$1.56
Main Seal	$2.34
Band Clamp	$3.12
3 x "O" Rings	$1.17
Screen	$2.34
Machine Recess, Slide Tube	$3.90
Top Spring	$0.78
Backwash Spring	$0.78
Labour	$3.90
Packaging	$2.34
Royalty	$20.00
Protective Cover	$5.60
Total	$64.99

Appendix D: Resumes and Organisational Chart

Andrew Thomas Maxwell

Age: 32

EDUCATION

1995 - 1996   Masters of Business Administration, Bond University.
Masters of Accounting, Bond University.

WORK EXPERIENCE

1985 -   Owner of Endeavour Inn Restaurant, Cooktown, North Queensland.

1993 - 1994   Owner and General Manager of United Distributors Cambodia, Phnom Penh, Cambodia.   Initiated a wholesale liquor and grocery distribution company in Cambodia and secured the South East Asian rights to international brands such as Hyram Walker spirits, Beck's Beer and Frexinet Champagne.

1992 - 1993   Founding partner in Angkor Brewery.   Commenced operations of Cambodia's only national brewery.

1992 - 1993   Business Adviser for Cape York Peninsula Development Association.   Advice given to entrepreneurs on new venture start ups and ongoing growth opportunities on behalf on the State Government.

1990 - 1992   National Marketing Manager (Retail and Allied business) for The Shell Company of Australia.   Part of the initial development team that set up a chain of 60 Shell Circle 'K' convenience stores nationally in the Australian market.

1990 - 1996   Business Development Manager for Collins and Leahy Pty. Ltd., Papua New Guinea.   Consultant and adviser for new venture initiations, continued market developments and viability assessment of ongoing business segments.   Also responsible for liaison with, and provodoring for, mining and exploration companies.

Kim Raymond Goriss

Age: 37

EDUCATION

1995- 1996   MBA, Bond University

1979   Bachelor of Surveying, University of Queensland.

WORK EXPERIENCE

Present   Financial Analyst within the Financial Policy and Management Division (FPMD) of the Queensland Department of Public Works and Housing, Brisbane, Australia.

1990 - 1994   Base Manager of Oceonics (Asia Pacific) Ltd., Abu Dhabi, United Arab Emirates. Divisional manager responsible for business activities in the Middle East region (GCC nations and India).

1988 - 1990   Operations Manager of Oceonics Asia Pacific) Pte. Ltd., Singapore. Responsible for operational activities of all projects undertaken in the Far East (ASEAN nations, Australia, PNG, Hong Kong, Peoples Republic of China and Taiwan).

1984 - 1988   Project Manager/Senior Surveyor for Geomex Surveys Pty. Ltd., Perth, Australia and Geomex Surveys (S) Pte. Ltd., Singapore. Responsible for coordination and execution of projects undertaken in the Far East (ASEAN nations, Australia, PNG, Hong Kong, Peoples Republic of China and Taiwan).

1982 - 1984   Senior Surveyor for the joint venture Nanhai Racal Survey And Positioning Company, Peoples Republic of China. Responsible for field projects undertaken in the Nanhai (south sea) areas of the Guangdong and Hainan Island provinces.

1980 - 1982   Senior Surveyor for Decca Surveys (S) Pte. Ltd., Singapore, and Racal-Decca Technical Positioning Services, Indonesia. Responsible for field projects undertaken in ASEAN counties (with particular emphasis on Indonesia), United Arab Emirates and India.

Prudence Jane Kellahan

Age: 22

EDUCATION

1996	Post Graduate Diploma of Legal Practice, Queensland University of Technology.
1996	Masters of Business Administration, Bond University.
1995	Masters of Accounting, Bond University.
1994	Bachelor of Laws, Bond University.

WORK EXPERIENCE

1990 - Legal Liaison and Office Manager with Kel Constructions. Responsible for the development and ongoing administration of the accounting and legal departments of this family business.

INTERNATIONAL EXPERIENCE

Travel throughout North America, South America, Canada, Singapore, Hong Kong, China, Thailand, Ireland and Europe.

EcoClear Inc. Organisational Chart Year's Two to Five

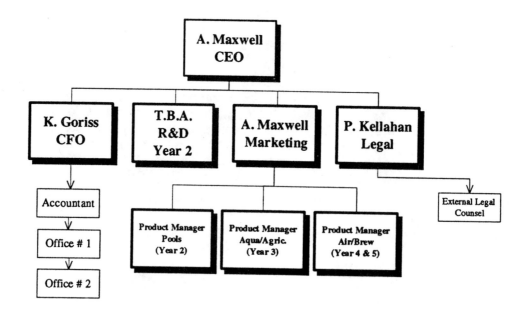

Appendix E: Research & Development Schedule

The following table outlines EcoClear Inc.'s projected R&D program and forecast product roll out schedule.

1997	1998	1999	2000	2001
Ongoing product development	Ongoing product development	Ongoing product development	Ongoing product development	Ongoing product development
Inline Mulcher development	Inline mulcher prototype	Inline Mulcher launch	Ongoing Inline mulcher develop.	Ongoing Inline mulcher develop.
Research commercial pools	Commercial pool development	Commercial pool prototype	Commercial pool launch	Commercial pool development
	Research other industries	Agriculture & Aquaculture development	Agriculture & Aquaculture prototype	Agriculture & Aquaculture launch
		Research other industries	Brewing & Air Conditioning development	Brewing & Air Conditioning prototype

EcoClear Inc.

Profit & Loss (Worst Case Scenario)

	Jan	Feb	Mar	Apr	May	Jun	Jul	Aug	Sep	Oct	Nov	Dec	1997	1998	1999	2000	2001
GROSS PROFIT FROM TRADING ACCOUNT																	
Fee Income	0	0	0	0	0	0	0	0	0	0	0	0	0	640,000	730,000	850,000	1,100,000
Other Operating Income	0	0	0	0	0	0	0	0	0	0	0	0	0	0	0	0	0
Total Operating Income	0	0	0	0	0	0	0	0	0	0	0	0	0	640,000	730,000	850,000	1,100,000
EXPENSES																	
Direct Costs - Services Entity	54,500	3,500	3,500	6,000	3,500	3,500	3,500	6,000	3,500	3,500	3,500	3,500	98,000	154,080	0	98,800	117,800
Research & Development Expense	118,042	23,292	8,292	17,042	8,292	8,292	14,542	10,792	8,292	14,542	8,292	8,292	248,000	198,600	102,575	221,400	241,750
Administration Costs	109,053	9,683	9,683	24,683	9,683	9,683	9,683	9,683	9,683	9,683	9,683	9,683	229,800	131,650	211,175	98,800	0
Selling & Distribution Costs	0	0	0	0	0	0	0	0	0	967	600	633	1,800	10,000	121,430	147,280	168,825
Interest Expense	0	1,833	1,833	1,833	1,833	1,833	1,833	1,833	1,833	1,833	1,833	1,833	20,167	9,167	9,167	0	0
Lease Expense	0	0	0	0	0	0	0	0	0	0	0	0	0	22,000	22,000	22,000	22,000
Depreciation	0	0	0	0	0	0	0	0	0	0	0	0	0	0	0	0	0
Movement in Provisions	0	0	0	0	0	0	0	0	0	0	0	0	0	0	0	0	0
Other Operating Costs	0	0	0	0	0	0	0	0	0	0	0	0	0	0	0	0	0
OPERATING PROFIT BEFORE TAX	(279,625)	(38,206)	(23,206)	(49,458)	(23,206)	(23,206)	(29,458)	(28,206)	(23,206)	(29,625)	(23,706)	(24,042)	(365,167)	23,700	263,653	300,520	532,225
Non-Operating Income	0	0	0	0	0	0	0	0	0	0	0	0	0	0	0	0	0
Non-Operating Costs	0	0	0	0	0	0	0	0	0	0	0	0	0	0	0	0	0
Income Tax Expense	(101,289)	(13,185)	(8,206)	(17,311)	(8,206)	(8,206)	(10,296)	(10,296)	(8,206)	(10,354)	(8,401)	(8,511)	(212,575)	(17,597)	70,081	112,570	195,247
Dividends	0	0	0	0	0	0	0	0	0	0	0	0	0	20,649	98,796	135,975	187,999
Extraordinary Profit	0	0	0	0	0	0	0	0	0	0	0	0	0	0	0	0	0
Amortisation of Intangibles	0	0	0	0	0	0	0	0	0	0	0	0	0	0	0	0	0
Transfer to Reserve	0	0	0	0	0	0	0	0	0	0	0	0	0	0	0	0	0
RETAINED EARNINGS	(178,336)	(25,022)	(14,972)	(32,147)	(14,972)	(14,972)	(19,160)	(17,910)	(14,972)	(19,271)	(15,307)	(15,530)	(362,592)	20,649	98,796	135,975	187,999

318

EcoClear Inc.

Cashflow (Worst Case Scenario)

Years ending 31-Dec-97

CASH INFLOWS
- Cash Sales
- Capital Subscriptions
- Loan Drawdowns – Secured
- – Unsecured
- Proceeds from Asset Sales
- Fee Income Services Entity
- Other Operating Income
- Non-Operating Income
- Receipts from Debtors

CASH OUTFLOWS
- Payments to creditors
- Cash Purchases/Additions
- Capital Expenditure
- Direct Cost Services Entity
- Other Operating & Non-Operating Costs
- Tax Payment
- Dividend Payments
- Research & Development Expense
- Administration and Selling Expense
- Loan Repayments – Secured
- – Unsecured
- Interest Payments
- Increase in Other Assets (incl. Investments)
- Lease Payments
- Reduction in Other Payables

NET CASH-FLOW

CLOSING OVERDRAFT OR CASH

EcoClear Inc.

Balance Sheet (Worst Case Scenario)

1997

As at 13-Dec-97

	Jan	Feb	Mar	Apr	May	Jun	Jul	Aug	Sep	Oct	Nov	Dec	1997	1998	1999	2000	2001
CURRENT ASSETS																	
Cash and Deposits	239,375	214,900	192,925	145,000	123,925	102,250	74,925	49,250	28,975	9,250	7,708	5,833	5,833	3,200	207,163	508,105	905,022
Debtors	0	0	0	0	0	0	0	0	0	0	0	0	0	45,000	60,833	73,333	91,667
Stock	0	0	0	0	0	0	0	0	0	0	0	0	0	0	0	0	0
Accrued Interest Receivable	0	0	0	0	0	0	0	0	0	0	0	0	0	0	0	0	1,833
Other	0	0	0	0	0	0	0	0	0	0	0	0	0	0	0	0	35,000
TOTAL CURRENT ASSETS	239,375	214,900	192,925	145,000	123,925	102,250	74,925	49,250	28,975	9,250	7,708	5,833	5,833	53,200	297,996	581,438	999,855
NON CURRENT ASSETS																	
Investments	0	0	0	0	0	0	0	0	0	0	0	0	0	0	0	0	0
Land and Buildings	110,000	108,167	108,333	104,500	102,667	100,833	99,000	97,167	95,333	93,500	91,667	89,833	89,833	67,833	45,833	23,833	0
Leased Assets	35,000	35,000	35,000	35,000	35,000	35,000	35,000	35,000	35,000	35,000	35,000	35,000	35,000	35,000	35,000	35,000	35,000
Plant and Equipment	0	0	0	0	0	0	0	0	0	0	0	0	0	0	0	0	0
Other	0	0	0	0	0	0	0	0	0	0	0	0	0	0	0	0	0
TOTAL NON-CURRENT ASSETS	145,000	143,167	141,333	139,500	137,667	135,833	134,000	132,167	130,333	128,500	126,667	124,833	124,833	102,833	80,833	58,833	35,000
TOTAL ASSETS	385,375	357,167	333,958	284,500	261,282	238,083	208,925	180,417	157,208	137,750	134,375	130,667	130,667	156,033	349,330	640,272	1,033,522
CURRENT LIABILITIES																	
Bank Overdraft – Secured	0	0	0	0	0	0	0	0	0	0	0	0	0	0	0	0	0
– Unsecured	0	0	0	0	0	0	0	0	0	0	0	0	0	50,000	0	0	0
Loans – Secured	0	0	0	0	0	0	0	0	0	0	0	0	0	0	0	0	0
– Unsecured	0	0	0	0	0	0	0	0	0	0	0	0	0	0	98,786	138,975	137,160
Creditors	0	0	0	0	0	0	0	0	0	0	0	0	0	20,849	0	0	187,988
Finance Lease Obligations	0	0	0	0	0	0	0	0	0	0	0	0	0	0	0	0	0
Provisions – Tax	0	0	0	0	0	0	0	0	0	0	0	0	0	0	0	0	0
– Dividend	0	0	0	0	0	0	0	0	0	0	0	0	0	2,500	2,292	0	0
– Employee Benefits	0	0	0	0	0	0	0	0	0	0	0	0	0	0	0	0	0
– Other	0	0	0	0	0	0	0	0	0	0	0	0	0	0	0	0	0
Accrued Interest Payable	0	0	0	0	0	0	0	0	0	167	500	833	833	73,148	99,078	138,975	325,148
Other Current Liabilities	0	0	0	0	0	0	0	0	0	0	0	0	0	0	0	0	0
TOTAL CURRENT LIABILITIES	0	0	0	0	0	0	0	0	0	167	500	833	833	73,148	99,078	138,975	325,148
NON CURRENT LIABILITIES																	
Loans – Secured	0	0	0	0	0	0	0	0	0	0	0	0	0	0	0	0	0
– Unsecured	0	0	0	0	0	0	0	0	0	10,000	30,000	50,000	50,000	0	0	0	0
Provisions	0	0	0	0	0	0	0	0	0	0	0	0	0	0	0	0	0
Future Tax Liability	0	0	0	0	0	0	0	0	0	0	0	0	0	0	0	0	0
Finance Lease Obligations	0	0	0	0	0	0	0	0	0	0	0	0	0	0	0	0	0
Other	0	0	0	0	0	0	0	0	0	0	0	0	0	0	0	0	0
TOTAL NON – CURRENT LIABILITIES	0	0	0	0	0	0	0	0	0	10,000	30,000	50,000	50,000	0	0	0	0
TOTAL LIABILITIES	0	0	0	0	0	0	0	0	0	10,167	30,500	50,833	50,833	73,148	99,078	138,975	325,148
NET ASSETS	385,375	357,167	333,958	284,500	261,282	238,083	208,925	180,417	157,208	127,583	103,875	79,833	79,833	82,895	249,752	501,297	708,373
SHAREHOLDERS FUNDS																	
Ordinary Capital	675,000	675,000	675,000	675,000	675,000	675,000	675,000	675,000	675,000	675,000	675,000	675,000	675,000	675,000	675,000	675,000	675,000
Preference Capital	0	0	0	0	0	0	0	0	0	0	0	0	0	0	0	0	0
Reserves – Revenue	(178,569)	(205,375)	(218,250)	(269,495)	(285,470)	(290,442)	(299,801)	(317,511)	(332,453)	(351,754)	(367,091)	(382,592)	(382,592)	(361,943)	(265,857)	(126,182)	61,806
– Asset Revaluation	469,844	471,822	459,860	424,593	409,530	394,558	375,398	357,498	342,517	323,246	307,959	292,408	292,408	315,067	499,843	549,818	730,906
– Other Capital	0	0	0	0	0	0	0	0	0	0	0	0	0	0	0	0	0
Retained Earnings	501,280	114,455	122,691	149,903	148,239	159,675	169,774	177,073	185,308	195,993	204,964	212,575	212,575	229,172	160,092	47,522	28,435
add : Minority Interests	0	0	0	0	0	0	0	0	0	0	0	0	0	0	0	0	0
less : Intangibles	0	0	0	0	0	0	0	0	0	0	0	0	0	0	0	0	0
SHAREHOLDERS EQUITY	385,375	357,167	333,958	284,500	261,282	238,083	208,925	180,417	157,208	127,583	103,875	79,833	79,833	82,895	249,752	501,297	708,373

Discussion Questions
for
EcoClear, Inc.

1. EcoClear, Inc. proposes to introduce an innovative, self-cleaning, swimming pool filter in the US which has been tested and launched in Australia.

    - How convincing is the evidence that the new filter is superior to those currently on the market?

    - How good is the market opportunity afforded by the new pool filter?

    - What is your assessment of EcoClear's proposed strategy to license an American manufacturer to produce and market the filter in the US?

    - What skills are required to carry-out EcoClear's proposed strategy?

    - Assuming EcoClear is successful in securing an American license, what business is EcoClear then in? What skills will be required?

    - What are the risks?

2. EcoClear has three management team members.

    - How well do the skills of the team members fit with skills required to launch the company successfully?

    - Who among the group is most critical to EcoClear's success?

    - Are any additional talent or skills needed?

3. Licensing a major manufacturer in the American pool industry is the critical step in EcoClear's launch strategy.

    - What are the benefits to the licensee?

    - What motivation does the licensee have to promote the new filter aggressively?

    - What are the relative merits of licensing one versus licensing several or all the major American manufacturers?

    - If EcoClear does not succeed in signing a licensee, what should the fall back strategy be?

4. Refer to EcoClear's Financial Plan.

    - Are the expenses shown in the income statements consistent with the actions discussed in the plan?

    - How does EcoClear manage to spend over $700,000 in 1997?

    - In Projected Cashflow, what is "Receipt from Debtors"?

    - In the Balance Sheet, what is included in "Plant and Equipment"?

    - How confident are you in 2001 projected "Operating Profit Before Tax" of nearly $3.5 million?

5. EcoClear is seeking $300,000 in exchange for 33% of the ownership.

    - What is the implicit valuation of the company? Does this valuation seem reasonable? How does it compare with the valuation at the time of the previous investments?

- How will the $300,000 be used by EcoClear?

- Can the management team proceed if no new investor is secured? Explain.

- Evaluate the proposed harvest strategies.

- Would you invest?

MOOT CORP®
Judge's Evaluation

Company: _____   Judge No: _____

I. Written Business Plan (40%)

Please evaluate the written <u>business plan</u> on the following aspects:

(Using this rating system: 1 = very poor, 2 = poor, 3 = fair, 4 = adequate, 5 = good, 6 = very good, 7 = excellent)

1. **Executive Summary (5%)**
   (Clear, exciting and effective as a stand-alone
   overview of the plan)   1   2   3   4   5   6   7
   Comments/Questions _____
   _____
   _____

2. **Company Overview (5%)**
   (Business purpose, history, genesis of concept,
   current status, overall strategy and objectives)   1   2   3   4   5   6   7
   Comments/Questions _____
   _____
   _____

3. **Products or Services (10%)**
   (Description, features and benefits, pricing, current
   stage of development, proprietary position)   1   2   3   4   5   6   7
   Comments/Questions _____
   _____
   _____

4. **Market and Marketing Strategy (10%)**
   (Description of market, competitive analysis, needs
   identification, market acceptance, unique
   capabilities, sales/promotion)   1   2   3   4   5   6   7
   Comments/Questions _____
   _____
   _____

5. **Operations (15%)**
   (Plan for production / delivery of product or
   services, product cost, margins, operating
   complexity, resources required)   1   2   3   4   5   6   7
   Comments/Questions _____
   _____
   _____

6. **Management (10%)**
   (Backgrounds of key individuals, ability to execute
   strategy, personnel needs, organizational structure,
   role of any non-student executive, which students
   will execute plan)   1   2   3   4   5   6   7
   Comments/Questions _____
   _____
   _____

In rating each of the above, please consider the following questions:
- Is this area covered in adequate detail?
- Does the plan show a clear understanding of the elements that should be addressed?
- Are the assumptions realistic and reasonable?
- Are the risks identified and the ability to manage those risks conveyed?

Company: _____ Judge No: _____

(Using this rating system: 1 = very poor, 2 = poor, 3 = fair, 4 = adequate, 5 = good, 6 = very good, 7 = excellent)

7. **Summary Financials (10%)**
Presented in summary form and follow U.S. generally accepted accounting principles.
Consistent with plan and effective in capturing financial performance; Quarterly for first two years, Quarterly/annually for years 3-5.

a. Cash Flow Statement	1 2 3 4 5 6 7
b. Income Statement	1 2 3 4 5 6 7
c. Balance Sheet	1 2 3 4 5 6 7
d. Funds Required/Uses	1 2 3 4 5 6 7
e. Assumptions/Trends/Comparatives	1 2 3 4 5 6 7

Comments/Questions _____
_____
_____

8. **Offering (10%)**
(Proposal/terms to investors—indicate how
much you want, the ROI, and the structure
of the deal; possible exit strategies)   1 2 3 4 5 6 7
Comments/Questions _____
_____
_____

9. **Viability (20%)**
(Market opportunity, distinctive competence,
management understanding, investment
potential)   1 2 3 4 5 6 7
Comments/Questions _____
_____
_____

10. **Brevity and Clarity (5%)**
(Is the plan approximately 25 pages with
minimal redundancy)   1 2 3 4 5 6 7
Comments/Questions _____
_____
_____

Additional Comments

MOOT CORP®
Judge's Evaluation

Company: _____ Judge No: _____

II. Presentation (20%)

(Using this rating system: 1 = very poor, 2 = poor, 3 = fair, 4 = adequate, 5 = good, 6 = very good, 7 = excellent)

1. **Formal Presentation (50%)**
   a. Materials presented in clear, logical and/or
      sequential form.   1   2   3   4   5   6   7
   b. Ability to relate need for the company with
      meaningful examples, and practical applications.   1   2   3   4   5   6   7
   c. Ability to maintain judges' interest.   1   2   3   4   5   6   7
   d. Quality of Visual Aids.   1   2   3   4   5   6   7

2. **Questions and Answers (50%)**
   a. Ability to understand judges' inquiries.   1   2   3   4   5   6   7
   b. Appropriately respond to judges' inquiries
      with substantive answers.   1   2   3   4   5   6   7
   c. Use of time allocated (minimal redundancy).   1   2   3   4   5   6   7
   d. Poise and confidence (think effectively on their
      feet).   1   2   3   4   5   6   7

Strengths of Presentation

Weaknesses of Presentation

MOOT CORP®
Judge's Evaluation

Company: _____ Judge No: _____

III. Viability of Company (40%)

		Definitely No				Definitely Yes		

1. **Market Opportunity (20%)**
   (There is a clear market need presented as well as
   a way to take advantage of that need.)   1   2   3   4   5   6   7
2. **Distinctive Competence (20%)**
   (The company provides something novel/unique/
   special that gives it a competitive advantage in its
   market.)   1   2   3   4   5   6   7
3. **Management Capability (20%)**
   (This team can effectively develop this company
   and handle the risks associated with the venture.)   1   2   3   4   5   6   7
4. **Financial Understanding (20%)**
   (This team has a solid understanding of the financial
   requirements of the business.)   1   2   3   4   5   6   7
5. **Investment Potential (20%)**
   (The business represents a real investment
   opportunity in which you would consider investing.)   1   2   3   4   5   6   7

Company Strengths

Company Weaknesses

Additional Comments